W9-BBU-447

WORLD CAPITAL MARKETS
CHALLENGE TO THE G-10

WORLD CAPITAL MARKETS
CHALLENGE TO THE G-10

WENDY DOBSON
GARY CLYDE HUFBAUER

ASSISTED BY
HYUN KOO CHO

INSTITUTE FOR INTERNATIONAL ECONOMICS
WASHINGTON, DC
MAY 2001

Wendy Dobson is professor at and director of the Institute for International Business at the University of Toronto. She was a visiting fellow at the Institute for International Economics in 1990-91. Between 1981 and 1987 she was president of the C.D. Howe Institute in Canada. From 1987 to 1989, she served as associate deputy minister of finance in the Canadian government with responsibility for international monetary affairs. Her most recent publications include *Financial Services Liberalization in the WTO* (Institute for International Economics, 1998) coauthored with Pierre Jacquet; *Fiscal frameworks and financial systems in East Asia: How much do they matter?* (University of Toronto Press, 1998); and *Multinationals and East Asia Integration* (1997) edited with Chia Siow Yue, which won the 1998 Ohira Prize.

Gary Clyde Hufbauer, Reginald Jones Senior Fellow, was formerly the Marcus Wallenberg Professor of International Finance Diplomacy at Georgetown University (1985-92); deputy director of the International Law Institute at Georgetown University (1979-81); deputy assistant secretary for international trade and investment policy of the US Treasury (1977-79); and director of the International Tax Staff at the Treasury (1974-76). He has written extensively on international trade, investment, and tax issues. He is coauthor of *NAFTA and the Environment: Seven Years Later* (2000); coeditor of *Unfinished Business: Telecommunications after the Uruguay Round* (1997); and coauthor of *Economic Sanctions Reconsidered* (2nd edition, 1990).

Hyun Koo Cho, research assistant, received his MA from the Johns Hopkins School of Advanced International Studies in Washington, DC.

INSTITUTE FOR INTERNATIONAL ECONOMICS
11 Dupont Circle, NW
Washington, DC 20036-1207
(202) 328-9000   FAX: (202) 328-5432
http://www.iie.com

C. Fred Bergsten, *Director*
Brigitte Coulton, *Director of Publications and Web Development*
Brett Kitchen, *Director of Marketing*

Printing by Kirby Lithographic Company, Inc.
Typesetting by Sandra F. Watts

Printed in the United States of America
03 02 01   5 4 3 2 1

Library of Congress Cataloging-in-Publication Data

Dobson, Wendy.
    World capital markets : challenge to the G-10 / Wendy Dobson, Gary Clyde Hufbauer; assisted by Hyun Koo Cho.
       p. cm.
    Includes bibliographical references and index.
    ISBN 0-88132-301-2
    1. Capital market. 2. Capital movements. 3. International finance.
    I. Hufbauer, Gary Clyde. II. Cho, Hyun Koo. III. Title.

HG4523.D63   2001
332'.042—dc21
                                    00-054019

The views expressed in this publication are those of the authors. This publication is part of the overall program of the Institute, as endorsed by its Board of Directors, but does not necessarily reflect the views of individual members of the Board or the Advisory Committee.

For **Anthony M. Solomon,**
*astute participant in the international economy
and wise supervisor of financial markets*

3   The Group of Ten and Financial Architecture   129

Tables

Spain are responsible for implementing major reforms, both to moderate the *actual* volatility of bank lending and to monitor the *potential* volatility of portfolio investment.

Dobson and Hufbauer recommend specific measures to change the rules of the game. Their major recommendations go further than the three "pillars" of the revised Basel Capital Adequacy Accord (also known as Basel II)—better alignment of bank capital with their risk profiles, stronger supervision, and more market discipline. Going beyond Basel II, Dobson and Hufbauer seek to influence the taste for, and management of, risk by banks and the financial institutions to which they lend. They emphasize the importance of further changes in the incentive structures for banks and for supervisors themselves. They also recommend changing the way liquidity crises are resolved, so as to create a clear *ex ante* framework for withdrawing the assurance of full and timely repayment when problems arise.

The Institute for International Economics is a private nonprofit institution for the study and discussion of international economic policy. Its purpose is to analyze important issues in that area and to develop and communicate practical new approaches for dealing with them. The Institute is completely nonpartisan.

The Institute is funded largely by philanthropic foundations. Major institutional grants are now being received from the William M. Keck, Jr. Foundation and the Starr Foundation. A number of other foundations and private corporations contribute to the highly diversified financial resources of the Institute. About 26 percent of the Institute's resources in our latest fiscal year were provided by contributors outside the United States, including about 11 percent from Japan. The Smith Richardson Foundation provided generous financial support for this project.

The Board of Directors bears overall responsibilities for the Institute and gives general guidance and approval to its research program, including the identification of topics that are likely to become important over the medium run (one to three years), and which should be addressed by the Institute. The Director, working closely with the staff and outside Advisory Committee, is responsible for the development of particular projects and makes the final decision to publish an individual study.

The Institute hopes that its studies and other activities will contribute to building a stronger foundation for international economic policy around the world. We invite readers of these publications to let us know how they think we can best accomplish this objective.

C. Fred Bergsten
Director
May 2001

Acknowledgments

The authors thank their colleagues at the Institute for International Economics and readers of this manuscript for their helpful comments: C. Fred Bergsten, Michael Dooley, Barry Eichengreen, Morris Goldstein, Ross Levine, Adam Posen, and John Williamson. The authors also benefited greatly from suggestions by Steven Canner (US Council for International Business), Steven Kamin (Federal Reserve Bank), Subir Lall (International Monetary Fund), James Lister (US Treasury), Thomas Palley (AFL-CIO), Alexis Rieffel (Institute of International Finance), and Howard Rosen. Subir Lall provided detailed comments on various versions of the study. We are indebted to Erika Wada for her help with statistical packages and Anita Rajan and Michael Wyman for research assistance at earlier stages of the project. Our special thanks go to the Institute's publication staff led by Brigitte Coulton. We thank Brigitte Coulton and Madona Devasahayam for arranging the editing of the book, Alfred R. Imhoff for editing, Marla Banov for ensuring rapid production, and Kara Davis for designing the book cover.

Supply-Side Criticism

In this book, our concern is the newer line of criticism. Notwithstanding the Latin American debt crises of the 1980s and 1994-95, and the Asian crisis of 1997-98, we think that trends from the 1970s to the 1990s preview a long upswing in private capital flows to emerging-market economies. Demographic factors, innovation, and deregulation in financial markets of countries belonging to the Organization for Economic Cooperation and Development (OECD) will continue to magnify the size and speed of capital flows across borders. These changes will markedly increase the efficiency with which capital is deployed around the globe—benefiting billions of people—but they also raise the risk of future financial collapse.

Mainstream analysis of the international financial architecture largely addresses problems in, and reform by, the debtor countries and the international financial institutions. We call this demand-side criticism, and although we agree with the more tempered critics (such as the Council on Foreign Relations 1999), the demand side is not the focus of this book. The much smaller literature on creditor institutions conveys an implicit assumption: Financial institutions and supervisors in the sophisticated Group of Ten (G-10) markets—players who set the rules of the game—have their monitoring and incentive systems about right. The flaws in these sophisticated financial markets are, in any event, being corrected.

The main debate within the G-10 is whether private-sector players should bear more of the responsibility for and costs of managing crises when they do occur. This somewhat relaxed attitude is sanctioned by the fact that G-10 countries were barely affected by the Asian and Russian collapses—between 1997 and 1999, jobs, growth, and financial markets in the leading OECD countries did rather well. For most Americans, Europeans, and Japanese, the financial crises were distant spectacles.

Our focus is *supply-side* criticism. The G-10 suppliers of international capital and their supervisors deserve more scrutiny. The G-10 is a convenient label for 11 rich industrial countries that dominate the supply side of international capital: Belgium, Canada, France, Germany, Italy, Japan, the Netherlands, Sweden, Switzerland, the United Kingdom, and the United States.[2] For the purpose of our policy recommendations, we add Spain to this group, because Spanish banks are major financial players in Latin America. We do not, however, address our policy

---

2. The ministers of finance and central bank governors of the G-10 usually meet twice a year, in the context of the spring and autumn meetings of the International Monetary Fund. In addition, the central bank governors meet monthly under the auspices of the Bank for International Settlements in Basel. The deputies of the G-10 meet as needed, normally two to four times a year. Ad hoc committees and working parties are established from time to time. G-10 communiqués are available at http://www.bis.org and http://www.imf.org.

recommendations to the entire OECD, because the 29 OECD members include many smaller countries (such as Denmark and New Zealand) and some not-so-wealthy countries (such as Mexico, Poland, and Turkey) that are not financial powerhouses.

Chapter Preview

Our account begins in this chapter with a comparative analysis of international capital flows since 1970, highlighting the crisis-prone nature of bank lending relative to other sources of capital, namely, portfolio investment and foreign direct investment (FDI). Although most financial crises are rooted in domestic mismanagement, the roots often draw nourishment from international capital. Strict capital controls (as urged, among others, by Eatwell and Taylor 2000) would sharply limit the extent of international nourishment—but at a high price. In this chapter, we make a case for the benefits of global capital flows—especially portfolio investment and FDI. In our view, the long-term growth benefits of these flows substantially outweigh crisis costs. Nevertheless, we argue that financial crises can be moderated in frequency and amplitude by measures that shift the composition of flows away from bank lending and toward portfolio equity and FDI.

In chapter 2, our focus shifts to why such measures are needed. We describe the market players—almost entirely based in the G-10 countries (plus Spain)—who dominate international markets and set the rules of the game. We note the special role banks play in any financial system. This special, somewhat anomalous role is both the rationale for, and the consequence of, public safety nets—created by national governments and in recent international crises by the international financial institutions. National and international safety nets were introduced to prevent bank runs and reduce the social costs of contagion by providing insurance.

Safety-net insurance, however, contributes to moral hazard, implicitly encouraging banking organizations to take more risks than they would if they had to accept the full cost of bad lending decisions. We examine the evidence for moral hazard and the efforts of national supervisors to offset it through prudential supervision—both at home and by cooperating with the Bank for International Settlements (BIS). We find that moral hazard is still an issue for banks, particularly in their short-term lending, and note that excessive leverage could become a similar problem in portfolio institutions.

In chapter 3, we explore ways G-10 governments might further reduce moral hazard and the volatility of short-term debt. One approach is for G-10 governments to change incentives and supervisory systems even more than they have. Our recommendations go further than the revised Basel Capital Adequacy Accord's three "pillars"—better alignment of banks' capital with their risk profiles, stronger supervision, and

of foreign investment. The main explanations: differences in human capital (one US worker may be the effective equivalent of five Indian workers), external economies in the use of human capital (when my colleagues are 10 percent more productive, I may be 3.6 percent more productive), and political risk in emerging markets.[6] Lucas concluded that the first two explanations probably explain a good part of the shortfall, but that the third explanation (the only one that is readily susceptible to policy intervention) must also be invoked.

A recent empirical study by Kraay and others (2000) examined gross and net foreign asset positions for a panel of 68 countries for the period 1966-97.[7] Their findings support Lucas (1990). Kraay and others reached three conclusions that are especially pertinent. First, a country's net foreign assets (on a per capita basis) are highly correlated with its wealth (domestic capital stock plus net foreign assets). Although most countries have negative net foreign assets, a few rich countries have positive net foreign assets. However, even the rich industrial countries with positive net foreign assets held less than 1 percent of their wealth abroad.

Second, although gross foreign assets are obviously larger than net foreign assets, the modest magnitudes for gross asset positions are surprising. Industrial countries hold about 3.3 percent of their gross equity wealth and 11 percent of their gross loan wealth in foreign assets. Conversely, developing countries issue about 2.8 percent of their gross equity and 8.8 percent of their gross debt to foreign holders. Third, the net and gross asset relationships are fairly persistent over time. The authors explain the modest size of these magnitudes, and their persistence over time, by the possibility of crises and default by emerging countries—in other words, political risk. The authors construct a model in which just two large-scale emerging-economy defaults in a century will generate magnitudes similar to those observed.

In other words, theoretical explanations, together with observed foreign asset stocks, suggest persistent low investment from rich to poor countries. Indeed, as recently as 1970, annual net-net flows of debt and equity capital (long-term and short-term, both public and private, net of repaid and repatriated capital, interest, and dividends) to emerging markets amounted to about 0.7 percent of the GDP of all emerging markets.[8] But the picture is slowly changing. In 2000, annual net-net flows may

---

6. Lucas (1990) also analyzed the effect of monopoly capital practices in limiting investment in the colonies (before 1945) as a way of suppressing real wages. According to his calculations, monopoly capital practices could increase returns in the colonies to about 2.5 times their level in the home country.

7. Foreign assets are defined to include bank loans, portfolio bonds, and equity and FDI.

8. By "net-net capital flows," we mean capital flows net of loan repayments and FDI repatriation, and also net of interest, dividends, and retained FDI earnings. However, the net-net concept does *not* mean net of capital outflows *from* emerging markets.

have approached 3 percent of their combined GDP (table 1.1).[9] In relation to the combined GDP of the G-10 countries, the 1970 flow figure was only 0.3 percent, whereas the 2000 flow figure may have approached 1.0 percent.

Flows during the 1990s

Detailed statistics on net capital flows during the 1990s are provided in tables 1.2 and 1.3, on the basis of International Monetary Fund sources. IMF capital flows are expressed on a net basis: They are net of repayments and repatriations; however (unlike the net-net concept used in table 1.1), interest and dividends are not subtracted. In table 1.2, official IMF estimates of capital inflows in the 1990s to emerging markets are grouped geographically. Table 1.2 gives dollar estimates of net private-capital inflows of all types (bank loans and deposits, portfolio investment, foreign direct investment), as well as official flows, the change in reserve assets, and the current account balance.[10] In table 1.3, the dollar figures for private and official capital inflows are related to emerging-market GDP, measured at market exchange rates.[11] When all regions are combined, the net flows averaged about 2.4 percent of emerging-market GDP in the 1990s.

The figures on cumulative capital flows for the period 1990-2000 (11 years), classified by type of flow, are revealing (table 1.2). Cumulative bank loans and deposits were a *negative* $135 billion. Cumulative portfolio investments (excluding bank loans and deposits) were a positive $612 billion. Cumulative FDI was $954 billion. Cumulative official flows were a positive $205 billion—mostly timed to offset negative bank loans and deposits. In other words, portfolio investment and FDI were the big positive private-capital flows to emerging markets during the 1990s.

Data collected by the private Institute of International Finance (IIF), shown in appendix A, shed more light on bank activity. The text of appendix A explains the major differences between IMF and IIF data on

---

9. Although the upward trend in capital flows to emerging economies is clear, precise calculations depend on the data source and accounting conventions. See appendix A for an explanation of alternative data sources.

10. A current account deficit equals a capital account surplus, and vice versa. A positive number for reserves indicates an increase in official holdings of foreign exchange; a negative number indicates a decrease.

11. In making the evaluation, it matters whether GDP is measured at purchasing power parity (PPP) exchange rates, or at market exchange rates. PPP rates can increase the dollar measure of GDP in emerging economies by more than 100 percent, thereby diminishing the apparent relative importance of a billion dollars of capital inflow. In order to compare like magnitudes, we compare capital inflows with GDP measured at market exchange rates.

Table 1.1 Net-net capital flows to emerging markets[a]

Flows	1970	1980	1990	1998
	(billions of dollars at current prices)			
All emerging markets				
Long-term capital (net-net)	3.9	36.6	41.6	182.5
Bank loans and other debt (net-net)[a]	4.7	32.1	(10.0)	(12.6)
Portfolio equity and bonds (net-net)[b]	(0.1)	0.2	1.0	15.3
FDI (net-net)[c]	(4.2)	(19.3)	7.2	119.7
Official net transfers	6.1	39.2	40.8	56.4
Private net transfers	(2.2)	(2.6)	0.8	126.1
Short-term capital (net-net)	2.0	26.2	4.0	(23.3)
	(percent of GDP of emerging markets)			
Long-term capital (net-net)	0.5	1.3	0.9	2.9
Bank loans and other debt (net-net)[a]	0.6	1.1	(0.2)	(0.2)
Portfolio equity and bonds (net-net)[b]	(0.0)	0.0	0.0	0.2
FDI (net-net)[c]	(0.5)	(0.7)	0.2	1.9
Official net transfers	0.8	1.3	0.9	0.9
Private net transfers	(0.3)	(0.1)	0.0	2.0
Short-term capital (net-net)	0.2	0.9	0.1	(0.4)
	(percent of GDP of G-10)			
Long-term capital (net-net)	0.2	0.5	0.3	0.9
Official net transfers	0.3	0.6	0.3	0.3
Private net transfers	(0.1)	(0.0)	0.0	0.6
Short-term capital (net-net)	0.1	0.4	0.0	(0.1)
Memorandum:[d]				
GDP of emerging markets	797	2,927	4,747	6,364
GDP of G-10	1,999	7,093	14,997	20,187

	High scenario[e]			Low scenario[f]		
Flows	2010	2020	2030	2010	2020	2030
	(billions of dollars at 2000 prices)					
Total capital flows (net-net)	400	750	1,300	370	530	660
Bank loans and trade credits	0	50	50	(30)	20	20
Portfolio and FDI	400	700	1,250	400	510	640
	(percent of GDP of emerging markets)					
Total capital flows (net-net)	4.0	5.0	5.9	3.7	3.5	3.0
Bank loans and trade credits	0.0	0.3	0.2	(0.3)	0.1	0.1
Portfolio and FDI	4.0	4.7	5.7	4.0	3.4	2.9

(*table continues next page*)

Table 1.1   (continued)

Flows	High scenario[e]			Low scenario[f]		
	2010	2020	2030	2010	2020	2030
	(percent of GDP of G-10)					
Total capital flows (net-net)	1.5	2.1	3.0	1.4	1.5	1.5
Bank loans and trade credits	0.0	0.1	0.1	(0.1)	0.1	0.0
Portfolio and FDI	1.5	2.0	2.8	1.5	1.5	1.5
Memorandum						
GDP of emerging markets[g]	10,000	15,000	22,000	10,000	15,000	22,000
GDP of G-10	26,000	35,000	44,000	26,000	35,000	44,000

Flows	1970	1980	1990	1998
Africa	(billions of dollars at current prices)			
Long-term capital (net-net)[a]	1.0	8.7	11.7	13.5
Short-term capital (net-net)	0.4	0.4	0.6	(1.0)
Memorandum: GDP[b]	62.0	253.0	291.0	338.0
	(percent of GDP)			
Long-term capital (net-net)	1.6	3.4	4.0	4.0
Short-term capital (net-net)	0.6	0.2	0.2	(0.3)
Middle East	(billions of dollars at current prices)			
Long-term capital (net-net)[a]	(1.6)	(4.2)	(0.1)	12.3
Short-term capital (net-net)	0.3	(1.1)	6.6	2.3
Memorandum: GDP[c]	45.0	456.0	475.0	600.0
	(percent of GDP)			
Long-term capital (net-net)	(3.5)	(0.9)	(0.0)	2.0
Short-term capital (net-net)	0.6	(0.2)	1.4	0.4
Asia Pacific	(billions of dollars at current prices)			
Long-term capital (net-net)[a]	3.0	13.1	20.0	81.1
Short-term capital (net-net)	0.5	4.6	6.2	(16.6)
Memorandum: GDP[b]	278.0	648.0	1,353.0	2,116.0
	(percent of GDP)			
Long-term capital (net-net)	1.1	2.0	1.5	3.8
Short-term capital (net-net)	0.2	0.7	0.5	(0.8)
Europe	(billions of dollars at current prices)			
Long-term capital (net-net)[a]	0.5	10.9	3.9	39.1
Short-term capital (net-net)	0.1	6.3	(7.9)	3.2
Memorandum: GDP[b]	568.0	804.0	1,480.0	1,176.0

(table continues next page)

Table 1.1   Net-net capital flows to emerging markets[a] (continued)

Flows	1970	1980	1990	1998
		(percent of GDP)		
Long-term capital (net-net)	0.1	1.4	0.3	3.3
Short-term capital (net-net)	0.0	0.8	(0.5)	0.3
		(billions of dollars at current prices)		
Latin America				
Long-term capital (net-net)[a]	0.9	8.2	(0.1)	36.6
Short-term capital (net-net)	0.7	16.1	6.6	(6.8)
Memorandum: GDP[b]	171.0	740.0	1,149.0	2,135.0
		(percent of GDP)		
Long-term capital (net-net)	0.5	1.1	(0.0)	1.7
Short-term capital (net-net)	0.4	2.2	0.6	(0.3)

FDI = foreign direct investment
G-10 = Group of Ten countries; see note below.

a. Bank loans and other debt include "loans from private banks and other financial institutions," and "credits from manufacturers, exporters, and other suppliers of goods, and bank credits covered by a guarantee of an export credit agency." Loan repayments of principal are subtracted to obtain net loans. Interest payments on long- and short-term debt are subtracted from new loans to calculate the net-net amounts. In 1998, for example, net new bank and other loans were $52.7 billion, but interest payments were $94.3 billion, resulting in net-net flows of ($41.6) billion.
b. Dividends and interest payments on portfolio equity and bonds are subtracted to obtain net-net amounts.
c. Profits on FDI are subtracted from new FDI flows to calculate the net-net FDI flows. In 1998, for example, profit remittances and reinvested earnings were $35.3 billion and new FDI flows (including reinvested earnings) were $155.0 billion.
d. GDP is expressed in dollars at market exchange rates (current prices).
e. In the high scenario, net-net capital flows from developed countries (mainly G-10 countries) to emerging markets are projected to rise gradually from about 1 percent of G-10 GDP in 2000 to 3 percent in 2030. Underlying the projected rise is our assumption that household savings rates in G-10 countries will rise (mainly through private pension funds), while the demand for physical capital will fall. The capital stock projections in table 1.4 are generated by the capital flow assumptions in table 1.1. In our projections, Bank loans and trade credits are limited to a small portion of total capital flows for two reasons: (1) we assume that regulators adopt a more cautious stance, for the reasons argued in this monograph; (2) in any event, we think banks will become more risk averse. Portfolio investment (equity and bonds) plus FDI flows are calculated as a residual between total capital flows and bank loans and credit.
f. In the low scenario, net-net capital flows are derived from the assumption that the foreign-owned capital stock in the emerging markets remains a fixed 70 percent of emerging market GDP (table 1.4). Bank loans and trade credits are limited to a small share of total capital flows for the reasons already given. Portfolio and FDI are calculated as a residual.
g. GDP in emerging markets is projected to grow at 4.0 percent per year in real terms.

Note: The World Bank terminology for "net-net" flows is "aggregate net transfers." The G-10 is made up of 11 industrial countries (Belgium, Canada, France, Germany, Italy, Japan, the Netherlands, Sweden, Switzerland, the United Kingdom, and the United States). The GDP of the G-10 is projected to grow at 2.5 percent per year in real terms.

Sources: World Bank, *Global Development Finance,* 1998, 1999; World Bank, *World Tables,* 1983. All projections by the authors.

capital flows. The biggest difference surrounds bank operations. The IIF data on "bank loans and other debt (net)" record loans made by (and repaid to) foreign banks (principally G-10 banks) in the emerging markets. Unlike the IMF, the IIF does *not* record deposits by local banks, other firms, or residents of the emerging markets in the G-10 banks and the banks based in other advanced countries. The result is a startling difference in the cumulative size of bank operations in emerging countries between 1990 and 2000. The IIF records a cumulative *positive* figure of $269 billion, in contrast to the IMF cumulative *negative* figure of $135 billion. Most of the difference reflects deposits by residents of emerging markets in the banks of G-10 countries. In other words, local banks, firms, and residents of emerging markets placed about $400 billion in deposits in G-10 banks during the 1990s.

There is nothing bad about "reverse" deposits from emerging markets into G-10 banks. Emerging-market firms and residents are perfectly entitled to bank where they find safety and convenience. We concur with Michael Dooley in making a stronger statement: Residents of emerging markets may do better by investing in G-10 financial and industrial firms than local institutions.[12] The competitive pressures created by giving each investor, wherever he or she lives, an array of investment opportunities could do a great deal to improve the performance of emerging-market firms.

But when "reverse" deposits are cumulated over a decade, the magnitudes underscore a important proposition: If both loans and deposits are counted, G-10 banks have not been, and are not likely to become, large net suppliers of funds to emerging markets during a sustained period of time. Well-managed banks can dramatically improve the efficiency of capital allocation, a contribution that deserves to be emphasized. At the same time, through their lending and deposit-taking patterns, G-10 banks can contribute to volatility, a problem that we explore later in this chapter.

Regional Experience

Turning to regional data, in dollar terms, Asia and the Pacific and Latin America attracted the most private investment (table 1.2). In relation to GDP, however, the picture is somewhat different (table 1.3). The Middle East was the winner (4.7 percent of GDP), with a few high years in the early 1990s. For the decade, Latin America was next best (3.2 percent of GDP, with a far steadier average rate of inflow than the Middle East), followed by Africa (2.3 percent), and Asia and the Pacific (1.7 percent).

---

12. Michael Dooley, personal comment, November 2000.

Table 1.2 Net capital flows to emerging markets, by area, 1990-2000
(official estimates, billions of dollars at current prices)

Flows	1990	1991	1992	1993	1994	1995
Emerging markets						
Total private capital inflows (net)	47.7	123.8	119.3	181.9	152.8	193.3
Bank loans and other debt (net)[d]	11.9	55.6	32.7	11.5	(35.5)	55.4
Portfolio investment (net)[e]	17.4	36.9	51.1	113.6	105.6	41.2
Foreign direct investment (net)	18.4	31.3	35.5	56.8	82.6	96.7
Net official flows	26.6	36.5	22.3	20.1	1.8	26.0
Change in reserve assets	66.1	75.1	31.5	83.9	90.9	123.1
Current account balance	(27.2)	(79.0)	(69.7)	(107.2)	(69.7)	(96.0)
Asia Pacific						
Total private capital inflows (net)	19.6	34.1	17.9	57.3	66.4	95.1
Bank loans and other debt (net)[d]	13.0	18.4	3.3	11.7	11.7	34.4
Portfolio investment (net)[e]	(2.7)	1.4	21.0	9.4	9.4	10.9
Foreign direct investment (net)	9.3	14.4	33.0	45.3	45.3	49.8
Net official flows	8.4	10.9	10.3	8.5	10.5	6.7
Change in reserve assets	47.4	45.9	6.9	43.0	78.3	47.7
Current account balance	1.7	4.5	3.6	(13.3)	(3.8)	(36.3)
Five affected countries[f]						
Total private capital inflows (net)	24.2	26.8	26.2	31.9	33.2	62.5
Bank loans and other debt (net)[d]	17.9	17.3	15.0	8.7	18.4	36.9
Portfolio investment (net)[e]	0.3	3.4	5.3	16.5	8.3	17.0
Foreign direct investment (net)	6.0	6.1	6.3	6.7	6.5	8.7
Net official flows	n.a.	4.4	2.0	0.6	0.3	0.7
Change in reserve assets	6.9	8.4	15.0	18.3	10.7	14.0
Current account balance	(16.0)	(25.2)	(16.1)	(13.5)	(23.2)	(40.5)
Other Asia						
Total private capital inflows (net)	(4.6)	7.3	(8.3)	25.4	33.2	32.6
Bank loans and other debt (net)[d]	(4.9)	1.1	(11.7)	3.0	(6.7)	(2.5)
Portfolio investment (net)[e]	(3.0)	(2.0)	15.7	(7.1)	1.1	(6.1)
Foreign direct investment (net)	3.3	8.3	26.7	38.6	38.8	41.1
Net official flows	n.a.	6.5	8.3	7.9	10.2	6.0
Change in reserve assets	40.5	37.5	(8.1)	24.7	67.6	33.7
Current account balance	17.7	29.7	19.7	0.2	19.4	4.2
Latin America						
Total private capital inflows (net)	13.7	24.1	55.9	62.6	47.5	38.3
Bank loans and other debt (net)[d]	(10.5)	(2.0)	11.7	(10.6)	(38.2)	10.6
Portfolio investment (net)[e]	17.5	14.7	30.3	61.1	60.8	1.7
Foreign direct investment (net)	6.7	11.3	13.9	12.0	24.9	26.0
Net official flows	1.8	2.7	(1.7)	0.7	(3.4)	21.1
Change in reserve assets	14.7	18.0	23.0	20.2	(4.3)	24.8
Current account balance	(1.0)	(16.9)	(34.5)	(45.7)	(50.9)	(35.9)

1996	1997	1998	1999[a]	2000[a]	Flows, 1990-2000 Total	Average	Absolute deviation[b]	Relative deviations (percent)[c] Own	Total
212.1	149.2	64.3	68.3	118.5	1,431.2	130.1	43.4	33	
16.3	(57.6)	(103.5)	(71.8)	(50.1)	(135.1)	(12.3)	43.8	>100	>100
80.8	66.8	36.7	21.6	40.2	611.9	55.6	28.6	51	66
115.0	140.0	131.0	118.5	128.4	954.2	86.7	15.3	18	35
(0.9)	24.4	41.1	9.4	(2.4)	204.9	18.6	18.1		
101.1	59.2	58.3	51.1	76.1	816.4	74.2	24.1		
(92.5)	(91.8)	(53.6)	(24.7)	(45.2)	(756.6)	(68.8)	25.4		
100.5	3.2	(55.1)	(29.6)	(3.3)	306.1	27.8	32.1	>100	
32.8	(60.3)	(89.7)	(62.8)	(43.5)	(131.0)	(11.9)	22.2	>100	69
12.6	0.9	(15.4)	(8.3)	(2.9)	36.3	3.3	7.9	>100	25
55.1	62.6	50.0	41.6	43.1	449.5	40.9	7.6	19	24
(0.5)	30.0	27.5	(0.4)	2.3	114.2	10.4	8.2		
61.4	23.5	63.3	42.2	47.3	506.9	46.1	26.0		
(37.5)	5.6	101.7	75.5	55.8	157.5	14.3	24.9		
62.4	(19.7)	(46.2)	(18.1)	(8.2)	175.0	15.9	18.6	>100	
32.9	(44.5)	(44.5)	(32.0)	(22.2)	3.9	0.4	14.1	>100	76
20.0	12.6	(6.5)	4.5	5.6	87.0	7.9	7.5	94	40
9.5	12.1	4.9	9.4	8.4	84.6	7.7	1.9	25	10
(4.6)	30.4	20.2	(4.5)	(0.6)	48.9	4.9	9.3		
14.5	(35.9)	47.1	39.9	29.9	168.8	15.3	17.3		
(53.4)	(27.0)	69.7	49.3	29.4	(66.5)	(6.0)	22.4		
38.1	22.9	(8.9)	(11.5)	4.9	131.1	11.9	14.1	>100	
(0.1)	(15.8)	(45.2)	(30.8)	(21.3)	(134.9)	(12.3)	11.9	97	84
(7.4)	(11.7)	(8.9)	(12.8)	(8.5)	(50.7)	(4.6)	7.4	>100	52
45.6	50.5	45.1	32.2	34.7	364.9	33.2	6.8	20	48
4.1	(0.4)	7.3	4.1	2.9	56.9	5.7	3.0		
46.9	59.4	16.2	2.3	17.4	338.1	30.7	25.6		
15.9	32.6	32.0	26.2	26.4	224.0	20.4	11.1		
82.0	87.3	69.0	47.2	62.7	590.3	53.7	17.8	33	
2.7	(3.1)	(18.1)	(7.7)	(4.0)	(69.2)	(6.3)	16.4	>100	92
40.0	39.7	33.0	12.0	23.6	334.4	30.4	18.7	61	>100
39.3	50.6	54.0	42.8	43.1	324.6	29.5	6.3	21	35
(14.1)	(8.4)	4.1	4.8	(0.1)	7.5	0.7	9.5		
26.2	13.5	(9.9)	(6.7)	4.1	123.6	11.2	11.6		
(39.0)	(65.1)	(89.5)	(56.5)	(56.5)	(491.5)	(44.7)	15.2		

(*table continues next page*)

Table 1.2   Net capital flows to emerging markets, by area, 1990-2000
(official estimates, billions of dollars at current prices) (*continued*)

Flows	1990	1991	1992	1993	1994	1995
Africa						
Total private capital inflows (net)	4.4	8.9	6.9	8.7	4.8	6.8
Bank loans and other debt (net)[d]	4.7	8.4	5.8	5.8	0.7	1.2
Portfolio investment (net)[e]	(1.5)	(1.5)	(0.6)	1.0	0.8	1.5
Foreign direct investment (net)	1.2	2.0	1.7	1.9	3.4	4.2
Net official flows	7.1	9.1	12.1	8.3	13.5	11.7
Change in reserve assets	4.6	3.7	(2.8)	1.6	4.6	1.9
Current account balance	(9.0)	(7.4)	(10.4)	(11.0)	(11.8)	(16.4)
Middle East						
Total private capital inflows (net)	10.0	73.0	30.9	27.3	17.9	5.0
Bank loans and other debt (net)[d]	5.8	50.8	19.6	5.9	2.6	(6.1)
Portfolio investment (net)[e]	3.5	21.9	11.3	18.1	12.1	8.3
Foreign direct investment (net)	0.6	0.3	0.1	3.2	3.1	2.8
Net official flows	(1.8)	3.9	(1.2)	2.2	(1.5)	(1.5)
Change in reserve assets	(2.9)	6.0	0.7	4.6	2.5	7.7
Current account balance	3.4	(64.2)	(25.5)	(24.6)	(10.8)	(3.9)
Europe						
Total private capital inflows (net)	0.0	(16.3)	7.6	26.0	16.1	48.1
Bank loans and other debt (net)[d]	(1.1)	(19.9)	0.3	7.0	(12.3)	15.2
Portfolio investment (net)[e]	0.5	0.4	2.3	12.4	22.5	18.9
Foreign direct investment (net)	0.5	3.2	5.1	6.7	6.0	13.9
Net official flows	0.5	9.3	3.6	(0.7)	(10.5)	(9.1)
Change in reserve assets	2.4	1.5	3.7	14.5	9.8	41.0
Current account balance	(22.2)	5.0	(2.9)	(12.7)	7.6	(3.6)

n.a. = not available

a. IMF estimates; IMF, World Economic Outlook, October 1999.
b. Average absolute value of year-to-year change.
c. The ratio of absolute deviation (note b) to the average flows for 1990-2000. The "own" figure relates the absolute deviation to average annual capital flows of the same type. The "total" figure relates the absolute deviation to the absolute deviation of total private capital flows. Negative signs are ignored in calculating relative deviations.
d. "Other" net investment includes trade credits and loans; currency and deposits; and other assets and liabilities.
e. Net portfolio investment includes both equity securities and debt securities (bond and notes; money market instruments; and financial derivatives).
f. Indonesia, Malaysia, the Philippines, South Korea, and Thailand.

1996	1997	1998	1999ª	2000ª	Flows, 1990-2000		Absolute deviationᵇ	Relative deviations (percent)ᶜ	
					Total	Average		Own	Total
7.6	16.3	10.3	11.7	18.3	104.7	9.5	3.8	40	
2.3	5.8	0.0	0.9	4.8	40.4	3.7	2.7	74	72
(0.2)	2.9	3.5	2.4	4.7	13.0	1.2	1.2	>100	32
5.5	7.6	6.8	8.4	8.7	51.4	4.7	1.0	21	26
0.2	(4.7)	2.2	4.8	(3.5)	60.8	5.5	5.0		
5.5	3.8	(1.5)	1.4	8.2	31.0	2.8	3.8		
(5.7)	(6.1)	(18.1)	(18.8)	(15.2)	(129.9)	(11.8)	3.8		
(3.1)	7.1	22.6	17.4	11.1	219.2	19.9	17.6	88	
(8.5)	1.8	9.6	7.1	(4.7)	83.9	7.6	13.7	>100	78
3.7	2.8	10.8	6.5	6.2	105.2	9.6	6.4	67	36
1.7	2.5	2.2	3.8	9.5	29.8	2.7	1.4	50	8
(1.1)	(0.8)	(1.1)	(1.7)	(2.0)	(6.6)	(0.6)	2.0		
5.1	11.8	2.4	6.8	5.1	49.8	4.5	5.0		
8.7	6.4	(25.0)	(8.9)	(9.2)	(153.6)	(14.0)	19.1		
25.2	35.3	17.5	21.6	29.7	210.8	19.2	16.4	85	
(13.0)	(1.8)	(5.4)	(9.3)	(2.8)	(43.1)	(3.9)	14.6	>100	89
24.8	20.5	4.8	9.0	8.6	124.7	11.3	5.6	50	34
13.4	16.6	18.2	21.9	23.9	129.4	11.8	2.6	22	16
(2.4)	8.2	10.8	1.9	1.1	12.7	1.2	6.0		
2.9	6.6	4.0	7.4	11.5	105.3	9.6	10.2		
(19.1)	(32.6)	(22.7)	(16.1)	(20.2)	(139.5)	(12.7)	12.6		

Note: According to the IMF's balance of payments reporting standards, interest payments, dividends, and retained FDI earnings are supposed to be recorded as current account debits. Hence, these items, in principle, should not be subtracted in calculating net bank loans, net portfolio investment, or net FDI.

Sources: Table adapted from IMF, International Capital Market, Developments, Prospects, and Key Policy Issues, September 1999, 92-93; IMF, World Economic Outlook, May 1998; October 1999.

Table 1.3 Net capital flows to emerging markets as a percentage of GDP, by area, 1990-2000 (official estimates)

Flows	1990	1991	1992	1993	1994	1995	1996	1997	1998	1999[a]	2000[a]	Average percentages
As share of GDP of the G-10[b]												
Total private capital inflows (net)	0.3	0.8	0.7	1.0	0.8	0.9	1.0	0.7	0.3	0.3	0.6	0.7
Bank loans and other debt (net)	0.1	0.3	0.2	0.1	(0.2)	0.3	0.1	(0.3)	(0.5)	(0.3)	(0.2)	(0.0)
Portfolio investment (net)	0.1	0.2	0.3	0.7	0.6	0.2	0.4	0.3	0.2	0.1	0.2	0.3
Foreign direct investment (net)	0.1	0.2	0.2	0.3	0.4	0.5	0.6	0.7	0.6	0.6	0.6	0.4
Net official flows	0.2	0.2	0.1	0.1	0.0	0.1	(0.0)	0.1	0.2	0.0	(0.0)	0.1
As share of GDP of all emerging markets[c]												
Total private capital inflows (net)	1.0	2.6	2.5	3.6	2.9	3.6	3.6	2.4	1.0	1.0	1.7	2.4
Bank loans and other debt (net)	0.3	1.2	0.7	0.2	(0.7)	1.0	0.3	(0.9)	(1.6)	(1.1)	(0.7)	(0.1)
Portfolio investment (net)	0.4	0.8	1.1	2.3	2.0	0.8	1.4	1.1	0.6	0.3	0.6	1.0
Foreign direct investment (net)	0.4	0.7	0.7	1.1	1.6	1.8	2.0	2.3	2.1	1.8	1.9	1.5
Net official flows	0.6	0.8	0.5	0.4	0.0	0.5	(0.0)	0.4	0.6	0.1	(0.0)	0.3
Asia Pacific												
Total private capital inflows (net)	1.4	2.4	1.2	3.5	3.7	5.1	4.9	0.2	(2.6)	(1.3)	(0.1)	1.7
Bank loans and other debt (net)	1.0	1.3	0.2	0.7	0.7	1.9	1.6	(3.0)	(4.2)	(2.8)	(1.9)	(0.4)
Portfolio investment (net)	(0.2)	0.1	1.4	0.6	0.5	0.6	0.6	0.0	(0.7)	(0.4)	(0.1)	0.2
Foreign direct investment (net)	0.7	1.0	2.1	2.8	2.5	2.7	2.7	3.1	2.4	1.9	1.8	2.2
Net official flows	0.6	0.8	0.7	0.5	0.6	0.4	(0.0)	1.5	1.3	(0.0)	0.1	0.6
Five affected countries[d]												
Total private capital inflows (net)	4.5	4.4	3.9	4.3	4.0	6.3	5.8	2.0	(6.9)	(2.6)	(1.1)	1.9
Bank loans and other debt (net)	3.3	2.8	2.2	1.2	2.2	3.7	3.0	(4.5)	(6.6)	(4.5)	(3.0)	(0.0)
Portfolio investment (net)	0.1	0.6	0.8	2.2	1.0	1.7	1.9	1.3	(1.0)	0.6	0.8	0.9
Foreign direct investment (net)	1.1	1.0	0.9	0.9	0.8	0.9	0.9	1.2	0.7	1.3	1.1	1.0
Net official flows	n.a.	0.7	0.3	0.1	0.0	0.1	(0.4)	3.1	3.0	(0.6)	(0.1)	0.6
Other Asia												
Total private capital inflows (net)	(0.6)	0.9	(0.9)	2.8	3.5	3.8	4.0	2.2	(0.6)	(0.8)	0.3	1.3
Bank loans and other debt (net)	(0.6)	0.1	(1.3)	0.3	(0.7)	(0.3)	(0.0)	(1.5)	(3.1)	(2.0)	(1.3)	(0.9)
Portfolio investment (net)	(0.4)	(0.2)	1.8	(0.8)	0.1	(0.7)	(0.8)	(1.1)	(0.6)	(0.8)	(0.5)	(0.4)
Foreign direct investment (net)	0.4	1.0	3.0	4.3	4.1	4.8	4.8	4.8	3.1	2.1	2.2	3.1
Net official flows	n.a.	0.8	0.9	0.9	1.1	0.7	0.4	(0.0)	0.5	0.3	0.2	0.6

Latin America

Total private capital inflows (net)	1.2	2.0	4.3	5.4	3.1	2.4	4.4	4.2	3.2	2.2	2.8	3.2
Bank loans and other debt (net)	(0.9)	(0.2)	0.9	(0.9)	(2.5)	0.7	0.1	(0.1)	(0.8)	(0.4)	(0.2)	(0.4)
Portfolio investment (net)	1.5	1.2	2.3	5.3	3.9	0.1	2.1	1.9	1.5	0.6	1.1	2.0
Foreign direct investment (net)	0.6	1.0	1.1	1.0	1.6	1.6	2.1	2.4	2.5	2.0	1.9	1.6
Net official flows	0.2	0.2	(0.1)	0.0	(0.2)	1.3	(0.8)	(0.4)	0.2	0.2	(0.0)	0.1

Africa

Total private capital inflows (net)	1.1	2.3	1.8	2.3	1.2	1.7	1.9	3.9	2.4	2.6	4.0	2.3
Bank loans and other debt (net)	1.2	2.2	1.5	1.5	0.2	0.3	0.6	1.4	0.0	0.2	1.0	0.9
Portfolio investment (net)	(0.4)	(0.4)	(0.2)	0.3	0.2	0.4	(0.0)	0.7	0.8	0.5	1.0	0.3
Foreign direct investment (net)	0.3	0.5	0.4	0.5	0.9	1.1	1.4	1.8	1.6	1.9	1.9	1.1
Net official flows	1.8	2.4	3.1	2.2	3.5	2.9	0.0	(1.1)	0.5	1.1	(0.8)	1.4

Middle East

Total private capital inflows (net)	2.7	18.5	7.8	6.5	4.2	1.1	(0.7)	1.5	4.5	3.4	2.1	4.7
Bank loans and other debt (net)	1.5	12.9	4.9	1.4	0.6	(1.4)	(1.9)	0.4	1.9	1.4	(0.9)	1.9
Portfolio investment (net)	0.9	5.6	2.8	4.3	2.9	1.9	0.8	0.6	2.2	1.3	1.2	2.2
Foreign direct investment (net)	0.2	0.1	0.0	0.8	0.7	0.6	0.4	0.5	0.4	0.7	1.8	0.6
Net official flows	(0.5)	1.0	(0.3)	0.5	(0.4)	(0.3)	(0.2)	(0.2)	(0.2)	(0.3)	(0.4)	(0.1)

Europe

Total private capital inflows (net)	0.0	(1.2)	0.6	2.3	1.4	4.4	2.3	3.1	1.5	1.8	2.4	1.9
Bank loans and other debt (net)	(0.1)	(1.5)	0.0	0.6	(1.1)	1.4	1.2	(0.2)	(0.5)	(0.8)	(0.2)	(0.3)
Portfolio investment (net)	0.0	0.0	0.2	1.1	2.0	1.7	2.2	1.8	0.4	0.8	0.7	1.0
Foreign direct investment (net)	0.0	0.2	0.4	0.6	0.5	1.3	1.2	1.5	1.5	1.8	1.9	1.0
Net official flows	0.0	0.7	0.3	(0.1)	(0.9)	(0.8)	(0.2)	0.7	0.9	0.2	0.1	0.1

n.a. = not available

a. IMF estimates.
b. The G-10 countries (actually 11 countries) supply most, but not all, of private and capital flows. The G-10 countries are Belgium, Canada, France, Germany, Italy, Japan, the Netherlands, Sweden, Switzerland, the United Kingdom, and the United States.
c. Emerging markets represent the rest of the world other than industrial countries. Industrial countries here include the G-10, Western Europe, Australia, and New Zealand.
d. Indonesia, Malaysia, South Korea, the Philippines, and Thailand.

Note: GDP is expressed in dollars at market exchange rates (current prices).

Sources: IMF, International Capital Market, Developments, Prospects, and Key Policy Issues, September 1999. IMF, *World Economic Outlook*, various issues. World Bank, *World Tables*, various issues.

The low rate for Asia and the Pacific mirrors negative private-capital outflows between 1997 and 2000 in the wake of the Asian crisis. If bank operations and portfolio investment are ignored, it is instructive to examine FDI flows relative to GDP for the decade as a whole. Asia and the Pacific was the clear winner (2.2 percent), followed by Latin America. The Middle East was the least-favored region for direct investment.

Categories of Capital

The dominant modes of finance to emerging markets have changed. Bond finance was very popular in the 1920s (until the Great Depression), whereas syndicated bank loans were popular in the 1970s (until the Mexican debt crisis in 1982). FDI became an important vehicle in the late 1980s and 1990s. During this period, an unprecedented volume of equity capital flowed to emerging markets through the auspices of institutional investors (Eichengreen and Fishlow 1996). The portfolio investment flows recorded in table 1.3 represent a mixture of equity and bonds; in recent history, bonds have been about 60 percent of portfolio investment and equity about 40 percent (see box 1.1 table), but the proportions differ from year to year and region to region.

Bonds and interbank loans have increasingly replaced syndicated bank loans as debt vehicles (table A.8 in appendix A). At the receiving end, private-sector debtors in the emerging markets have outpaced sovereign debtors (Frankel and Roubini 2000).[13] Sovereign debtors borrow both from private-capital sources and from official institutions such as the World Bank and IMF. Flow figures during the 1990s portray the declining role of official finance: Net official flows to emerging markets amounted to only one-seventh of net private flows—$200 billion versus $1,400 billion (table 1.2). But for some regions (especially Africa) and in some crisis years (especially 1997 and 1998 in the crisis countries), official flows were significant.[14]

Econometric evidence, although limited, suggests that the pro-growth benefits of portfolio equity and FDI are substantially higher than the benefits of bank loans and portfolio bonds. (The evidence is discussed later in this chapter.) The question, as Hausmann and Fernandez-Arias put it,[15] is whether a valid distinction can be made between "good cholesterol" and "bad cholesterol," and between "safe" and "unsafe" foreign capital. Having flagged this question for later exploration, we return

---

13. Private-sector borrowers grew from 19 percent of all emerging-economy borrowing in the decade 1980-89 to 53 percent in 1990-98, whereas public-sector borrowing correspondingly contracted (Mussa and Richards 1999, 8).

14. These same relationships emerge in the IIF data in appendix A.

Box 1.1   G-10 Portfolio Investment Assets in Emerging Markets

Evolving financial innovation and liberalization of financial markets increased portfolio investment flows in the 1980s and 1990s. However, the statistical measurement of certain portfolio flows (e.g., financial derivatives) is still in its infancy. At the end of 1993, global net transactions in portfolio investment showed an imbalance of $220 billion: measured assets were $220 billion smaller than measured liabilities.

To improve the statistical picture, the IMF set up a task force in October 1994. The first results of the IMF *Coordinated Portfolio Investment Survey* (CPIS, 29 countries) (IMF 1999a) came out in 1999. The CPIS encompassed equity and debt securities and disaggregated debt securities by bonds and notes, money market instruments, and financial derivatives.

The total value of portfolio investment assets around the world reached $6,074 billion at the end of 1997: $2,562 billion in the form of equity securities; $3,409 billion long-term debt securities; $98 billion short-term debt securities; and $4 billion financial derivatives. The table below illustrates the portfolio holdings of G-10 countries (excluding Germany and Switzerland).

As of 1997, most portfolio investment from the G-10 countries was placed in other industrial countries, with around 20 percent placed in emerging markets. Equity securities accounted for 43 percent ($370 billion out of $860 billion) of the total portfolio stock in emerging economies, based on available data from the G-10 countries. Long-term debt securities (long-term bonds and notes) was 47 percent of the total, and short-term debt securities (money market instruments) accounted for about 10 percent.

The share of emerging markets in G-10 portfolio investment stocks placed abroad, at end—December 1997 (billions of dollars)

Selected G-10 Investors	Bel-gium	Canada	France	Italy	Japan	Nether-lands	Sweden	United Kingdom	United States	Total
Equity securities	65	106	100	75	159	127	52	462	1,197	2,343
Share in emerging markets (percent)	2	14	11	9	9	9	4	12	21	16
Long-term debt securities	87	18	206	172	712	115	17	483	543	2,353
Share in emerging markets (percent)	8	19	12	42	18	4	2	16	50	23
Short-term debt securities	11	5	n.a.	10	31	n.a.	3	27	n.a.	87
Share in emerging markets (percent)	5	14	n.a.	19	27	n.a.	2	25	n.a.	22

n.a. = not available

Sources: IMF (1999a, 1999g).

to the datapresented in our tables, organized according to traditional categories.

Foreign Assets Relative to GDP

Looking at asset stocks, in 1970, combined debt and foreign direct investment placed in emerging economies amounted to about 21 percent of their combined GDP (table 1.4). By 2000, the figure reached 58 percent of combined GDP. In comparison with the combined GDP of the G-10, assets placed in emerging economies amounted to 19 percent of GDP in 2000.

Between 1970 and 2000, the components of the total stock of debt shifted dramatically (table 1.4). In relation to emerging-economy GDP, long- and medium-term debt grew four times, from 7.5 to 32.2 percent. Short-term debt stock, however, has remained at about 5 percent of emerging-economy GDP. Foreign direct investment grew about three times, from 7.0 to 21.1 percent. What these figures say is that short-term debt, the hottest of hot money, has shrunk relative to longer-term debt and FDI. Nevertheless, short-term debt can still create troublesome waves. The conventional story, illustrated by recent events, is told in box 1.2.

Much of so-called medium- and long-term debt has short-term characteristics, in substance if not in form. Loans that were originally medium- or long-term become short-term as they age. Loan conditions may enable a nervous lending bank to accelerate principal payments. These features tend to color medium- and long-term debt with the same volatility characteristics as short-term debt.

Aging Populations in the OECD Countries

An inescapable demographic feature of the United States, Europe, and Japan during the next generation is their aging populations. By 2030, 33 percent of Americans age 15 years and above will qualify as senior citizens—as older than age 65. The figures for other industrial countries are more worrisome: Germany, 40 percent; France, 40 percent; Italy, 48 percent; the United Kingdom, 37 percent; and Japan, 44 percent.[16] The prospective burden of aging populations is so severe that OECD countries

---

15. Two papers by the same authors examine these questions: Hausmann and Fernandez-Arias (2000) and Fernandez-Arias and Hausmann (2000).

16. Group of Ten (1998). For a short account, see *Washington Post*, 26 April 2000, 1.

Table 1.4 Total foreign capital stock in emerging markets

Capital stock	1970	1980	1990	2000[a]	1970	1980	1990	2000[a]
	(billions of dollars at current prices)				(percent of GDP of emerging markets)			
Foreign capital stock	176	770	2,164	4,937	22.1	26.3	45.6	72.6
Long- and medium-term debt stock	60	457	1,203	2,192	7.5	15.6	25.3	32.2
Official	33	182	630	977	4.1	6.2	13.3	14.4
Private	28	275	573	1,215	3.5	9.4	12.1	17.9
Share of official debt (percent)	54	40	52	45				
Share of private debt (percent)	46	60	48	55				
Short-term debt stock[b]	50[b]	147	241	352	6.3	5.0	5.1	5.2
Portfolio investment stock	10[c]	60[c]	364	959	1.3	2.0	7.7	14.1
FDI inward stock	56[d]	106	356	1,434	7.0	3.6	7.5	21.1

					(percent of GDP of G-10)			
Foreign capital stock					8.8	10.9	14.4	23.2
Long- and medium-term debt stock					3.0	6.4	8.0	10.3
Official					1.6	2.6	4.2	4.6
Private					1.4	3.9	3.8	5.7
Short-term debt stock					2.5	2.1	1.6	1.7
Portfolio investment stock[b]					0.5	0.8	2.4	4.5
FDI inward stock					2.8	1.5	2.4	6.8

Memorandum:[e]								
GDP of emerging markets	797	2,927	4,747	6,798				
GDP of G-10	1,999	7,093	14,997	21,208				

	High scenario[f]			Low scenario[g]		
Capital stock	2010	2020	2030	2010	2020	2030
	(billions of dollars at 2000 prices)					
Foreign capital stock	7,300	12,700	21,800	7,000	10,500	15,400
Bank loans and trade credits	2,500	3,000	3,500	2,200	2,400	2,600
Portfolio and FDI	4,800	9,700	18,300	4,800	8,100	12,800
	(percent of GDP of emerging markets)					
Foreign capital stock	73.0	84.7	99.1	70.0	70.0	70.0
Bank loans and trade credits	25.0	20.0	15.9	22.0	16.0	11.8
Portfolio and FDI	48.0	64.7	83.2	48.0	54.0	58.2
	(percent of GDP of G-10)					
Foreign capital stock	28.1	36.3	49.5	26.9	30.0	35.0
Bank loans and trade credits	9.6	8.6	8.0	8.5	6.9	5.9
Portfolio and FDI	18.5	27.7	41.6	18.5	23.1	29.1
Memorandum:						
GDP of emerging markets[h]	10,000	15,000	22,000	10,000	15,000	22,000
GDP of G-10	26,000	35,000	44,000	26,000	35,000	44,000

(table continues next page)

Table 1.4   Total debt stock and FDI stock in emerging markets (continued)

Capital stock	1970	1980	1990	2000[a]	1970	1980	1990	2000[a]
	(billions of dollars at current prices)				(percent of GDP)			
Africa								
Long- and medium-term debt stock[c]	6	62	168	191	10.0	24.4	57.9	52.2
Official	4	27	116	146	6.9	10.8	39.9	39.8
Private	2	34	52	46	3.1	13.6	18.0	12.4
Share of official debt (percent)	69	44	69	76				
Share of private debt (percent)	31	56	31	24				
Short-term debt stock	8[d]	23	28	50	12.8	8.9	9.6	13.5
FDI inward stock	1[f]	11	36	92	1.6	4.5	12.2	25.1
Memorandum: GDP[g]	62	253	291	366				
Middle East								
Long- and medium-term debt stock[c]	4	63	138	179	9.3	13.7	29.1	28.4
Official	3	32	82	114	6.9	7.1	17.2	18.1
Private	1	30	57	65	2.4	6.6	11.9	10.3
Share of official debt (percent)	74	52	59	64				
Share of private debt (percent)	26	48	41	36				
Short-term debt stock	7[d]	21	44	37	15.5	4.6	9.2	5.9
FDI inward stock	n.a.[f]	13	48	59	n.a.	2.9	10.1	9.3
Memorandum: GDP[g]	45	456	475	629				
Asia								
Long- and medium-term debt stock[c]	18	86	318	713	6.3	13.2	23.5	30.4
Official	14	55	202	337	5.0	8.6	14.9	14.3
Private	4	30	117	376	1.3	4.7	8.6	16.0
Share of official debt (percent)	79	65	63	47				
Share of private debt (percent)	21	35	37	53				
Short-term debt stock	6[d]	17	51	71	2.2	2.6	3.8	3.0
FDI inward stock	22[f]	32	140	715	7.9	5.0	10.4	30.5
Memorandum: GDP[g]	278	648	1,353	2,348				
Europe								
Long- and medium-term debt stock[c]	4	58	180	416	0.7	7.3	12.1	33.7
Official	3	21	66	171	0.5	2.6	4.5	13.9
Private	1	38	114	245	0.2	4.7	7.7	19.8
Share of official debt (percent)	68	35	37	41				
Share of private debt (percent)	32	65	63	59				
Short-term debt stock	6[d]	17	41	78	1.1	2.1	2.8	6.4
FDI inward stock	0[f]	0	3	142	0.0	0.0	0.2	11.5
Memorandum: GDP[g]	568	804	1,480	1,234				

(table continues next page)

Table 1.4 (continued)

Capital stock	1970	1980	1990	2000ᵃ	1970	1980	1990	2000ᵃ
	(billions of dollars at current prices)				(percent of GDP)			
Latin America								
Long- and medium-term								
debt stockᶜ	28	189	398	694	16.2	25.5	34.6	31.2
Official	8	46	165	209	4.8	6.3	14.3	9.4
Private	20	142	234	485	11.4	19.2	20.3	21.8
Share of official debt								
(percent)	30	25	41	30				
Share of private debt								
(percent)	70	75	59	70				
Short-term debt stock	23ᵈ	69	77	119	13.5	9.3	6.7	5.3
FDI inward stock	18ᶠ	48	126	486	10.5	6.5	11.0	21.9
Memorandum: GDPᵍ	171	740	1,149	2,220				

n.a. = not available

a. For 2000, figures are extrapolated from table 1.2 (flow table). For long-term and medium-term private debt stock, net portfolio investment flows for 2000 are added to the 1999 stock figure to obtain the 2000 stock figure. For short-term debt stock, net bank loans (flow) for 2000 are added to the 1999 stock figure to obtain the 2000 figure.

b. Short-term debt stock for all emerging markets is arbitrarily estimated at $50 billion in 1970, reflecting the surge in short-term petrodollar loans during 1970s, especially to Latin America. The total figure was then apportioned between regions according to its share in 1980.

c. Figures are arbitrarily assumed by authors.

d. FDI stock figures for 1970 are estimated by subtracting average inflows of FDI to each region.

e. GDP figures are evaluated at market exchange rates.

f. In the high scenario, net-net capital flows from industrial countries (mainly G-10 countries) to emerging markets are projected to rise gradually from about 1 percent of G-10 GDP in 2000 to 3 percent in 2030. Underlying the projected rise is our assumption that household savings rates in G-10 countries will rise (mainly through private pension funds), while the demand for physical capital will fall. The capital stock projections in table 1.4 are generated by the capital flow assumptions in table 1.1. In our projections, Bank loans and trade credits are limited to a small portion of total capital flows for two reasons: (1) we assume that regulators adopt a more cautious stance, for the reasons argued in this book; (2) in any event, we think banks will become more risk averse. Portfolio investment (equity and bonds) plus FDI flows are calculated as a residual between total capital flows and bank loans and credit.

g. In the low scenario, net-net capital flows are derived from the assumption that the foreign-owned capital stock in the emerging-markets remains a fixed 70 percent of emerging market GDP (table 1.4). Bank loans and trade credits are limited to a small share of total capital flows for the reasons already given. Portfolio and FDI are calculated as a residual.

h. The GDP of emerging markets is projected to grow at 4 percent per year in real terms.

Notes: The G-10 is made up of 11 industrial countries (Belgium, Canada, France, Germany, Italy, Japan, the Netherlands, Sweden, Switzerland, the United Kingdom, and the United States). GDP of the G-10 is projected to grow at 2.5 percent per year in real terms.

Sources: UNCTAD, *World Investment Report*, 1995, 1997. World Bank, *Global Development Finance*, 1998, 1999, 2000.

Box 1.2 Short-term Capital Flows

In conventional analysis, short-term capital flows (mainly short-term bank loans) are the most readily reversible capital flows, hence quickest to react to panic in a crisis. Did short-term capital flows play a role in the recent Asian, Russian, and Brazilian crises? A recent study by the World Bank (2000a, chap. 4) reinforces the conventional analysis.

- Short-term lending by international banks increased rapidly in the run-up period, despite a falling share of international bank lending in total private-capital flows to emerging markets.
- G-10 policy measures, such as capital adequacy regulations, favored shorter-term lending by banks, and international rescue efforts gave precedence to short-term bank claims.
- Short-term bank lending to emerging markets is procyclical with respect to economic expansion and contraction, especially with respect to adverse shocks.
- A country whose ratio of short-term debt to central bank reserves significantly exceed unity appeared vulnerable to financial crisis, more so if it ran a significant current account deficit and had an overvalued currency.

When the Bank for International Settlements' definition of short-term debt is applied (the BIS uses remaining maturity, whereas the World Bank uses the original maturity to classify short-term debt), short-term debt grew nearly 160 percent in the 1990s, from $176 billion (1990) to $454 billion (1997). In East Asia, the ratio of short-term debt to reserves increased from 124 percent (1990) to 214 percent (1997). The rising share of short-term flows reflected private borrowing, channeled though interbank lending. This shift toward short-term financing in emerging markets took place against a backdrop of a falling share of bank lending to emerging markets relative to other kinds of capital flows. Foreign direct investment and portfolio investment grew sharply in the 1990s.

are likely to welcome many more immigrants than they do today. Even so, within a generation, the aging OECD countries will either need to boost their savings rates and build funded retirement systems, or compel younger workers to pay remarkably high payroll taxes. Payroll taxes to pay retirement benefits are already 12 percent in the United States, 18 percent in France, 21 percent in Germany, and 28 percent in Italy. If the OECD countries coast on policy autopilot, these tax rates will need to increase by 50 percent during the next 30 years to pay for annual retirement benefits in the year 2030.[17]

Pension Prudence

If the industrial countries are prudent—both in private and public behavior—they will aggressively pre-fund their pension systems to pay the costs of an aging society (Peterson 1999, chap. 4). Econometric analysis

---

17. These illustrative figures say nothing about the costs of medical care for the elderly. On that sobering subject, see Peterson (1999).

by Higgins (1998) casts a gloomy pall over the prospects for prudent pension behavior. Higgins finds that a high ratio of persons over 60 in a society strongly predicts lower national savings. His coefficients suggest that the average savings rate as a share of GDP in OECD countries will drop by 5.8 percentage points between the 1985-89 level and 2025, simply because of aging populations.

On this important dimension, we are unwilling to buy into a gloomy prognosis. We think private and public attitudes toward pension funding are dramatically changing in all OECD countries.[18] We think there is a reasonable prospect that OECD countries will heed leaders like Peter G. Peterson (1999) and accumulate large financial balances in their private and public pension plans—balances that can be drawn down as retirement costs mount.

Physical Capital Demands

Meanwhile, it seems very likely that aging societies will have a reduced demand for physical capital—less new infrastructure, fewer new homes and office buildings. Higgins (1998) suggests that the average investment rate as a share of GDP in OECD countries will fall by 7.5 percentage points between the 1985-89 level and 2025. If the prospective savings and investment rates projected by Higgins are combined, the collective current account balances of OECD would rise by 1.7 percentage points between the 1985-89 level and 2025. In other words, according to the demographic evidence assembled by Higgins, OECD countries taken together may increase their current account balance with the rest of the world from a negative 0.4 percent of GDP (1985-89 average) to a positive 1.3 percent of GDP.[19]

Current Account Forecast

We think the collective current account surplus of OECD countries with the rest of the world rise will be somewhat larger than 1.3 percent of GDP, perhaps 1 or 2 percentage points higher, because we hold a more

---

18. The National Bureau of Economic Research (NBER) has already published, and has in progress, several books drawn from conferences on social security and retirement systems. NBER research illuminates concrete changes that can be made to encourage pension prudence. See, e.g., Gruber and Wise (1999, 2001).

19. The 1985-89 average current account balance for all OECD countries (negative 0.4 percent) is taken from OECD (2000, annex table 52). The current account surplus figure of 1.3 percent in 2025 is calculated by adding Higgins's estimate of a 1.7-percentage-point rise in the current account balance to the 1985-89 current account deficit of 0.4 percent. Note that Higgins projects a collective OECD current account surplus of 2.8 percent in 2010 before the onset of serious aging in the OECD countries (2.8 percent is calculated by adding his estimate of a 3.2 percentage-point rise to the 1985-89 current account deficit).

optimistic view about pension funding. Although we cannot forecast the political dynamics that will shape pension debates in the G-10 countries, a few statistical observations are worthwhile. Among the G-10 nations, the United Kingdom has most aggressively encouraged funded private pensions (and, starting with Prime Minister Margaret Thatcher, has aggressively discouraged sole reliance on the pay-as-you-go state system). In 2004, as a consequence, British pensions will hold approximately $2 trillion in pension assets, approximately 115 percent of projected GDP. In the same year, the United States will hold $10 trillion, about 90 percent of projected GDP, whereas Japan will hold $2 trillion, about 40 percent of projected GDP.[20]

On average, the other G-10 countries have more disappointing pension funds: In 2004, their total will reach $2.4 trillion, about 30 percent of GDP. If all G-10 countries acquired the current pension virtues of the United Kingdom by 2030 (115 percent of GDP), G-10 pensions together would total about $50 trillion (in 2000 prices) by 2030. The bold forecasts in table 1.4 (discussed just below) imply that a substantial fraction of those pension assets (perhaps a fifth, or $10 trillion), would be invested directly and indirectly in emerging markets. This whole arithmetic depends, of course, on a revolutionary change in public attitudes toward pension funding.

The combination of more prudent retirement systems and reduced demand for physical capital in the OECD countries could push down rates of return and energize the search for investment opportunities in emerging markets. As emerging economies embrace market principles, they are becoming more attractive places to invest. Together, the push and pull forces could raise the annual net private capital outflows from OECD countries to the emerging markets. Instead of 1 percent of G-10 GDP, private-capital outflows might reach 3 percent in 2030. This would mean annual inflow rates approaching 6 percent of emerging-market GDP. Foreign-owned debt and FDI could reach 100 percent of emerging-market GDP and 50 percent of G-10 GDP. These are large magnitudes. Only half these amounts would have enormous policy consequences.

Portfolio Diversification

Contrary to our optimism, OECD countries may not practice pension prudence. If attitudes toward savings stay where they now are, OECD countries will not significantly increase their collective *net* capital flows to emerging markets. However, portfolio *diversification* by itself could lead to substantial *gross* investment in emerging markets by OECD asset holders, offset by *gross* investment in the other direction by emerging-market asset holders. Up to now, foreign assets have roughly balanced foreign liabilities for most OECD nations (Kraay et al. 2000). This story could persist: Large

---

20. The pension figures are from *The Economist*, 20 May 2000, 127. The original source is InterSec Research.

gross investments in both directions between the emerging markets and OECD countries, and much smaller net investments. By itself, gross investment in both directions could bring substantial benefits, particularly to residents of emerging economies, who would have access to a wider range of investment opportunities.

What would be the magnitude of G-10 investments in emerging markets in a portfolio-diversification scenario? The projections in table 1.4 suggest that the combined GDP of all G-10 countries will be about 67 percent of the world total in 2030 (against 76 percent in 2000), whereas the combined GDP of emerging markets will be about 33 percent (against 24 percent). For portfolio-diversification reasons alone, G-10 investors should at least maintain the current ratio of their emerging-economy assets to emerging-economy GDP.[21] Under this conservative assumption, gross assets in emerging economies would then amount to about 36 percent of G-10 GDP, against 23 percent in 2000 (table 1.4). Meanwhile, asset holders in the emerging markets could be acquiring comparable stakes in the G-10. At the level of national arithmetic, *net* holdings could be modest in both directions, but cross-border gross holdings could be enormous. Sudden shifts in gross holdings could drive financial manias and panics just as easily as sudden shifts in net holdings.

Heroic Forecasts

Our speculations are expressed as heroic forecasts in tables 1.1 and 1.4. We give a high and a low scenario for the placement of capital flows and stocks by OECD nations in emerging markets. Before turning to these scenarios, we must emphasize that the vast majority of international capital will continue to represent flows *between* OECD countries. Most international capital, in whatever form, will flow from one rich country to another. In this book, we focus on capital flows to emerging markets, but we do not want to convey the misleading impression that these flows will become the centerpiece of the international capital-markets story.

High and Low Scenarios

The high scenario in tables 1.1 and 1.4 assumes that OECD nations increase their annual net-net capital flows to emerging markets from roughly 1 percent of OECD GDP to 3 percent. (Recall that net-net flows are defined as net of repaid and repatriated capital, and net of interest and

---

21. Ahearne, Griever, and Warnock (2000) observe that foreign equities accounted for only about 2 percent of equity portfolios held by US residents in the late 1980s, but the share rose to about 10 percent in the late 1990s. On the basis of a cross-country analysis of foreign equities in US portfolios, the authors conclude that information barriers are an important reason for the "home country bias" of investment portfolios. These barriers, which retard investment in emerging markets, should fall sharply in the next 30 years.

dividends.) The capital stock figures are calculated by cumulating the annual capital flows. The low scenario assumes that OECD countries just maintain the present ratio of their capital stock to emerging-economy GDP, for portfolio diversification reasons. Annual capital flow figures are calculated so as to maintain this ratio.

In both the high and low scenarios, emerging-market residents are accumulating assets in the OECD countries (as well as in each other). We do not attempt to forecast the magnitude of these holdings. In the low scenario, however, emerging-market residents would hold assets in OECD countries nearly the size of converse holdings. In the high scenario, emerging-market residents would hold far fewer assets in the OECD countries than holdings the other way.

If our guesses are roughly right, in the high scenario net-net flows would reach $1.3 trillion annually in 30 years (at 2000 prices), and industrial countries would hold an investment stock of more than $20 trillion in emerging economies. In the low scenario, net-net flows would approach $700 billion annually, and the investment stock would be about $15 trillion. In both scenarios, after 2030, the inflows might reverse, and assets held in emerging markets might diminish, as older generations in the OECD nations draw down their savings, and as younger generations in emerging markets acquire financial assets.

Bank Flows

The forecasts in table 1.4 project that, in dollar terms, net bank flows to emerging markets will grow much more slowly than either portfolio investment (equity and bonds) or FDI. The compositional magnitudes embodied in these forecasts are influenced by our normative analysis in chapters 2 and 3. We think there is a strong normative case against net bank flows growing as fast as other capital flows to emerging markets. Hence, we forecast that prudential regulation, both in the G-10 countries and the emerging markets, will slow the tide of bank debt, even if G-10 banks are once again willing to lend on a large scale.[22] In the future, G-10 banks will more and more play the role of efficient allocators of bank deposits and other funds *within* emerging economies, and also of facilitators of portfolio investment and FDI from OECD countries *to* emerging economies.

Institutional Reforms

Dramatic institutional reforms would necessarily precede capital inflows and foreign ownership on the scale and composition we have

---

22. Cline (2000), among others, observes that the Asian crisis diminished the appetite of G-10 banks for net lending to emerging markets. More lending is being done through syndicated loans and bonds.

envisaged, in both the high and low scenarios. We emphasize four critical changes:

- A world where high-quality financial standards are the norm, not the exception;

- A world where the economic principles now at work in such economies as Taiwan and Hong Kong, and such countries as Mexico, and Chile, become commonplace throughout the emerging markets;

- A world of free trade and investment, where flows of goods and services are far larger (relative to GDP) than the figures observed today;

- Finally, a world where private prudence and public incentives ensure that the bulk of capital flows take the form of portfolio investment and FDI, rather than bank lending.

In this book, our core concern is the design of appropriate measures addressed to the last condition. The goal is to attenuate financial shocks in an environment of much larger capital flows to emerging economies. With that goal in mind, we continue our tour of the benefits associated with international investment.

Spreading Technology

Multinational enterprises (MNEs), through foreign direct investment, move major sums of capital around the world. At the same time, and equally important, they spread technology along with capital. As table 1.4 indicates, FDI stocks in emerging markets amounted to $1.4 trillion in 2000, nearly 30 percent of the total foreign capital stock in these countries. Although $1.4 trillion is considerable, MNE activities raise two puzzles. First, why do MNEs exist on a substantial scale? Why does international capital not predominately move through financial markets, as it did in the 19th century? The answer to the first puzzle raises a second: Why is *so little* of the world's FDI placed in emerging markets?

Two Puzzles

Hymer (1976), of course, answered the first puzzle. Markets are highly imperfect for firm-specific technology. In principle, well-managed local firms, drawing on their home-court advantage, should be able to squeeze higher returns out of good technology than distant firms grounded in unfamiliar cultures. But successful foreign firms are reluctant to license their technology to local firms. Foreign firms have a hard time teaching local firms the management lore of a successful operation. Licensing arrangements are not only immensely cumbersome, but their value to prospective local buyers is often less than their value to potential foreign sellers: The foreign seller thinks it is surrendering the crown jewels; the local buyer wonders what it is buying. For these reasons, successful firms exploit their proprietary technology on a global basis by launching operations abroad rather than licensing. Hence, large-scale MNE operations are practically synonymous with globalization.[23]

Hymer's answer poses the second puzzle. If FDI offers the magic carpet for conveying technology to developing countries, why do they not have more of it? In 2000, the world stock of FDI amounted to about $5 trillion, but less than 30 percent was placed in the emerging markets, although they account for more than 80 percent of the world's population (tables 1.5 and 1.6; UNCTAD 1999). To be sure, the share of world FDI in emerging markets approximately equals their share in world GDP. But simpleminded arithmetic suggests that MNEs should earn far higher profit rates by operating in emerging markets than in OECD countries. After all, *if* similar technology can be operated anywhere in the world, and countries trade freely with one another, the returns to capital should be far higher in the country with abundant labor and lower wage rates—the developing country, not the OECD country. This reasoning suggests that we should observe a lopsided extent of FDI activity in emerging markets. We do not.

Consider the example of a representative manufacturing enterprise.[24] In the United States, purchased inputs may be 40 percent of the cost structure; wages, salaries, and fringe benefits may be 35 percent; depreciation charges may be 10 percent; and returns to capital (interest plus profits) may be 15 percent. If the capital-output ratio is 1.5, interest plus profits will work out to a 10 percent return on capital. Suppose the wage and salary rate in Mexico is one-third the US level. Also suppose that, thanks to the North American Free Trade Agreement, free trade prevails between the United States and Mexico, and the product in question fetches the same price in both countries (the Law of One Price operates).[25]

If the same enterprise could operate with exactly the same technology in Mexico, and *if* it could purchase the required inputs at the same overall cost—two big ifs—the return to capital from operating in Mexico would be much higher than the 10 percent US figure. Two-thirds of the US

---

23. For rounded accounts of forces driving multinational firms, see Dunning (1988) and Vernon (1998).

24. See Lucas (1990) for sophisticated calculations, using a neoclassical production function, of the high implied profit rates in emerging markets, consistent with the assumption of equivalent technology between rich and poor countries.

25. Hufbauer, Wada, and Warren (2001) summarize the literature, and present fresh evidence, showing that the Law of One Price is an exception in the world economy today.

Table 1.5 FDI-associated production, 1983-98 (percentages)

Year	Value added of all foreign affiliates as percent of world GDP^a	Exports of all foreign affiliates as percent of world exports^b	Export propensity of foreign affiliates as percent of sales^c	FDI stock in emerging markets as percent of total FDI stock
1983	5.0	27.7	23.7	
1984	5.1	31.5	25.8	
1985	5.2	31.9	27.5	30.3
1986	5.5	28.6	24.4	
1987	4.3	25.6	21.0	
1988	5.7	26.9	21.3	
1989	6.2	26.3	19.8	
1990	6.4	27.5	22.1	21.0
1991	6.2	22.7	19.3	
1992	5.8	26.6	23.3	
1993	5.7	27.7	21.4	
1994	6.1	28.3	22.0	
1995	6.3	32.3	23.5	27.6
1996	6.8	28.2	19.6	
1997	6.9	30.3	20.9	
1998	7.0	35.6	20.5	29.8

FDI = foreign direct investment

a. Worldwide value added is estimated assuming that the value added by non-US foreign affiliates bears the same relation to non-US FDI stock as the relation between value added and US FDI stock.
b. Worldwide exports are based on the worldwide exports of foreign affiliates of Japan and US MNEs and their share of the worldwide inward FDI stock. In calculating the exports of Japanese affiliates, exports by wholesale affiliates are excluded to avoid double counting.
c. Share of exports of foreign affiliates in total sales of foreign affiliates.

Source: Adapted from United Nations, *World Investment Report*, 1998, 6; 1999, 9.

labor cost (assumed to be 35 percent of overall costs) would be shifted into the capital earnings column in the Mexican enterprise. The overall return to capital would rise to 25 percent in Mexico, relative to 10 percent in the United States.[26]

Where Is the "Giant Sucking Sound?"

If this hypothetical US-Mexican example accurately described current world conditions, and if rates of return to capital were truly that high in emerging economies, the world would be deafened by Perot's "giant sucking sound"

---

26. The hypothetical 25 percent return to capital in Mexico is calculated as follows: The US capital-share figure is 15 percent of enterprise revenues. Hypothetically add two-thirds of the 35 percent of revenues that, in the United States, are paid to wages. The total share of revenues paid to capital in Mexico would then be 38 percent. Divided by a capital-output ratio of 1.5, the hypothetical return to capital in Mexico is 25 percent.

Table 1.6 FDI inward stock per capita, 1997

Region or group	FDI inward stock (billions of dollars)	Population (millions)	FDI stock per capita (dollars)
World	3,437	5,820	591
Industrial countries	2,312	927	2,494
G-10	1,921	723	2,658
European Union	1,230	373	3,296
Austria	18	8	2,230
Belgium and Luxembourg	143	11	13,516
Denmark	25	5	4735
Finland	9	5	1751
France	141	59	2,406
Germany	209	82	2,547
Greece	21	11	1,996
Ireland	17	4	4,645
Italy	81	58	1,408
Netherlands	127	16	8,141
Portugal	18	10	1,837
Spain	101	39	2,569
Sweden	42	9	4,746
United Kingdom	276	58	4,742
North America	819	298	2,747
United States	681	268	2,542
Canada	138	30	4,556
Others	263	256	1,029
Japan	27	126	214
Australia	101	19	5,454
New Zealand	32	4	8,511
Emerging-market economies	1,056	4,893	216
Africa	68	775	88
Middle East	43	117	368
Asia	581	3,032	191
Five affected countries[a]	136	401	338
Others	445	2,631	169
Europe	78	474	165
Latin America	346	494	700

FDI = foreign direct investment
G-10 = Group of Ten countries; see table 1.1 note for definition.

a. Indonesia, Malaysia, South Korea, the Philippines, and Thailand.

Sources: UNCTAD (1999); World Bank, World Development Indicators, 1999; IMF, International Financial Statistics, Yearbook, 1999.

(Perot and Choate 1993, especially chap. 4). Firms everywhere would pull up stakes in high-wage Japan, Europe, and the United States, and flock to Brazil, China, Mexico, Poland, and Turkey. But it is no easy matter for firms to replicate successful operations in emerging markets. There are various reasons why they do not. And these reasons explain why MNE activity is concentrated in the rich OECD countries.

It is not easy for a firm to transfer its in-house technology to an emerging economy with less skilled technical and managerial personnel. Moreover, effective protection of intellectual property is often lacking in emerging economies. And the firm may have a hard time purchasing the vast array of inputs it needs to operate—everything from specialized telecommunications to high-purity chemicals—at the same cost and with the same prompt delivery.

Hence the bulk of FDI represents cross-investment within the OECD family. Lipsey (2000) has calculated the relationship between annual FDI outflows and annual FDI inflows for industrial countries during the period 1970-95. The coefficient of FDI outflows on FDI inflows is 0.868 (meaning $86.8 million of outflows for every $100 million of inflows), with a high level of significance. This is a statistical way of describing a persistent fact: The vast bulk of FDI represents investment by one rich country in another rich country.

Gravity Models of FDI

Measured in terms of FDI stock per capita, densities in OECD countries are multiples of the densities found in emerging markets (table 1.6). Equations that analyze the location of FDI, using pooled data from *both* industrial and emerging countries, show that the size of host-country GDP, and the level of GDP per capita, are the strongest attracting forces (UNCTAD 1998, annex to chap. 4; Hausmann and Fernandez-Arias 2000).[27] The more open the economy (measured by the relation between merchandise trade and GDP), the larger the stock and flows of inward FDI (Lane and Milesi-Ferretti 2000; Lipsey 2000; Hausmann and Fernandez-Arias 2000). Adding these forces together, and making general observations about industrial and emerging economies pooled together, most

---

27. However, when economies are divided into two groups, industrial and developing, economic size and per capita income are no longer significant. For estimates that *separately* analyze industrial and developing countries, see Lane and Milesi-Ferretti (2000). These authors do not find statistically significant coefficients for GDP size or GDP per capita in explaining inward FDI stocks *within* each group. Lipsey (2000) examines inward FDI stocks and flows for industrial countries *relative* to GDP. Even though FDI stocks and flows increase with national GDP, they do not increase percent for percent. Hence, his observed coefficients for GDP size are negative. Hausmann and Fernandez-Arias (2000) likewise normalize FDI inflows by GDP and find a small negative coefficient for GDP size (pooling both industrial and developing countries).

FDI goes to big, high-income, open countries—another way of saying that most FDI circulates within the OECD family.[28]

FDI and Development

This picture is changing at the margin. The annual FDI flow figures for 1997 and 1998 combined (table 1.7) show that about 32 percent of US FDI, about 37 percent of Japanese FDI, and about 20 percent of European FDI went to emerging markets. New FDI dollars are directed to emerging economies to a greater extent than the average for old FDI dollars. There are two big reasons why an even larger share of FDI will be invested in the emerging markets in the future. First, investment climates are getting better as market principles spread. Second, new technology decidedly favors fragmentation of production, snipping the "value-added chain" into smaller parts, and locating the parts where the combination of cost and productivity is highest. JP Morgan, for example, is spending $300 million to locate all its Asian back-office operations in Bangalore, India.[29] Multiply the example a thousand times, and that is the future of FDI.

No one should claim that FDI offers a magic bullet for development.[30] Indeed, Hausmann and Fernandez-Arias (2000) argue that a high FDI stock relative to total *private*-capital liabilities in an emerging economy indicates an unhappy economic environment. When an emerging economy exhibits macroeconomic stability, open trade policies, and strong property rights, private firms have greater access to foreign bank credit and portfolio capital. Rather than being good cholesterol, FDI simply represents the most readily available form of external finance for private firms in "bad countries."

Challenging this thesis, Smarzynska and Wei (2000) and Wei (2000) find that FDI is negatively affected by the extent of corruption. Wei (2000) contends that a high ratio of bank loans to FDI reflects poor governance, not the reverse. Moreover, Lane and Milesi-Ferretti (2000) point out that

---

28. The same general observations can be made about portfolio investment. But in a pooled regression with both industrial and developing countries, portfolio investment and bank loans exhibit much stronger income, size, and openness coefficients than FDI (Hausmann and Fernandez-Arias 2000). Moreover, when countries are divided into two groups (industrial countries and emerging markets), the estimated coefficients are very different for variables that explain inward FDI stocks and inward portfolio investment stocks (Lane and Milesi-Ferretti 2000, tables 5a, 5b, 6a, 6b).

29. Oral interview, Daniel Zelikow, managing director, JP Morgan, 16 May 2000.

30. McKinnon (1973) sounded an early cautionary note on FDI, warning that trade and financial repression in emerging markets could create lucrative opportunities for multinational corporations—in contexts where the private returns to foreign investment substantially exceeded the social returns. Of course, the policy environment in most emerging markets has vastly changed since the 1970s, and price signals are now much better matched with social returns.

Table 1.7 Net FDI flows to emerging markets, 1990-98 (billions of dollars)

Flows	1990 United States	1990 Japan	1990 European Union-13[a]	1991 United States	1991 Japan	1991 European Union-13[a]	1992 United States	1992 Japan	1992 European Union-13[a]
All countries	31.0	56.9	129.2	32.7	41.6	110.4	42.6	34.1	105.2
All emerging markets	13.5	11.6	21.5	11.4	10.7	21.6	19.3	10.4	22.0
Africa	(0.5)	0.6	0.5	0.1	0.7	1.2	(0.1)	0.2	1.2
Middle East	0.5	0.0	0.6	0.5	0.1	0.9	0.8	0.7	0.3
Asia Pacific	2.9	7.1	1.4	3.3	5.9	2.4	4.9	6.4	2.9
China	0.0	0.3	0.0	0.0	0.6	0.2	0.1	1.1	0.2
India	n.a.	0.0	0.1	0.1	0.0	0.0	0.1	0.1	(0.0)
Asian 5[e]	1.7	3.5	0.4	1.1	3.3	1.1	1.2	3.4	1.4
Europe	n.a.	0.0	0.2	0.2	0.1	0.8	0.2	0.0	1.1
Russia	n.a.	n.a.	n.a.	n.a.	n.a.	0.0	0.0	0.0	0.1
Latin America	10.1	3.6	6.4	7.2	3.3	3.4	12.8	2.7	5.5
Argentina	0.4	0.2	0.2	0.4	0.0	0.3	0.6	0.0	0.4
Brazil	0.9	0.6	0.6	0.9	0.2	0.5	2.1	0.5	0.7
Mexico	1.9	0.2	0.3	2.3	0.2	0.1	1.3	0.1	0.4

Flows	1993 United States	1993 Japan	1993 European Union-13[a]	1994 United States	1994 Japan	1994 European Union-13[a]	1995 United States	1995 Japan	1995 European Union-13[a]
All countries	78.2	36.0	91.4	73.3	41.1	114.6	92.1	52.7	156.1
All emerging markets	26.2	10.9	19.4	30.8	15.6	35.6	23.4	17.3	19.5
Africa	0.8	0.5	1.5	0.8	0.3	0.8	0.4	0.4	2.1
Middle East	0.8	0.2	0.3	0.7	0.3	0.4	0.9	0.2	0.8
Asia Pacific	5.7	6.6	4.7	10.3	9.7	5.9	5.7	12.7	6.7
China	0.6	1.7	0.2	1.2	2.6	0.7	0.3	4.6	0.9
India	0.1	0.0	0.3	0.3	0.1	0.3	0.2	0.1	0.4
Asian 5[e]	1.8	2.6	1.6	4.1	4.3	2.5	3.6	4.7	2.2
Europe	0.7	0.2	1.2	1.2	0.1	1.4	0.4	0.0	1.7
Russia	0.2	0.0	0.1	0.1	0.0	0.4	0.5	0.0	0.4
Latin America	16.9	3.4	3.5	17.7	5.8	8.4	16.0	4.0	7.3
Argentina	1.1	0.0	0.4	1.5	0.0	0.9	2.0	0.1	1.4
Brazil	3.3	0.4	0.3	3.3	1.2	1.4	7.0	0.3	1.9
Mexico	2.5	0.1	0.1	4.5	0.6	0.4	3.0	0.2	1.0

(table continues next page)

Table 1.7 Net FDI flows to emerging markets, 1990-98 (billions of dollars) (continued)

Flows	1996			1997			1998			Average absolute year-to-year deviation		
	United States	Japan	European Union-13[a]	United States	Japan[b]	European Union-13[a,c]	United States	Japan	European Union-13[a]	United States	Japan	European Union-13[a]
All countries	74.8	49.7	148.0	114.5	54.7	175.4	18.3	7.0	19.7	16.9	8.0	41.3
All emerging markets	29.9	17.5	39.5	42.9	21.9	47.4	6.9	1.8	9.0	7.5	2.7	10.2
Africa	0.7	0.2	3.3	3.8	0.3	4.0	0.8	0.2	0.7	0.8	0.2	1.0
Middle East	0.5	0.2	0.3	1.1	0.5	0.6	0.2	0.2	0.3	0.3	0.3	0.5
Asia Pacific	8.9	12.0	9.5	11.8	12.4	9.0	2.6	1.3	1.2	2.8	1.8	1.6
China	0.9	2.6	1.9	1.2	2.0	1.9	0.4	1.0	0.3	0.4	1.0	0.3
India	0.3	0.2	0.5	0.4	0.4	0.5	0.1	0.1	0.1	0.1	0.1	0.1
Asian 5[d]	3.6	5.6	(2.5)	2.1	6.2	3.0	0.8	0.7	1.8	0.7	0.9	2.3
Europe	1.6	0.2	2.3	1.7	0.2	3.7	0.5	0.1	0.5	0.6	0.1	0.1
Russia	n.a.	0.0	0.6	n.a.	0.0	0.7	0.2	0.0	0.1	0.2	0.0	0.3
Latin America	16.1	4.6	13.7	23.8	6.4	20.4	3.3	1.2	3.7	3.6	1.0	4.5
Argentina	0.0	0.0	1.2	1.8	0.1	2.6	0.8	0.1	0.4	0.8	0.1	0.5
Brazil	3.8	0.9	3.9	6.5	1.2	4.9	1.7	0.5	0.7	1.8	0.5	2.1
Mexico	2.7	0.1	0.6	5.9	0.3	1.7	1.4	0.2	0.4	1.6	0.2	0.7

n.a. = not available

a. EU-15 except for Ireland and Greece.
b. For Japan's 1997 FDI flows, data from the Japanese Ministry of Finance is used.
c. For the United Kingdom and the Netherlands, due to lack of data, we assume that 1997 flows are the same as 1996 flows.
d. Indonesia, South Korea, Malaysia, the Philippines, and Thailand.

Sources: OECD, International Direct Investment Statistics Yearbook, 1998; Statistics, Ministry of Finance of Japan, http://www.mof.go.jp.

official external liabilities are a very large share of total external liabilities in "bad countries." They argue that the ratio of official external liabilities to total external liabilities provides a more accurate indicator of poor economic health than capital ratios involving FDI.

Whatever the relationship between FDI and national virtue, "bad countries" cannot pray their way to a state of grace. They need specific policies. Pro-investment policies—reduced corruption, better FDI incentives, and fewer FDI restrictions—are all useful tools (Wei 2000). Direct investment brings new technology to domestic production and better access to foreign markets. Borensztein, De Gregorio, and Lee (1998) demonstrate that the combination of more FDI and higher schooling levels makes a statistically significant contribution to per capita GDP growth. This finding is reproduced by UNCTAD (1999, annex to chap. 11). Moreover, when direct investment is combined with the cross-border integration of fragmented value-added chains, the gains can be large. Moran (2001) cites the example of the Mexican automotive industry. Even though its output accounts for only 3 percent of Mexican GDP, the gains from integrated FDI and free trade could reach 0.9 percent of Mexican GDP.

Never mind the debates in the 1960s and 1970s, multinational enterprises became welcome guests in the 1990s. From the vantage of emerging economies, the biggest problem with FDI is that there is not enough of it. The good news is that, in 2030, emerging economies will enjoy much more FDI than they have today. Currently, the FDI stock per capita in the industrial world is about $2,500, whereas the stock per capita in emerging economies is about $220 (table 1.6). By 2030, the FDI stock per capita in emerging countries might reach $1,500 (in 2000 dollars). Already, the FDI stock in emerging countries is about 20 percent of GDP (table 1.4). Under our high scenario (table 1.4), that ratio could approach 40 percent in 30 years (assuming that FDI and portfolio equity stocks are about the same size).

Building Financial Institutions

International capital can help build better financial institutions, and thereby create more efficient capital markets. During the 20th century, numerous countries grew out of poverty through the brute force of capital accumulation. Communist countries were the first to practice this strategy on a grand scale. After the Second World War, Europe was reconstructed with massive investment, Japan pursued the same strategy, and other Asian countries followed in Japan's wake. Before the 1980s, when the socialist model ran into severe problems of weak incentives and excessive corruption, the USSR and Eastern Europe had good growth rates, driven by heavy capital spending. During a longer period, Japan and South Korea proved to be the most successful practitioners of this style.

Inefficient Capital Markets

Solow's (1956, 1957) pioneering work showed the limitations of brute capital accumulation. Technology contributes more to economic growth than sheer investment. Hollis Chenery and his World Bank colleagues (1986) confirmed these limitations in developing countries. Many countries had high investment rates but poor growth rates. This was true in Brazil, Eastern Europe, India, and the USSR. In the 1990s, the malaise of high investment and low growth spread to more countries in Asia, Europe, and Latin America. Although each country had unique characteristics, the common theme was inefficient capital markets.

"Inefficiency" can be grouped into two large categories: too much capital flowing to some sponsors, too little to others. Scarce capital may be wasted on public show projects; overbuilding of offices and hotels; or white-elephant industries (steel, autos, aircraft, petrochemicals, etc.). Wasteful uses are often associated with government-directed investment, credit assessments based on sponsorship and asset values rather than cash flows, and negative real interest rates paid to bank depositors.

At the same time, there may be a shortage of funding for new enterprises and smaller firms. For example, in a bank-dominated system with limited competition, if the local bank says no, the venture is limited to its internal funds. When securities markets are run in a traditional fashion, with listing hurdles and tough restrictions on pension funds, access may not be much better.

Later in this chapter, we survey the overwhelming evidence that financial development augments economic growth. Ross Levine has pioneered the modern analysis.[31] Here a simple illustration will suffice. A country with inefficient capital markets may require 150 units of investment, accompanied by other inputs, to produce 100 units of additional output. By contrast, a country with efficient capital markets may require 100 units of investment or less. The difference in investment efficiency could readily translate into the difference between a 10 percent return on investment and a 15 percent return. During a period of years, that difference in returns could easily diminish economic growth.[32]

Rx for Capital-Market Inefficiency

The remedies for capital-market inefficiency entail privatization of public enterprises; modern banking, insurance, and pension systems; flourishing

---

31. See the numerous works under Levine in the references, and the discussion later in this chapter.

32. Illustrating this possibility, Pomerleano and Zhang (1999) find evidence that the return on invested capital seldom exceeded its opportunity cost throughout much of Asia in the early 1990s.

stock and bond markets; and markets for corporate control. These remedies are easy to enumerate and hard to accomplish.[33] They require a massive shift of power toward professional regulators, trained managers, and the rule of law—and away from politicians, well-connected families, and the exercise of discretion.[34] They also require enormous technical expertise. International capital can nudge a country toward a managerial or legal style, but more concretely, it can provide the technical expertise that underpins efficient capital markets. Commercial banks, investment banks, insurance firms, accounting firms, and others bring an array of experience when they establish a presence in a new environment.

Mexico's banking system illustrates the transition. For decades, Mexican banks have been synonymous with connected-lending, nonperforming loans, and public bailouts. The system is now consolidating toward five large banks, most of them foreign owned.[35]

Evidence from various sources suggests that the transition to a "good" financial system, exemplified by Mexico, is worthwhile. (Foreign domination is not essential to create a good system.) In the period 1980-95, for example, Levine (2000) estimates that the difference between the "good" Chilean financial system, on the one hand, and the "bad" systems operating in Peru and Argentina, on the other, penalized the bad countries with about 1 percent of GDP growth annually.[36] Dobson and Jacquet (1998, table 1.1) estimate that the benefits of phased liberalization to users of financial services residing in low- and middle-income countries would amount to about 1 percent of GDP in 2010.

The proposition that financial development and openness contribute to growth (examined in more detail below) argues for capital account liberalization. But just as trade liberalization is phased to smooth adjustment, so should capital account liberalization be sequenced to ensure

---

33. By today's standards, even US capital markets were relatively inefficient 20 years ago. See *Wall Street Journal* (Money-Go-Round, 1 February 2000, A1) for an account of the dramatic change in the structure of US capital markets in the 1990s.

34. The market for corporate control is particularly sensitive. Various techniques, tolerated or even encouraged by public policy, are commonly used to discourage hostile takeovers. Among them are cross-shareholdings between affiliated corporations, extra voting rights for shares held by the control group, various kinds of poison pills, bankruptcy systems that barely work, and government veto on mergers and acquisitions. Many of these are reminiscent of feudal laws that worked to thwart transactions in real property.

35. *The Economist* (1 April 2000, 70). In the most recent takeover, Banco Bilbao Vizcaya Argentaria (Spain) announced it would acquire control of Bancomer, Mexico's second largest bank.

36. Barth, Caprio, and Levine (2000) do not find a significant relationship between the costs of a banking crisis (expressed as a percentage of GDP) and the ratio of bank assets to equity market capitalization. This result reinforces Levine's (2000) prescription that what matters most for financial development is a strong legal system, not the distinction between bank-based finance and capital-market finance.

adequate managerial and regulatory skills (Johnston and Sundararajan 1999). And just as trade flows are sometimes interrupted to cope with industrial stress, so must capital flows be occasionally interrupted to cope with economic crisis.[37]

Manias and Panics

Critics of international capital during the era of European expansion were not foremost concerned with manias and panics. They were outraged by predatory practices. In the colonial era, when European capital traveled overseas, it was too often associated with plunder, slavery, and opium. As Hernán Cortés was reported to have told the envoys of Montezuma, "I and my colleagues suffer from a disease of the heart that be cured only with gold."[38] Between the mid-15th and mid-19th centuries, 12 million Africans were shipped to the New World.[39] The opium war of 1840-42, and the ensuing Treaty of Nanjing, enabled British merchants to sell Indian opium and other wares through the five "treaty ports" of China. It also confirmed the United Kingdom's perpetual claim on Hong Kong.

By the end of the 19th century, these atrocities were fading, but a new source of criticism emerged. Building on Marx and Engels (1959; originally published 1867-94), as well as Hobson (1902), Lenin (1939; originally published 1917) characterized international capital as the propagator of imperialism. The colonial rush to Africa in the second half of the 19th century informed Lenin's analysis. The flavor of Lenin's appraisal, if not the specifics, influenced commentators for 50 years. The imperialist critique, however, shifted from a diplomatic story to a commercial story. In the 1950s and 1960s, multinational firms were often equated with enclaves isolated from the rest of the economy and monopolies that appropriated economic rents.[40]

Apart from these citations, we pass over the predatory capital debate. It is now ancient history. By the mid-1970s, most Europeans and even the French were inviting US multinationals. By the mid-1980s, developing countries were putting out a warm welcome, and with the fall of the Berlin Wall, Eastern Europe and the former Soviet Union joined the courting game.

In the 1980s and 1990s, concern shifted to a different aspect of international capital: bank lending and portfolio investment (see table 1.8).

---

37. For a comparison of shock responses in the trading and financial systems, see Hufbauer and Wada (1999a).

38. Quoted in *The Economist*, 31 December 1999, 55.

39. *The Economist*, 31 December 1999, 69.

40. Baran and Sweezy (1966) authored the leading critique. Lall and Streeten (1977) wrote a less strident analysis.

Table 1.8 Net bank lending to emerging markets, 1994-98 (official estimates, billions of dollars at current prices)

	1994				1995				1996			
Lending	United States	Canada	Japan	EU 13[a]	United States	Canada	Japan	EU 13[a]	United States	Canada	Japan	EU 13[a]
All countries	6.1	n.a.	8.5	59.6	9.1	2.3	16.2	20.4	26.1	3.1	4.1	65.6
All emerging markets	8.3	n.a.	12.1	60.0	7.8	2.2	18.0	16.9	23.4	2.3	5.7	54.2
Africa	0.7	n.a.	0.4	10.8	0.7	0.2	0.4	(1.7)	0.5	(0.0)	0.5	(2.3)
Middle East	(0.8)	n.a.	(1.2)	6.8	(0.7)	0.1	(1.6)	(4.9)	0.2	0.0	(0.8)	(1.2)
Asia and Pacific	2.7	n.a.	20.6	28.2	6.0	1.5	19.6	19.4	8.4	1.8	5.7	34.8
China	0.2	n.a.	1.2	5.8	0.7	0.1	3.5	2.7	1.0	0.3	0.2	5.6
India	0.5	n.a.	(0.4)	3.4	0.4	0.1	(0.4)	(1.6)	(0.1)	0.1	(0.1)	1.4
Asian 5[c]	1.9	n.a.	18.4	13.8	4.4	0.9	18.6	14.3	7.0	1.2	6.1	26.3
Europe	0.9	n.a.	(2.6)	0.3	1.3	0.0	(1.0)	4.8	5.6	(0.0)	(0.8)	6.0
Russia	0.3	n.a.	(0.9)	2.4	0.1	0.0	(1.0)	2.8	4.9	0.0	(0.6)	(0.3)
Latin America	4.8	n.a.	(5.1)	13.9	0.4	0.4	0.7	(0.7)	8.6	0.5	1.1	17.0
Argentina	0.2	n.a.	(0.5)	4.9	1.3	0.3	0.0	(0.6)	2.0	0.4	0.1	4.5
Brazil	2.0	n.a.	(4.7)	(0.3)	3.1	0.1	0.4	2.3	4.0	(0.3)	0.4	4.3
Mexico	2.9	n.a.	0.4	4.4	(4.3)	(0.2)	0.4	(4.4)	(0.4)	0.3	0.9	1.5

(table continues next page)

Table 1.8 Net bank lending to emerging markets, 1994-98 (official estimates, billions of dollars at current prices) (continued)

Lending	1997				1998				Average absolute year-to-year deviation			
	United States	Canada	Japan	EU-13[a]	United States	Canada	Japan	EU-13[a]	United States	Canada	Japan	EU-13[a]
All countries	(3.2)	9.0	(6.3)	108.6	(13.1)	(2.1)	(35.9)	42.7	14.8	5.9	14.9	48.3
All emerging markets	(4.5)	4.3	(4.4)	76.4	(15.7)	(0.8)	(29.6)	5.4	13.8	2.4	13.4	43.4
Africa	0.9	0.4	(0.7)	6.7	(1.7)	0.6	(0.9)	0.9	0.8	0.3	0.4	7.0
Middle East	1.3	0.1	0.6	(0.0)	0.6	0.2	0.5	7.6	0.7	0.1	0.6	6.0
Asia and Pacific	(4.8)	1.4	(3.8)	21.2	(9.2)	(1.7)	(28.8)	(25.8)	5.9	1.3	12.4	21.2
China	(0.2)	0.3	1.8	6.4	(0.6)	(0.5)	(4.5)	(3.2)	0.6	0.3	3.4	4.1
India	0.2	0.2	0.4	1.6	(0.1)	0.0	(0.5)	(0.9)	0.3	0.1	0.5	2.5
Asian 5[b]	(3.9)	0.5	(7.0)	9.1	(7.3)	(0.7)	(21.9)	(19.0)	4.8	0.7	10.2	14.4
Europe	1.2	0.1	0.2	9.0	(4.1)	(0.0)	(0.2)	10.9	3.6	0.1	0.8	2.7
Russia	2.2	0.1	0.1	5.0	(5.3)	(0.0)	0.2	0.1	3.8	0.0	0.3	3.4
Latin America	(3.1)	2.3	(0.7)	39.5	(1.3)	0.2	(0.2)	11.8	6.5	1.4	2.1	20.6
Argentina	(2.7)	0.5	(0.2)	16.8	0.7	1.1	0.4	(0.2)	2.5	0.3	0.4	9.9
Brazil	(2.6)	0.1	(0.2)	8.4	(3.1)	(0.8)	(0.8)	4.9	2.3	0.5	1.6	3.0
Mexico	(0.8)	0.4	(0.7)	3.8	1.5	(0.0)	(0.0)	2.2	3.5	0.3	0.7	4.6

n.a. = not available
EU = European Union.

a. EU-15 except for Portugal and Greece.
b. Indonesia, Malaysia, the Philippines, South Korea, and Thailand.

Source: Bank for International Settlements, Semi-Annual International Banking Statistics.

Nonfinancial corporations have a long history of shifting short-term funds from country to country and currency to currency, in search of lower taxes, better yields, and appreciating exchange rates.[41] But in the 1980s and 1990s, bank lending and portfolio flows came to dwarf the short-term funds moved from place to place by nonfinancial MNEs. Moreover, the explosion of derivative markets brought high-powered leverage to financial flows.

Crisis History

These developments set the stage for a new look at an old concern: manias and panics, driven or augmented by international capital. Using Kindleberger's count (including four recent episodes not covered in his 1996 edition), 46 world-class manias and panics have occurred since 1618.[42] Manias and panics can erupt in any asset market—tulips, shares, bonds, property, and money itself.[43] By contrast with many of the early episodes, recent world-class manias and panics have involved an admixture of securities, property, and currency markets.[44]

Many financial crises never rise to the level of world-class panics. The majority of crises are either small, or they ensnare small countries. Between 1970 and 1998, 64 banking crises and 79 currency crises afflicted various countries (some countries were hit more than once, and some were simultaneously hit by banking and currency crises).[45] Only a handful of these episodes were part of world-class panics.

How deeply implicated are international capital flows—either in world-class manias and panics, or in smaller scale crises? Taking the long view, and focusing only on world-class events, the international dimension of manias and panics, if not international capital flows per se, has gained prominence. During the three centuries from 1600 to 1900, only 7 of the 31 episodes identified by Kindleberger had significant international dimensions. In the 20th century, international dimensions characterized 9

---

41. See, e.g., Bergsten, Horst, and Moran (1978) and Caves (1996).

42. If purely national episodes were recorded, the total count would be much larger. For example, the IMF has identified 143 banking and currency crises between 1970 and 1998 (IMF 1999e).

43. One of the earliest asset booms involving money itself revolved around the German thaler in the 17th century (Kindleberger 1996). Large exchange rate misalignments are today's expression.

44. In Kindleberger's list (augmented by our additions), 6 of the 45 world class episodes involved security, property, and currency admixtures: 3 in the 19th century and 3 in the 20th. The 3 admixture episodes in the 20th century were the Latin American debt crisis of the 1980s, the Mexican crisis of 1994-95, and the Asia-Russia-Brazil crisis of 1997-99.

45. See Hufbauer and Wada (1999b, table 3).

of 15 episodes. A global economy means that booms and busts are more likely to spill across national borders. Apart from the world-class manias and panics that drew Kindleberger's attention, many of the smaller financial crises, involving one or two countries, may have an international banking or portfolio dimension. Indeed, because international capital flows have blossomed since 1970, their contribution to local crises has probably expanded, often intertwined with local mismanagement.

The Cost of GDP Volatility

Whether small-scale or world-class, financial volatility enlarges GDP volatility. If that were the end of the story, financial shocks would be a matter of regret, but they might be accepted as a necessary growing pain in a capitalist system. However, evidence assembled by Ramey and Ramey (1995), and confirmed by Gavin (1997), persuasively demonstrates that higher GDP volatility is associated with substantially lower growth rates in GDP per capita.

Ramey and Ramey (1995) examined the growth experience between 1960 and 1985 of 92 countries. After controlling for the usual variables, they estimated a negative coefficient of 0.21 (with a standard error of 0.08) on the standard deviation of the annual growth rate. The mean standard deviation of annual growth rates in these 92 countries was 3.58 percent, and that degree of volatility was associated with a reduction of 0.8 percent in average annual growth for the period. The experiences of Mexico and other Latin American countries in the early 1990s, and Asia in the late 1990s, reinforce the proposition that volatility exacts a toll on growth.[46]

Balance Sheets and Momentum Investment

Manias and panics feed on the interaction of two forces: balance sheet values and momentum investment. Both forces can have an international component. Bank loans and bond issues are often extended on the basis of balance-sheet values—assets minus liabilities, both roughly assessed at current market prices. As share and property prices rise, they create stronger balance sheets—on a rough "mark-to-market" basis.[47] The result is more collateral that can support additional bank loans or bond

---

46. Gavin (1997) asserts that if Latin American volatility in the early 1990s had been no higher than industrial-country volatility, Latin American growth would have been 1 percentage point a year higher.

47. In mark-to-market accounting, a firm values both its assets and its liabilities at their current market values, not at their historic costs. The resulting difference between assets and liabilities provides a rough estimate of the firm's current equity value. When asset prices are rising fast, and the value of liabilities is stable, the estimated equity value will

issues. Firms with improved balance sheets draw on their new strength, take on more debt, and buy additional assets (Minsky 1982). International banks may loan directly to these firms. Most important, they may expand their credit lines wholesale to local financial houses, and bypass the time-consuming process of evaluating primary borrowers.

Portfolio holdings of bonds and equity can follow a similar trajectory. The initial rise in security prices might reflect improved fundamentals that raise prospective cash flows—the traditional manner of valuing investments. Rising share and bond prices enable wealthy individuals and institutions to leverage their holdings. The next rise of asset prices could be inspired by sheer momentum: These firms and individuals, aided by fresh liquidity, buy tomorrow because prices rose yesterday. Foreign portfolio investors may follow suit, some because they are conscious momentum investors, others because they index their holdings to market capitalization and thereby become inadvertent momentum investors. According to Harvey and Roper (1999), the total dollar capitalization of Asian markets tripled between 1990 and 1996, from $300 billion to $1.1 trillion. Part of the rise can plausibly be attributed to international momentum investors.[48]

Banks in a Crisis

When events sour, the stories are told in reverse—often at a faster pace. Balance sheets reach a threshold characterized as "weak," and financial institutions turn cold. Whatever the loan documents may say, a collapsing balance sheet transforms short-term bank loans—unwittingly and unwillingly—into long-term bonds and equity investments.[49] By definition, banks are leveraged custodians of liquidity. They perform an immensely valuable role by issuing liquid demand deposits and other short-term liabilities and acquiring longer-term, less liquid assets. But banks cannot hold large amounts of clearly illiquid investments and retain public confidence that depositors will be paid on demand. To avoid a liquidity crunch—or worse, insolvency—banks will abruptly cut credit lines and call loans when their borrowers get in trouble.

---

soar. Conversely, when asset prices are falling fast, or when liabilities are denominated in foreign currency and the exchange rate depreciates sharply, the estimated equity value will plunge. When bank lending is influenced by mark-to-market equity valuations, the availability of credit will fluctuate sharply with changes in asset and liability values.

48. See, e.g., the work of Kaminsky, Lyons, and Schmukler (2000). Reisen and von Maltzan (1999) find that when the rating agencies (Moody's, Standard & Poor's, and Fitch IBCA) change their assessment of emerging-economy bonds, that affects the price and yield. However, in the period 1989-97, they find that rating changes were not made sufficiently far in advance to moderate booms in emerging-economy bonds.

49. The formal transformation of short-term bank loans into long-term bonds or equity required years of negotiation in the debt crisis of the 1980s. See Cline (1995).

If corporate balance sheets were highly leveraged before the panic, only a small cushion separates the majority of firms from the perilous threshold defined by the line between a "strong" and a "weak" balance sheet. Even a large cushion will quickly disappear when local firms have borrowed heavily in dollars, euros, or yen and the local currency is then sharply devalued.

Beyond cutting credit decisions to firms in a troubled emerging-market country, bankers may withdraw funds from other countries in the same region, or other countries that share similar profile, but do not necessarily have adverse fundamentals. Below, we discuss the evidence for bank contagion.

Portfolio Investors in a Crisis

Is portfolio investment subject to similar swings and contagious influences? Institutional portfolio investors are generally not highly leveraged. Unlike banks, they face losses, but not insolvency, when the market turns. Hence they are not forced to sell shares and bonds in the same fashion that banks are forced to withdraw credit to troubled borrowers. Box 1.1 wrestles with the statistical problems encountered in measuring portfolio flows. The bottom line, summarized in the table at the foot of box 1.1, is that portfolio investors hold somewhat larger amounts of long-term debt securities than equity securities in emerging markets. Their holdings of short-term debt in emerging markets are very small. This profile reinforces the overall proposition that institutional investors, in contrast with banks, may be less likely to liquidate their position when crises strike emerging-market economies.

Not all portfolio institutions ride out financial storms. To the extent that institutional investors are momentum players, they will sell when a downtrend emerges, even though the urgency to sell is less. It is commonplace to assert that contagion and herding haunt stock exchanges—particularly among less knowledgeable investors during bear markets. In a careful study of stock trades by foreign portfolio investors in South Korea during the 1997-98 crisis, Kim and Wei (2000), for example, found that foreign institutions without branches in Korea were more likely to engage in herding than those with local branches.

Below, we examine the econometric evidence for contagion among portfolio investors. Here it is worth repeated the estimates gathered by Cline (2000) for the Asian and Russian crises. According to his figures, banks lost $60 billion, bondholders lost another $50 billion, and portfolio equity investors lost $240 billion—on a mark-to-market basis. Whereas banks called their loans, realizing moderate losses in the process, many portfolio investors held their investments, absorbing big paper losses in 1997 and 1998 on the way down, but substantially recouping in the 1999 recovery.[50]

---

50. Barth and Zhang (1999) confirm this account.

Hedge funds attracted enormous attention in the wake of the Asian crisis, because of high-profile accusations by Malaysian Prime Minister Mohamad bin Mahathir Mohammed and the near-collapse of the giant hedge fund Long Term Capital Management (LTCM).[51] Edwards (1999) and Eichengreen (1999a) tell the hedge fund saga. Hedge funds are high-risk, leveraged portfolio investment vehicles, catering to institutions and wealthy individuals.[52] Although their size and daily operations are closely guarded secrets, Edwards (1999) suggests that hedge funds in 1998 may have managed $200 billion in client-owned capital. With an average 2-to-1 leverage ratio, the total borrowed and client-owned capital under hedge fund control may have been about $600 billion.[53] This figure is modest in comparison with the $6.4 trillion controlled by the mutual fund industry in 1998 (table 2.4).

Hedge funds may have exacerbated the Asian crisis, although some incurred heavy losses (Blustein 2001 has good anecdotes). Eichengreen (1999a) is skeptical that hedge funds systematically made money on the Asian debacle. All in all, in terms of their influence of capital markets, hedge funds were probably second-string players. To quote Martin Baily and his colleagues (2000, 99): "The hot money in the recent crises came mostly from bank lending, not from hedge funds or other nonbank investments such as pension and mutual funds."

"Good Cholesterol" versus "Bad Cholesterol"

To summarize the story so far, international capital flows may contribute to national and regional manias and panics. Bank lending may be more prone to run than portfolio capital, because banks themselves are highly leveraged, and they are relying on the borrower's balance sheet to ensure repayment. These features lead to the cyclical extension and withdrawal of bank credit, as the probability of repayment rises and falls.

---

51. LTCM had an extraordinary 20-to-1 leverage ratio. When LTCM collapsed, the New York Federal Reserve strong-armed 16 of LTCM's creditor banks to put an additional capital of $3.6 billion in exchange for 90 percent of LTCM's equity.

52. In 1998, the number of hedge funds may have exceeded 3,000, in comparison with fewer than 1,000 at year-end 1992. However, the attrition rate for hedge funds between 1989 and 1996 was nearly 40 percent, and the average annual return of "surviving" funds was about 18 percent versus about 11 percent for "nonsurviving" funds (Edwards 1999).

53. Estimated on the basis of rough leverage ratios suggested by Edwards (1999) and Eichengreen (1999a): 12 percent of hedge funds may have leverage of more than 8 to 1, 55 percent may have leverage of 1 to 1, and 33 percent may have no leverage.

When portfolio managers act as momentum investors, they can have the same procyclical effect. But a portfolio manager who places funds in a country during a boom pays a premium for shares. Likewise, a portfolio manager who pulls funds during a bust absorbs a steep discount. Multinational corporations (aside from banks) have received practically no blame for booms and busts. Perhaps they get off too easily. But multinationals that build new plants or acquire nonfinancial assets abroad typically invest for the long haul. Project decisions are supposedly made on the basis of anticipated sales, dividends, and royalties over a period of years. Cyclical events should accordingly have little weight.[54]

Does the available evidence support these generalizations? Does it support the notion that bank lending tends to "fly away" in a crisis, whereas FDI is "bolted down?" Does it support the idea that portfolio investment is perched between the fly-away and bolted-down modes?

Econometric Evidence

Our review of the econometric literature starts with two skeptics, Sarno and Taylor (1999). Using sophisticated econometric techniques, they distinguished between permanent and temporary components in four types of private capital flows to nine Latin American and nine Asian developing countries during the period 1988-97. Their analysis confirmed that FDI is indeed bolted down—the permanent component absolutely dominates FDI flows. But surprisingly, they found that commercial bank credit displayed a permanent component that exceeded the temporary component. By contrast, portfolio bonds and equity flows seemed largely temporary and reversible. Sarno and Taylor explained the apparent permanence of bank credit as the outcome of bank efforts to learn the characteristics of debtor countries.[55]

Events subsequent to 1997 showed that the previous "permanence" of bank lending was illusory. A glance at tables A.1 and A.2 in appendix A reveals that bank credit collapsed after 1996, especially to Asia. Additional data in appendix A indicate that bank lending to emerging markets was anything but permanent in the second half of the 1990s.

Economists are quick to disdain anecdotal evidence, unless it sustains their prior beliefs. In this spirit, we commend the newly published volume

---

54. Econometric analysis (reported by UNCTAD 1998) shows only a weak connection between annual FDI flows and past GDP growth. Some multinationals may be caught up in boom fever, and they may put investment plans on hold when a crisis strikes, but they do not appear to be prime generators of manias and panics.

55. Sarno and Taylor (1999) include syndicated bank loans in bank credit, and syndicated loans are the most stable component, whereas interbank lending is the least stable. They also report that official flows have a large temporary component. This can be explained by the role of official flows in offsetting volatility in private flows. Also see table 1.2 above and the tables in appendix A.

by our colleague Paul Blustein (2001). He interviewed key actors in the Asian drama, both in government circles and financial markets. His anecdotes illustrate the exuberance of bankers in the early 1990s, and their flight when trouble brewed.

Warning Indicators

But we need not rely on anecdotes. Econometric research points to the volatile character of bank lending. Eichengreen and Rose (1997) were in the forefront of scholars stressing that short-term external debt increases the vulnerability of a nation's banking sector. Rodrik and Velasco (1999) later reported that when short-term foreign bank loans exceed reserves, the chances of a massive reversal of capital increase by a factor of 3.[56]

Comparing the Latin American debt crisis in the wake of Mexico's default in 1982 with the Latin American financial crisis of 1994-95, Gilibert and Steinherr in Goldstein et al. (1996) found more pluses than minuses in the shift from bank credit to capital markets.[57] In 1994-95, there was little danger of a bank "meltdown," and the rapid drop in Latin American share and bond prices accelerated adjustment.[58]

In their systematic study of early-warning indicators, Goldstein, Kaminsky, and Reinhart (2000) listed rising short-term capital inflows (i.e., predominantly interbank loans) as a harbinger of future disaster. The authors examined 87 currency crises and 29 banking crises in 25 emerging economies and small industrial nations during the period 1970-95. They analyzed 25 monthly and 9 annual indicators to discover country-specific thresholds where the signals flashed "crisis ahead!"[59]

Although the majority of signals have domestic origins, a few emanate from international capital flows—particularly bank operations. The three best monthly indicators of a currency crisis were an appreciating real exchange rate, a prior banking crisis, and a fall in stock prices. In turn, the best monthly indicators of a banking crisis were an appreciating real exchange rate, a fall in stock prices, and a rising M2 money multiplier (i.e., more bank credit). Appreciating real exchange rates are

---

56. Radelet and Sachs (1998) and Ito (1999) emphasize the same themes.

57. At year-end 1982, Latin America's external debt was $330 billion, of which $225 billion (68 percent) was bank credit (4 percent of the assets of G-7 banks), and only $66 billion (20 percent) was owed to nonbank creditors. In 1994, Latin America's external debt was $524 billion, of which $197 billion (40 percent) was owed to nonbank creditors (Gilibert and Steinherr 1996).

58. In 1994-95, portfolio losses on Latin American securities were widespread and had no adverse impact on US stock and bond markets—an outcome that was repeated in the Asia crisis of 1997-98 (Gilibert and Steinherr 1996).

59. The technique used by Goldstein, Kaminsky, and Reinhart to distinguish a good indicator of future crises from a bad indicator is the "noise-to-signal" ratio. This is basically the ratio of bad calls to total calls (Goldstein, Kaminsky, and Reinhart 2000, 32).

often associated with an inflow of foreign loans and portfolio investment.

Turning to annual indicators, Goldstein and his colleagues found that the best-performing signals for both currency and banking crises (but with differing noise-to-signal ratios) are rising short-term capital inflows (relative to GDP), a rising current account deficit (relative to investment and GDP), and a rising budget deficit (relative to GDP). Interestingly, a high ratio of FDI inflows to GDP has no value as a crisis predictor.

Goldstein and his colleagues did not include portfolio investment as a possible crisis indicator. However, studies by Taylor and Sarno (1997) and Chuhan, Claessens, and Mamingi (1998), using the same dataset, reached some interesting conclusions. These two sets of authors examined monthly US portfolio flows (bonds and equity) to nine Latin American and nine Asian countries between January 1988 and September 1992. They found significant coefficients on both "push" and "pull" factors.

The main push factor is the level of US interest rates—when rates are high, less capital goes to emerging-economy bond and equity markets. The main pull factors are the country's credit rating, the black-market premium on its exchange rate, the price-earnings ratio on shares, and the total return on equities relative to the US stock market. These push and pull factors can obviously reverse their sign within 6 months, imparting a fair degree of volatility to portfolio investment.

Contagious Banks and Investors

Another way of looking at the fly-away versus bolted-down characterization of different capital categories is to examine their proclivity to contagion. Briefly, there is substantial evidence that bank lending decisions within a region are contagious during a crisis; there is moderate evidence that portfolio investment decisions are contagious; and there is no evidence that FDI decisions are contagious.

After the Asian crisis, several analytic papers documented the "common banker" as a transmission mechanism for spreading financial contagion.[60] In a sophisticated analysis, Fratzscher (2000) analyzed quarterly data from 1989 to 1998 for 24 emerging markets. If two countries shared common bankers, financial pressure was significantly transmitted between them—regardless of their distinct fundamentals. Moreover, the estimated transmission coefficient rose sharply in periods when financial pressure turned into financial crisis.

Turning to portfolio investors, the evidence is mixed. Using monthly data for the period 1958-96, Longin and Solnik (2000) uncovered a tendency for the five largest equity markets (the United States, the United

---

60. Leading papers are by Van Rijckeghem and Weder (1999), Kaminsky and Reinhart (2000), and Caramazza, Ricci, and Salgado (2000). Typically, the common banker is a group of international banks based in the same city, e.g., Tokyo or New York.

Kingdom, France, Germany, and Japan) to exhibit extreme correlation during sharp bear markets, but not during sharp bull markets. Kaminsky, Lyons, and Schmukler (1999) likewise found that 13 US mutual funds dedicated to Latin American equities exhibited a stronger tendency toward contemporaneous momentum strategies (buying current winners and selling current losers) during crisis periods than during noncrisis periods.[61] Kim and Wei (2000) find that foreign portfolio investors with branches in Korea are less likely to engage in positive feedback trading than similar investors who do not have a Korean presence.

Forbes and Rigobon (1999) question some of the published studies that truly identify contagion among portfolio investors. They argue that the conventional measure of contagion—higher price correlation between stock prices—is biased. When volatility rises, the price correlation between two stock indexes will increase, even if there is no change in the underlying structural connection between the two markets.

By making an appropriate adjustment in the standard price correlation measure, Forbes and Rigobon found higher "comovement," but no contagion between stock prices in the 1997 East Asian crisis, the 1994 Mexican peso crisis, or the 1987 US stock market crash. Stulz (1999) is another skeptic. He claims that unadjusted share price correlation coefficients rose in the OECD bear market of 1973-74, when no one thought contagion was at work.[62]

The case is stronger for portfolio contagion at a regional than at a global level.[63] Froot, O'Connell, and Seasholes (1998) report statistical evidence of strong contagion *within* regions, using high-frequency data. Fratzscher (2000) finds evidence of contagion during crisis episodes between countries that exhibit more highly correlated share price movements in tranquil

---

61. Other studies on institutional investors with the same flavor include Brown, Goetzmann, and Park (1998), Eichengreen and Mathieson (1998), Kim and Wei (1999), and Frankel and Schmukler (1998). On a different but related aspect, Coppejans and Domowitz (2000) found that foreign equity ownership in emerging markets, *accompanied* by cross-listing (e.g., on the New York Stock Exchange), increases the variance of returns.

62. Evidence on the behavior of some investors also runs contrary to the contagion thesis. For example, Choe, Kho, and Stulz (1999) found that foreign portfolio investors were momentum *buyers* when the South Korean market was rising, but they were *not* momentum sellers during the crisis (the last 3 months of 1997). At the level of mutual fund investors, one study found that individuals decreased their net inflows to Mexican and Asian funds during the crises, but did not increase their net outflows (Froot, O'Connell, and Seasholes 1998). An earlier study by Sachs, Tornell, and Velasco (1996) argued that the 1994-95 "tequila crisis" had no lasting effect on Latin American countries with strong fundamentals.

63. Moreover, it should not be assumed that high *price* correlation between securities in different regions implies high correlation in capital flows. For example, it would be wrong to infer from the high price correlation, in late 1998, between plunging Russian debt values and soaring Brazilian Brady bond spreads that capital *flows* were highly correlated between Eastern Europe and Latin America.

times. In tranquil times, share price movements are more highly correlated within regions than between regions (Fratzscher 2000, table 3).

FDI: "Bolted Down"

Before Goldstein and his colleagues published their work on crisis warning indicators, Frankel and Rose (1996) had established that a *high* ratio of FDI inflows to external debt stock consistently decreased the likelihood of a currency crash. Their work was based on panel data for 100 developing countries between 1971 and 1992.

Fernandez-Arias and Hausmann (2000) extended the Frankel and Rose (1996) dataset to 1997, included several industrial countries, and used FDI stocks rather than FDI inflows as a crisis predictor. In their provocatively titled paper ("Is FDI a Safer Form of Financing?") Fernandez-Arias and Hausmann reach a conventional result, but offer an unconventional rationale. They contend that, although FDI stocks have a record of being bolted down by comparison with bank loans and portfolio investments, multinational companies can just as readily move liquid funds abroad in anticipation of a crisis. MNEs are not inherently virtuous.

Fernandez-Arias and Hausmann do not give much credence to the argument that MNE operations have long horizons. Nor do they emphasize the structural variables confirmed again and again by econometric analyses of FDI.[64] Instead, they argue that MNE operations are typically hedged in terms of currency and maturity risk, whereas bank loans are likely to be characterized by currency and maturity mismatch. Portfolio investment may embody some degree of mismatch. As a result of these characteristics, bank loans and portfolio investments exhibit a greater tendency to fly away when crisis brews.

Year-to-Year Deviations

The data on private-capital flows assembled in table 1.2 (IMF sources) and appendix A (IIF sources) can also be used to evaluate the fly-away and bolted-down characterizations. This evaluation is a good deal simpler than the econometric evidence reported above. It has the virtue of being easily understood, and the vice of less sophistication. Our analysis has no control variables to exclude extraneous influences on particular capital flow categories.

We use the annual data to calculate simple year-to-year deviations in capital flowing to emerging markets; from these deviations, we draw inferences about the stability of different types of flows. At the outset, it is important to emphasize that we are examining flows, not stocks. To

---

64. See, e.g., UNCTAD (1998), Lane and Milesi-Ferretti (2000), Lipsey (2000), and Hausmann and Fernandez-Arias (2000).

be precise, we are examining the volatility of flows, which is somewhat different than the question of whether capital stocks are permanent. On the basis of official IMF estimates (table 1.2), the average *absolute* year-to-year deviation of "bank loans and other debt (net)" to all emerging markets was $44 billion between 1990 and 2000. This figure includes bank loans, trade credits, and resident deposits. By contrast, on the basis of IIF estimates (table A.1), the average absolute year-to-year deviation of only bank loans and trade credits (excluding resident deposits) to all emerging markets was $35 billion. By inference, year-to-year swings in the bank deposits held by residents of emerging markets added about $10 billion annually to the overall volatility of bank operations.

The average absolute deviation of portfolio flows (bonds and equity) to all emerging markets was between $29 billion (IMF data, table 1.2) and $34 billion (IIF data, table A.1). The average absolute deviation of FDI was about $15 billion (both sources).

Relative Deviations

To put these absolute deviations in perspective, we calculate two relative magnitudes. The first relative deviation, labeled "own" in table 1.2 and the tables in appendix A, is the ratio between the average absolute deviation and the average annual flow of the particular category of capital (e.g., bank loans and other debt). The second relative deviation, labeled "total" in table 1.2 and the tables in appendix A, is the ratio between the average absolute deviation of the particular category of capital and the average absolute deviation of *total* private capital. Because the year-to-year changes in flows of particular categories offset each other, the sum of total relative deviations for all categories exceeds 100 percent.[65]

The own and total relative deviation of all bank operations (bank loans, trade credits, and resident deposits) in emerging markets exceeded 100 percent in the period 1990-2000 (table 1.2). Excluding resident deposits, the own relative deviation still exceeded 100 percent, but the total relative deviation dropped to 63 percent (table A.1). By contrast, the own relative deviation for portfolio investment was about 50 percent, whereas the total relative deviation was somewhat more than 60 percent (tables 1.2 and A.1). For FDI, the own relative deviation was about 18 percent,

---

65. A simple measure of offsetting changes in capital flows is the difference between the sum of total relative deviations and 100 percent. If the sum equals 100 percent, there are no offsetting tendencies. If the sum exceeds 100 percent by large margin, offsetting tendencies are stronger. For the three kinds of capital flows identified in table 1.2, the sum of total relative deviations is about 200 percent. In rough terms, this means about half the annual changes in one category of flows are offset by opposite annual changes in another category (or categories) of flows. But for individual regions, offsetting tendencies may be much weaker. For example, in the five affected Asian countries, the sum of total relative deviations was only 126 percent.

and the total relative deviation figure was about 30 percent (again, tables 1.2 and A.1).

From this overview of year-to-year changes in capital flows to all emerging markets, we deduce there is solid evidence that FDI flows are easily the most stable component. Bank operations are the least stable, but in terms of the absolute size of annual deviations, portfolio flows are a close second. An important reason why annual absolute deviations in portfolio flows loom large is that average annual portfolio flows are nearly three times the size of net new bank loans (table A.1).

Individual regions and components of bank operations (appendix A), and the experience in the second half of the 1990s, follow the same overall pattern (table 1.2 and appendix A). Own relative deviations for bank flows almost always exceed portfolio flows, sometimes by a large margin. Total relative deviations are similar (although bank flows generally exceed portfolio flows). FDI flows to all regions are very stable.

Contrary Results

In an earlier study that was based on quarterly capital flow data from the mid-1970s to 1992 for five industrial countries and five emerging markets, Claessens, Dooley, and Warner (1995) argued that there was no important difference in the time-series properties of FDI, portfolio equity, long-term debt, and short-term debt. All were equally volatile. Claessens and his colleagues concluded that the labels "short-term" and "long-term" convey no useful information. Their findings were challenged by Chuhan, Perez-Quiros, and Popper (1996), who examined quarterly capital flow data between 1985 and 1994.[66] In any event, both studies focused on events before the Asian crisis. We think the IMF data analyzed in table 1.2, buttressed by the IIF data analyzed in appendix A, reveal important differences in the volatility of different kinds of capital flows to emerging markets—especially when the turmoil of the late 1990s is factored into the evaluation.

How Bad Is International Volatility?

Earlier in this chapter, we remarked that financial volatility contributes to GDP volatility. We also presented evidence that larger fluctuations in GDP translate into slower GDP growth over an extended period. Obviously, to the extent year-to-year deviations in international capital flows contribute to financial volatility, those deviations are not helpful. No one

---

66. Chuhan, Perez-Quiros, and Popper (1996) tried out a model specification in which capital flows of one category (e.g., portfolio investment) were allowed to influence capital flows of another category (e.g., bank loans). They found that short-term flows were sensitive to other categories, but that FDI was not.

Table 1.9   Correlation between activity indicators and capital flows (first difference in capital flows versus annual percentage change in activity indicators, 1990-2000)

Type of capital flow (annual change)	Activity indicator (annual change)		
	Exchange rate[a]	Stock market indexes	Real GDP
Total private capital	(0.12)	0.24	0.01
Bank loans	(0.06)	0.15	(0.06)
Portfolio investment	(0.07)	0.16	0.03
Foreign direct investment	(0.14)	(0.04)	0.16
Official capital	0.02	(0.18)	0.03
Reserves	0.40*	0.13	(0.16)
Current account balance	0.42	(0.12)	(0.25)

* Indicates the coefficient is significant at the 95 percent or better level of confidence.

a. The exchange rate observations for Brazil (1990-94), Argentina (1990-91), and Mexico (1995) are excluded, because of hyperinflation conditions (see table A.6).

Note: This table is based on data in table 1.2 and table A.6.

asserts that rapidly shifting capital flows are good for emerging markets. The subtle question is how bad they might be.

Small Standard Deviations

Fernandez-Arias and Hausmann report (2000, table 1) that the standard deviation of total capital flows to emerging economies in the 1990s was only 1 percent of GDP.[67] It is not obvious that a swing of plus or minus 1 percent of GDP (the implied range for two-thirds of the country-years) would induce national mania or panic. The far less frequent, but far more ominous, 2-standard-deviation and 3-standard-deviation swings are the ones likely to bring turmoil.

Table 1.9 illuminates the influence of international financial flows on activity variables—exchange rates (local currency per US dollar), stock market indexes (expressed in dollar terms), and GDP growth rates. The interesting point is how small the correlation coefficients are, none of them significant. Judging from the signs of the coefficients, on average, private flows decrease during years of exchange rate depreciation and increase during years of appreciation—an expected association. Annual data are not sufficiently detailed to determine causation, but capital flows are probably driving exchange rates, rather than vice versa. Official flows rise with exchange rate depreciation and fall with appreciation, again as might be expected. Private-capital flows are positively associated with

67. For FDI, the standard deviation was 0.6 percent of GDP in the 1990s; for portfolio investment, 0.6 percent; and for bank loans, trade credits, and official finance together, 1.2 percent (Fernandez-Arias and Hausmann 2000).

real GDP changes. International capital flows of all kinds show little association with stock market indexes (expressed in dollars). There is only small surprise in the indicated association between the activity variables and the capital flow variables. The bigger surprise is that none of the coefficients is significant.

Whether national activity drives international capital, or vice versa, the correlation coefficients in table 1.9 are all fairly weak. These weak coefficients, in combination with the modest standard deviation of capital inflows, suggest that international capital volatility has been a secondary contributor to national financial volatility—at least so far.

Past Not Necessarily Prologue

But the past may not be prologue. Fernandez-Arias and Hausmann (2000) calculate that the coefficient of variation (the standard deviation divided by the mean) of total capital flows to developing countries was about 0.3 in the 1990s. If this relationship holds in the future, and if capital flows rise in line with our high scenario (table 1.1), the standard deviation of capital flows would increase from 1 percent of GDP in emerging markets to 2 percent. Moreover, if residents of emerging markets act like G-10 financial institutions, increasing their *outflows* from developing nations just when G-10 institutions are decreasing their *inflows* to developing nations, the fluctuations would be magnified. Even in our low scenario (table 1.1), these fluctuations could become a frequent source of crisis in the world economy.

Sizing Up Costs and Benefits

On the basis of this array of data, we reach three main conclusions about capital flows and emerging markets in the 1990s:

■ Fluctuations in bank operations (loans and deposits) have a troublesome record, because they usually dominate year-to-year changes in private-capital flows, because they can drive exchange rate in a procyclical way, because extreme inflows often presage a crisis, and because extreme outflows often worsen a financial collapse.

■ Fluctuations in portfolio investment have been a lesser problem for emerging markets. A key feature of these flows was their growing size. Because the stock of portfolio capital in emerging markets is large and growing, the potential for future troublesome fluctuations cannot be dismissed.

■ FDI fluctuations have not been a source of financial volatility in emerging markets. Strong reasons can be given for why FDI flows are fairly stable: Currency and maturity mismatch is low; projects typically have a long life. The historical record confirms the bolted down hypothesis.

This review leads us to conclude that the boom-and-bust aspect of capital flows is an *episodic* problem concentrated in bank operations, but a problem that could become more prominent in portfolio investment. However, we must emphasize that boom and bust is not a *persistent disease* associated with all international capital. The distinction is important. Observers who detect a persistent disease are quick to condemn financial institutions in general and advocate broad capital controls.

Leading Critics, and a Counter-Critic

Four examples of open capital markets may be cited: Bhagwati (1998), Krugman (1998), Eatwell and Taylor (2000), and Rodrik (1998). Among the four, Bhagwati (1998) is the most restrained. The title of his essay tells the message: "Yes to Free Trade, Maybe to Capital Controls." He argues that the evidence for free trade is overwhelming, and the evidence for free capital is weak. Hence, capital controls might not be such a bad way of addressing crises in particular, and antiglobalization sentiments in general.

Coming out of the Asian crisis, Krugman (1997) detected seven perverse "habits" in financial markets: Think short term. Be greedy. Believe in the greater fool. Run with the herd. Overgeneralize. Be trendy. Play with other people's money. This characterization leads him to conclude that financiers during the crisis formed "an extremely dangerous flock of financial sheep" (Krugman 1997).

In less colorful language, Eatwell and Taylor (2000) generalize Krugman's criticism to cover the whole field of international capital in the post-Smithsonian era. They ascribe multiple sins to the free flow of capital: high and variable real interest rates, volatile asset prices, contagiously spreading market instabilities, waves of currency crises, and declining rates of growth and investment.

This brand of criticism leads Rodrik, among others, to conclude (1998, 60):

> Think of capital flows as a medicine with occasionally horrific side effects. The evidence suggests we have no good way of controlling the side effects. Can it be good regulatory policy to remove controls on the sale and use of such a medicine?

From a completely different ideological standpoint, Dooley (2000) argues that the "horrific side effects" (to use Rodrik's colorful phrase) are a *necessary complement* for substantial international private bank loans and bond placements. Private lenders have no credible means of seizing assets from sovereign borrowers. As recent experience in Indonesia has shown, they in fact may have no means of collecting debts from private foreign borrowers. In the event of default, the only effective response by private lenders is to withhold fresh credit and force an economic crisis. In Dooley's view, misguided "reforms" that blunt this threat will, in the long run, encourage mischievous political leaders and finance ministers to pursue bad policies. Then they, or their successors, will engage in "strategic defaults" on foreign obligations. This behavior, in turn, will significantly diminish the flow of private capital to emerging markets.

We reject the broad condemnation of open capital markets voiced by the four distinguished authors first cited. In our view, the benefits of international capital for emerging markets already outweigh the costs— and we think the balance will become more favorable in the decades ahead. In contrast to Rodrik, we believe that there are good ways of controlling the side effects. In contrast to Bhagwati, we think the case for international capital flows is inherently as strong, if not yet as well documented, as the case for international trade.[68]

With Dooley, we believe that emerging-market crises need not be an inevitable complement to international capital flows. Correctly structured reforms that curtail moral hazard (both in financial institutions and emerging markets) will limit the frequency of crises and avert "strategic defaults."[69]

To support our position on the balance between costs and benefits, we first summarize some empirical findings on the costs and benefits of financial development in general and international capital flows in particular. We then offer rough calculations that juxtapose the gains from foreign trade, the gains from foreign capital, and the costs of banking and currency crises.

Finance and Growth

Starting at the most general level, a rich literature supports the strong connection between financial development (including the rule of law in financial affairs) and income growth. The basic idea can be traced to

---

68. Stanley Fischer, the IMF's deputy managing director, made a telling remark at a luncheon sponsored by American University on 13 April 2000. The econometric case for capital flows today is approximately where the econometric case for international trade was in the 1980s, when Bela Balassa and Anne Krueger were carrying out pioneering studies at the World Bank. The evidence on capital is beginning to come in, and some of it is cited in this chapter, but much more work needs to be done.

69. Australia, Canada, and the United States, among other countries, have at points in their history been large net borrowers, but their regulatory institutions kept pace with their financial development. The same can happen during the next few decades in emerging markets. On the *demand side* of the capital flow account, the IMF is working to improve policy in general and financial surveillance in particular.

Alexander Hamilton (1781), Walter Bagehot (1862; originally published 1873), and Joseph Schumpeter (1934; originally published 1912).[70] After a long dormancy during the Keynesian heyday, the financial connection was rediscovered by Goldsmith (1969) and McKinnon (1973). Reviewing the experience of 35 countries between 1860 and 1963, Goldsmith was persuaded that finance and development go together. But he was agnostic on the direction of causality: "Whether financial factors were responsible for the acceleration of economic development or whether financial development reflected economic growth whose mainsprings must be sought elsewhere" (Goldsmith 1969, 48).[71]

In an important study published a few years later, McKinnon (1973) argued that financial development often leads economic growth. He contended that, when strong financial institutions pay positive real returns, households and firms will entrust those institutions with their savings—thereby improving the allocation of capital. Examining the postwar experience of Japan and Germany, McKinnon observed that ratios of broad monetary aggregates to GDP rose sharply, whereas the same ratios were low and stagnant in a number of poorly performing semi-industrial countries.

What Causes What?

Using a then-novel approach to establish the direction of causality and sidestep the post hoc ergo propter hoc fallacy, King and Levine (1993) showed that previous financial development predicted income growth during the next 10 to 30 years. Subsequently, Levine (1997, 1998, 2000), Levine and Zervos (1998), and Rajan and Zingales (1998), among others, published persuasive papers establishing the causal importance of finance, using time-series and cross-country data. Levine and Zervos (1998), for example, found that a 1-standard-deviation increase in the extent of bank credit to the private sector at the beginning of the period 1976-93 was associated with an increase in annual per capita GDP growth of 0.7 percent during the period. A 1-standard-deviation increase in the extent of stock market liquidity was associated with an increase in annual per capita GDP growth of 0.8 percent during the period. Similarly, Khan

---

70. The early literature is cited in Levine, Loayza, and Beck (2000). As they point out, Alexander Hamilton claimed that "banks were the happiest engines that were ever invented" for creating wealth (Hamilton 1781).

71. De Soto (2000) places responsibility for the failure of capitalism in many developing countries on very weak legal systems that fail to protect real property rights: "The total value of the real estate held but not legally owned by the poor of the Third World and former communist nations is at least $9.3 trillion. . . . [But the developing countries lack] formal property systems with a variety of mechanisms [that enable these assets to be sold or pledged] in such a way that [they] can be converted into [financial] capital" (De Soto 2000, 46).

(2000) found that a 1-percentage-point increase in the national level of financial development (measured as the ratio of stock market capitalization plus domestic bank credit to GDP) was associated with a 1.86 percent increase in annual growth during the period 1976-91.

Levine, Loayza, and Beck (2000) and Beck, Loayza, and Levine (2000) applied sophisticated econometric techniques, including instrumental variables, to panel data for 71 countries for the period 1960-95. The first paper (Levine, Loayza, and Beck 2000) demonstrated that the development of financial intermediaries causes economic growth. Their estimated coefficients suggest, for example, that if Argentina had enjoyed the same level of financial intermediaries as the average developing country between 1960 and 1995, its per capita GDP would have grown 1 percent a year faster. The second paper (Beck, Loayza, and Levine 2000) showed that banks in particular exert a large causal impact on total factor productivity growth, which feeds into overall GDP growth.

Levine, Loayza, and Beck (2000) also show that legal and accounting systems help determine differences in financial development. Shareholder rights, creditor rights, common law (as opposed to civil law) traditions, low corruption, and strong accounting standards all condition the extent of financial development.[72] These are all matters that governments can alter by policy initiatives. In well-run financial systems—whether dominated by securities markets or banks—capital markets become more efficient (Demirgüç-Kunt and Levine 1999, table 4). Bank loans fund the best projects, rather than the best-connected firms. New capital sources spring up: private placements, venture capital, and public offerings. An array of new vehicles—such as securitized loans, swaps, and futures contracts—enable risk to be divided and spread.

Financial development not only promotes faster income growth, it also helps to reduce the volatility of per capita GDP. Denizer, Iyigun, and Owen (2000), for example, estimate that a 1-standard-deviation increase in the ratio of claims on the nonfinancial private sector to total domestic credit reduces the standard deviation of real per capita GDP growth by about 14 percent.

Sequencing Financial Development

The fact that financial development promotes growth does not, of course, imply that every conceivable measure in the direction of financial

---

72. Supplementary evidence is the study by Morck, Yeung, and Yu (2000), suggesting that highly synchronized individual share-price changes within stock markets in developing countries can be partly explained by a measure of "poor governance." The implication is that, when good or bad information is revealed about one company, investors assume (because of poor disclosure, bad accounting practices, etc.) that similar good or bad information characterizes other companies. Individual share-price changes are synchronized to a much lower extent in industrial countries with "good governance."

liberalization is a "good thing." Demirguç-Kunt and Detragiache (1998), for example, examined interest-rate deregulation between 1985 and 1995. The probability of a banking crisis was high during the next 3 or 4 years, especially where the domestic regulatory environment was weak. Such findings underpin a cottage literature on "financial sequencing" (e.g., Johnston and Sundararajan 1999). As with almost anything else in economic life, financial development can be pursued in a way that creates harm. That said, overwhelming evidence demonstrates that financial development by and large promotes economic growth.

International Capital and Growth

In comparison with the mature body of work on the connection between financial development and economic growth, empirical research on *international* capital flows, growth, and volatility is at an infant stage. In an early theoretical paper, Obstfeld (1994) calculated the potential wealth gains for several regions of the world assuming complete financial integration of the world economy. The potential wealth gains in emerging-market economies seem unbelievably large—ranging from a gain of 22 percent in East Asia to one of 238 percent in South America.[73] Subsequent empirical studies shed further light.

Quinn (1997) examined the connection between average real long-run per capita income growth (1960-89) in 64 countries and changes in their international financial regulation between 1958 and 1988. He constructed two measures: one for capital account liberalization (*capital*) and one for overall financial liberalization (*openness*). He created the measures by numerically coding laws and regulations affecting capital transactions, current transactions, and exchange regimes. He used the change in the numerical scales between 1958 and 1988 as independent variables. Both measures are statistically significant in explaining long-run economic growth, and capital proved more robust than openness. Similarly, Françoise and Schuknecht (1999) found that moving from a closed to a relatively open financial service regime is associated with an annual rise in GDP growth of more than 1 percent.

Less sweeping studies focused on components of the capital account. Henry (2000) studied the experience of six Asian and six Latin American countries in the late 1980s and early 1990s. He estimated that the prospect of opening a closed stock market to foreign investors boosts equity prices on average by 25 percent (after eliminating the general influence of world equity price changes). This, of course, lowers the cost of equity capital. In the 2 years following the stock market opening, domestic

---

73. In a subsequent essay, published after the Mexican and Asian crises, Obstfeld (1998) surveyed the literature on the balance and benefits of international capital. At that time, the literature was still heavier on argument than evidence.

investment rose about 20 percent on average. In a similar analysis, Bekaert, Harvey, and Lundblad (2000) estimated that opening equity markets to foreign investors is associated with an increase in annual real growth of between 0.7 and 1.4 percentage points, after accounting for other influences. They do not claim a cause and effect relationship, but they suggest that a lower cost of capital and more venturesome investment decisions might be at play.

Portes and Rey (1999) applied a gravity model to analyze a large dataset (of 1,500 observations) on bilateral cross-border equity flows. They find that market size, distance, transaction efficiency, and the quantity and quality of information explain 70 percent of the variance.[74] Interestingly, language, currency, and trading bloc membership do not seem to matter. A country cannot do much about its market size or distance from financial centers. However, even small and medium-sized countries can favorably shape some of the factors assessed by Portes and Rey—for example, transaction efficiency and quality of information.[75]

Goldberg, Dages, and Kinney (2000) found that foreign banks operating in Mexico and Argentina between 1994 and 1999 compared favorably with their domestic counterparts. They had higher loan growth rates and lower loan volatility. Most important, during crisis periods, foreign banks showed notable credit growth relative to their domestic counterparts. The authors conclude that these differences reflect bank health rather than ownership per se. A major detriment to bank health is loan concentration, and it is hard for banks that do all of their business in an economy that is smaller and more concentrated than California (the case for Argentina, Mexico, and many other emerging markets) to field a diversified loan portfolio. Add to concentration the problems of policy-based loans, connected lending, and less-than-frontier technology, and it is easy to see why foreign banks have better performance records.

The Benefits—Rough Calculations

Although scholars and public officials agree that foreign capital augments the GDP of emerging-market countries, the possibility of financial crises—in which foreign capital plays a role—must be placed on the other side of the ledger. To form a judgment about the broad direction of policy, it is useful to size up, in a rough way, the benefits and costs. We start with the benefits. Table 1.10 offers our rough calculations of the GDP

---

74. They measure information quantity by telephone call traffic and multinational bank branches; they measure information quality by the extent of insider trading.

75. The authors did not draw on Quinn's (1997) empirical work to include, as explanatory variables, measures of capital account regulation or financial openness. Future work may show that Quinn's measures—which reflect policy determinations by each country—influence the magnitude of portfolio investment.

Table 1.10 Contributions of foreign trade and capital to emerging-market GDP (billions of dollars or percent)[a]

Contribution	1970	1980	1990	2000	2010
GDP of emerging markets	797	2,927	4,747	6,798	10,000
Foreign trade					
Trade value (merchandise exports plus imports)[b]	157	1,262	1,796	3,972	8,182
Trade as percentage of GDP	20	43	38	59	82
Trade expansion as percentage of GDP[c]	n.a.	23	(5)	21	23
GDP gains from trade expansion[d] (billions of dollars)	n.a.	n.a.	282	358	1,452
Foreign capital					
Foreign capital stock (billions of dollars)	176	770	2,164	4,937	7,300
Bank loans and trade credits	110	604	1,444	2,544	2,500
Portfolio investment (bonds and equity)	10	60	364	959	2,000
Foreign direct investment	56	106	356	1,434	2,800
Foreign capital stock as percentage of GDP	22	26	46	73	73
Bank loans and trade credits	14	21	30	37	25
Portfolio investment (bonds and equity)	1	2	8	14	20
Foreign direct investment	7	4	7	21	28
Foreign capital stock expansion as percentage of GDP	n.a.	4	19	27	0
Bank loans and trade credits	n.a.	7	10	7	(12)
Portfolio investment (bonds and equity)	n.a.	1	6	6	6
Foreign direct investment	n.a.	(3)	4	14	7
GDP gains from foreign capital expansion (billions of dollars)	n.a.	(35)	127	457	394
Bank loans and trade credits[e]	n.a.	0	0	0	0
Portfolio investment (bonds and equity)[f]	n.a.	5	53	88	118
Foreign direct investment[g]	n.a.	(40)	73	370	276

n.a. = not available

a. Values are in nominal dollars (at current year prices), except for 2010 figures, which are expressed in 2000 prices.
b. The 2000 trade value is calculated by assuming 5 percent annual growth on the 1998 figure. The 2010 trade value is extrapolated by assuming the same real decade growth rate (106 percent) as in the 1990s.
c. Calculated as the decade-to-decade difference in the ratio of merchandise trade (exports plus imports) to GDP.
d. Calculated as a steady-state gain of 3.3 percent in GDP for each 10-percentage-point increase over the previous two decades in the trade to GDP ratio. The 3.3 coefficient is based on the relationship between trade expansion and GDP gains estimated by Frankel and Rose (2000). Also see Frankel and Romer (1999) for a smaller coefficient (0.8 percent) based on cross-country experience over a shorter time frame within East Asia.
e. Soto (2000) finds a negative short-term relationship between debt flows (bank loans and trade credits) and GDP. We assume the relationship is zero.
f. Calculated as a GDP gain of 0.2 percent for each 1-percentage-point increase over the previous decade in the ratio of the stock of portfolio investment to GDP. The 0.2 coefficient is based on the relationship between portfolio inflows and GDP estimated by Soto (2000).
g. Calculated as a GDP gain of 0.4 percent for a 1-percentage-point increase over the previous decade in the ratio of the stock of FDI to GDP. The 0.4 coefficient is based on the relationship between FDI inflows and GDP estimated by Borensztein, De Gregorio, and Lee (1998) and Soto (2000).

Note: This table is based on data in table 1.4 and the assumptions noted below.

Sources: IMF, *International Financial Statistics, Yearbook,* 1999; IMF, *Results of the 1997 Coordinated Portfolio Investment Survey,* 1999; World Bank, *World Tables,* various issues; Frankel and Romer (1999); Frankel and Rose (2000); Soto (2000); Borensztein, De Gregorio, and Lee (1998).

gains for emerging markets from participation in the international economy, contrasting benefits both from the expansion of merchandise trade and foreign capital. The coefficients built into our calculations for the gains from trade expansion are drawn from the work of Frankel and Romer (1999). The coefficients for the gains from foreign capital are based on the work of Borenszstein, De Gregorio, and Lee (1998) and Soto (2000).

Trade and Growth

Trade expansion is defined as a rising ratio between merchandise trade (exports plus imports) and GDP. As long as the ratio does not change, the external economy is more or less preserving the status quo. A rising ratio means that underlying economic forces, perhaps augmented by a liberal commercial policy, are encouraging greater integration with the global economy.[76] According to the conservative estimates made by Frankel and Romer (1999) for East Asia, steady-state GDP rises by about 0.78 percentage points for each 10 percent rise in the ratio of merchandise trade to GDP. A more recent gravity model estimate by Frankel and Rose (2000) suggests that each 10 percent rise in the merchandise trade ratio increases GDP by 3.3 percentage points after 20 years. The 3.3 percent coefficient finds ample support in computable general equilibrium (CGE) and computable partial equilibrium (CPE) estimates of the benefits of trade liberalization.[77] This is the coefficient we use in the calculations presented in table 1.10. Applying this coefficient to merchandise trade growth between 1980 and 2000 suggests that trade expansion may have contributed $358 billion, or 5.3 percent, to emerging-market GDP, in 2000. On the basis of current trends—if trade continues to boom—the GDP contribution could exceed $1 trillion, more than 10 percent of emerging-market GDP, in 2010.

To size up the contribution of foreign capital, we separately consider foreign debt capital (bank loans and trade credits) and foreign equity capital (FDI and portfolio equity). These categories follow the available econometric evidence.

Bank Loans and Growth

Examining annual data for a panel of 44 developing countries for the period 1986-97, Soto (2000) estimated the impact of different kinds of

---

76. See Edwards (1997) for a range of estimates demonstrating that trade openness, variously measured, significantly contributes to total factor productivity growth.

77. A recent CGE analysis of world trade by Brown, Deardorff, and Stern (2001) concluded that the welfare benefits of Uruguay Round trade liberalization were 49 percent ($75 billion) of the induced increase in world merchandise imports plus exports ($157 billion). They go on to calculate the potential welfare benefits of a "Millenium Round" as 92 percent ($612 billion) of the potential increase in world merchandise imports plus exports ($668 billion). See Hufbauer and Wada (1999c) for a summary of other calculations.

foreign capital on GDP growth in emerging markets. According to his estimated coefficients, foreign bank loans and trade credits are associated with GDP *losses* in emerging markets. Like Soto, we think these debt coefficients are misleading. They capture the greater willingness of G-10 banks and exporters to lend when times are good and growth is not capital-constrained, and their lesser willingness to lend when times are bad. For the purpose of table 1.10, we assume bank loans and trade credits make a *zero* contribution to GDP levels in emerging markets. This assumption totally discounts the benefits we foresee from the improved long-term efficiency in the internal allocation of capital with the rise of G-10 financial institutions in emerging markets (see Dobson and Jacquet 1998).

FDI and Growth

Turning to FDI, two studies lend themselves to rough calculations of the benefits for emerging markets. The first is the study by Borensztein, De Greogrio, and Lee (1998). They examined the impact of average FDI inflows (as a percentage of GDP) on average real per capita GDP growth in 69 developing countries during the period 1970-89. They entered a large number of control variables in the more elaborate model specifications.[78] In a simple specification, they found that a 1-percentage-point increase in the average FDI inflow ratio was associated with an increase in the average per capita annual GDP growth rate of 0.66 percent (with a standard error of 0.46 percent). Assuming that the same relationship holds for FDI stocks, a 1-percentage-point rise in the ratio between the FDI stock and GDP would imply a 0.66 percent increase in the GDP level. Because it is estimated on the basis of average relationships during nearly two decades, this coefficient can be interpreted as the long-run GDP benefit of FDI, taking into account various externalities.

The second study that lends itself to a quantitative estimate of the GDP contribution from FDI is Soto's (2000) work. On the basis of annual panel data, he estimated that a 1-percentage-point rise in the ratio of FDI inflows to GDP increases the short-term level of GDP by 0.16 percent (with a standard error of 0.02 percent). Assuming that this coefficient applies to FDI stocks, a 1-percentage-point increase in the ratio of FDI stock to GDP will increase the short-term level of GDP by 0.16 percent. Using a Solow growth model, Soto then calculates that the long-term, steady-state gain in the GDP level is 0.60 percent for each

---

78. The most interesting control variable is the country's average level of schooling. It turns out that an interactive term between FDI and schooling is highly significant: FDI raises per capita income to a much greater extent in countries where secondary schooling is more prevalent. The analysis by UNCTAD (1999, annex to chap. 11) reaches the same conclusion.

1-percentage-point rise in the ratio of FDI stock to GDP. This is practically the same as the long-run coefficient of 0.66 directly estimated by Borensztein, De Gregorio, and Lee (1998).

As a conservative assessment of FDI benefits, we average Soto's short-run coefficient of 0.16 with the Soto and Borenszstein, De Gregorio, and Lee long-run coefficient (taken to be 0.66). The simple average is a 0.4 percent rise in the GDP level for each 1-percentage-point rise in the ratio of FDI stock to GDP. We assume that this coefficient applies to changes during a decade in the ratio of FDI stock to GDP. For example, if the ratio rises from 10 to 15 percent, the indicated rise in the decade-end GDP level would be 2.0 percent (0.4 times 5 percent equals 2.0 percent).

Portfolio Investment and Growth

We turn now to portfolio investment, where econometric estimates are sparse. The only ones we have found are Soto's. He calculates that a rise of 1 percentage point in the ratio of portfolio equity stock to GDP will increase the level of GDP by 0.68 percent (with a standard error of 0.05 percent). This coefficient seems unbelievably high.[79]

Conversely, Soto calculates that a rise of 1 percentage point in the ratio of portfolio bond stock to GDP will *decrease* the level of GDP by 0.06 percent (with a standard error of 0.06). Assuming a 60 percent weighting for portfolio bonds and a 40 percent weighting for portfolio equity, we blend Soto's two portfolio coefficients to arrive at a weighted average: Each percentage point increase in the ratio of portfolio investment stock to FDI increases the GDP level by 0.2 percent. Again, we assume this coefficient applies to changes during a decade. For example, if the portfolio investment ratio rises from 8 to 12 percent, the indicated GDP gain would be 0.8 percent (0.2 times 4 percent equals 0.8 percent).

Sizing Up Trade, Capital, and Growth

What are the results of this sizing-up exercise, using coefficients to assess the contribution of trade and capital to emerging-economy GDP? The calculations shown in table 1.10 indicate that the induced GDP growth gains from foreign capital in 2000 may have been in the same ballpark as the gains from expanded trade. In rough terms, the gains from expanded trade may be GDP levels that are 5 percent higher than otherwise, and the gains from expanded foreign capital could be similar.

Now the caveats. There is a lot at "play" in these calculations. Coefficients linking trade and investment expansion to GDP growth are far from settled in the econometric literature. Moreover, trade and capital

---

79. Soto's calculation implies a 68 percent return on portfolio equity. Even taking into account external efficiencies from privatization and the like, this seems much too high (as John Williamson has pointed out; personal communication).

are close complements: Policies that encourage commerce encourage investment. It is possible that separate estimates of trade and investment growth coefficients double count the other factor. GDP growth gains from trade expansion during the next 10 years, as suggested in table 1.10, could be substantially larger than gains from additional foreign investment. We conclude with a cautious assertion: On the basis of the available evidence, foreign capital confers gains on emerging economies in the same range as the gains conferred by foreign trade.

Skeptics and a Counter-Skeptic

Not every economist will agree with our cautious assertion. A contemporary skeptic, Dani Rodrik, dismisses evidence that FDI has been associated with faster growth. He writes (1999, 37):

> Today's policy literature is filled with extravagant claims about positive spillovers from FDI. These spillovers include technology transfer, marketing channels, superior management, and labor training. Once again, the hard evidence is sobering. Systematic plant-level studies from countries such as Morocco and Venezuela find little in the way of positive spillovers.

Rodrik's "hard evidence" is based on plant-level studies involving Côte d'Ivoire, Morocco, and Venezuela in papers that have, as a common author or coauthor, Ann Harrison.[80] Ted Moran (2001) has closely examined these studies. He concludes that the countries chosen for study by Harrison and her coauthors were ones with places and contexts where only small positive spillovers could be expected from FDI to begin with. Côte d'Ivoire, Morocco, and Venezuela are not countries with good policy regimes or strong connections to world markets. Indeed, as Moran (2001) points out, a companion study by Aitken, Hanson, and Harrison (1997) of Mexican manufacturing plants finds positive spillovers from FDI in Mexico.

Obviously, the benefits of FDI in emerging markets remain a matter of contention among economists. The benefits (if any) from portfolio investment have barely been investigated. Provisionally, we stick with our cautious assertion: Foreign capital confers benefits in the same range as the benefits of foreign trade.

The Costs—Rough Calculations

Turning to the other side of the ledger, how do the costs of crises compare with the calculated benefits from foreign capital? Table 1.11 gives

---

80. The earliest paper, on Morocco, is Haddad and Harrison (1993). The next paper, by Harrison (1996), surveys Côte d'Ivoire, Morocco, and Venezuela. The most recent paper, by Aitken and Harrison (1999), focuses on Venezuela.

Table 1.11 GDP losses from banking and currency crises

	1980s	1990s	2000s
	(billions of dollars)		
GDP of emerging markets[a]	3,837	5,773	8,445
Asia	1,000	1,850	
Latin America	945	1,684	
Africa	272	328	
Europe	1,142	1,357	
Middle East	466	552	
	(billions of dollars)		
Decade's GDP loss from financial crises in emerging markets[b]	249	419	250[c]
Asia	13	260	
Latin America	207	123	
Africa	15	18	
Europe	n.a.	11	
Middle East	14	7	
	(percent of GDP)		
Average annual GDP loss in emerging markets	0.6	0.7	0.3
Asia	0.1	1.4	
Latin America	2.2	0.7	
Africa	0.5	0.6	
Europe	n.a.	0.1	
Middle East	0.3	0.1	

n.a. = not available

a. Average of values for beginning and end years. For example, the 1980s figure for emerging markets as a whole is the average of $2,927 billion (1980) and $4,747 billion (1990). See table 1.4.

b. Unless a specific loss figure was estimated by Caprio and Klingebiel (1996) or Goldstein, Kaminsky, and Reinhart (2000) (for Asian crisis figures), we assume that a banking crisis results in a GDP loss of 2 percent per year throughout its duration. Caprio and Klingebiel estimated loss figures for 24 major banking or currency crises in the 1980s and 1990s. We use these estimates where available. When not available, the assumed impact figures are based on: (1) In the case of a banking crisis, the loss figure of 2 percent per year is based on the average loss of 2.4 percent a year for 22 major crises identified by Caprio and Klingebiel (all 24 crises except for the shattering events in Argentina (1980-82) and Chile (1981-83). (2) In the case of a currency crisis, we assume that such a crisis results in a GDP loss of 5.6 percent per year for high-inflation countries (with more than 100 percent inflation for the crisis years—10 cases), and 2.6 percent GDP loss per year for low-inflation countries (with less than 100 percent inflation—16 cases), again unless a specific loss figure was estimated by Caprio and Klingebiel. Differing GDP loss experience depending on the previous rate of inflation is based on Goldstein, Kaminsky, and Reinhart (2000). Thus, we make a distinction between high (more than 100 percent inflation during the crisis years) and moderate (below 100 percent inflation during the crisis years).

c. Forecast by authors, assuming policy changes outlined in this book.

Note: Goldstein (1997) defines a banking crisis as (1) a bank run that leads to the closure, merger, or public takeover of one or more financial institutions; and (2) an event that requires large scale government assistance to one or more important financial institutions. The identification of banking crises is usually consistent across different studies. Kaminsky and Reinhart (1999) define a currency crisis by an index that combines significant exchange rate depreciation and decline of foreign reserves.

Sources: Caprio and Klingebiel (1996); Goldstein (1997); Goldstein, Kaminsky, and Reinhart (2000); IMF, International Financial Statistics, Yearbook, 1999.

estimates of GDP losses from all banking and currency crises recorded in the 1980s and 1990s. The calculations reflect 24 banking crises and 36 currency crises (many of them overlapping). The impacts of crises were of course uneven: A few countries were hit very hard; many escaped altogether. Added up, the crises cost all emerging markets about 0.6 percent of GDP per year in the 1980s, and 0.7 percent per year in the 1990s.[81]

These losses—bad and concentrated as they may be—were substantially less than conservatively estimated gains from international capital. Latin American suffered in the 1980s, Asia in the 1990s, and Africa throughout. But by no stretch of rhetoric can all financial crises be laid at the doorstep of international capital. Even if international capital is responsible for half the damage (an exaggeration, in our opinion), the benefits overall easily outweigh the costs.

Costs are nevertheless important, especially because they hit a few countries hard. It would be fatuous to suppose that crises can be eliminated, but we think they can be reduced in frequency and severity. Crisis amelioration is the theme of chapters 2 and 3.

Complements or Substitutes?

In this chapter, we have examined the costs and benefits of various forms of international capital. In chapters 2 and 3, we will examine why banks supply volatile short-term debt and how this problem might be addressed. Of course, one of the key questions that follows is whether different capital flows to emerging markets are complements or substitutes.

If, in fact, there is little substitution between different kinds of capital (bank loans, portfolio bonds, portfolio equity, and FDI), policy measures that discourage bank loans may diminish, one for one, the overall flow of resources to emerging markets. Even worse, if different kinds of capital strongly complement one another, policy measures that discourage bank loans may reduce not only those loans but also portfolio investment and FDI. Finally, there is a practical problem: Capital flows with a particular character may fly under different flags. General Electric (GE), for example, runs a virtual bank (GE Capital), and is one of the top FDI firms in the world. GE thus has multiple avenues to move capital in and out of emerging markets. If G-10 policy works to restrain interbank loans, firms like GE may instead supply equally unstable short-term funds to local borrowers.

The broad flavor of our recommendations is to shift the composition of capital inflows toward more permanent forms—exemplified, in the case

---

81. If the magnitude of crises in the 2000s can be held to the same dollar level as those in the 1980s and 1990s, the costs would fall to 0.3 percent of emerging-market GDP (table 1.11).

of debt finance, by a longer maturity on loans, but also exemplified by more portfolio investment and FDI in the investment mix. These recommendations are akin to knocking on an open door. Finance ministers in emerging markets are now fully familiar with the hazards of excessive reliance on short-term foreign debt. As Rodrik and Velasco (1999, abstract) observe, "The empirical analysis shows that the short-term debt to reserves ratio is a robust predictor of financial crises, and that greater short-term exposure is associated with more severe crises when capital flows reverse." Yet short-term capital may be the only kind of capital some countries can attract (Jeanne 2000).[82]

Banks and Capital Markets

Levine and Zervos (1998) examined evidence from 47 countries, averaged over the period 1976-93. In terms of the share of GDP, they found a strong positive correlation of 0.647 between *domestic* bank credit and *domestic* stock market capitalization.[83] They found a lesser positive correlation of 0.324 between *domestic* bank credit and *domestic* capital stock growth. This evidence suggests that bank credit and stock markets are relatively strong complements, even though real investment and the financial markets are less tightly linked.[84] This observation about complementary *domestic* financial markets does not, however, demonstrate that *foreign* bank lending, portfolio investment, and FDI are strong complements.

Domestic and Foreign Capital

Table 1.12 illustrates the wide range of experience in the respective roles of foreign banks and FDI, using financial market data assembled by Beck, Demirgüç-Kunt, and Levine (1999), and FDI data reported by UNCTAD (1999). The ratios of financial magnitudes to GDP in table 1.12 are compiled for long periods of time, as explained in the table notes. Even so, there is considerable variation between countries. Within the banking sector, foreign banks sometimes play a large role, and sometimes a very small role. In Latin America, for example, the share of foreign bank assets in total bank assets has historically ranged from nearly zero to 30 or 40

---

82. Debt maturities are often kept short *because* bank lenders fear the worst—a crisis.

83. Nevertheless, as table 1.12 shows, there is considerable variation between countries. For example, within the five Asian crisis countries, the ratio of total bank assets to share market capitalization ranges from 0.40 in Malaysia to 2.72 in Indonesia. In Latin America, the same ratio ranges between 0.54 in Chile to 1.94 in Brazil.

84. Analysis by Levine (2000) also suggests that the world has different "styles" of finance—some dominated by bank finance and others where capital markets play a large role. But by and large the two kinds of financial markets are complements.

Table 1.12   Financial structures in emerging markets

Country	GDP per capita, 1990-95	Bank assets[a]	Market cap[b]	FDI stock[c]	Bank/ market[d]	Bank/ FDI[e]	Foreign bank/ total bank[f]
Five affected Asian countries							
Indonesia	610	0.49	0.18	0.27	2.72	1.83	0.23
South Korea	3,909	0.55	0.37	0.02	1.49	22.36	n.a.
Malaysia	2,629	0.82	2.01	0.28	0.41	2.95	0.06
Philippines	734	0.37	0.52	0.08	0.71	4.86	0.30
Thailand	1,503	0.82	0.57	0.07	1.44	11.17	0.05
Other Asia							
Bangladesh	194	0.31	0.04	0.01	7.75	44.29	0.20
Hong Kong	10,538	1.49	1.96	0.95	0.76	1.56	n.a.
India	385	0.34	0.28	0.01	1.21	26.15	0.06
Nepal	200	0.22	0.05	0.01	4.40	26.40	0.96
Pakistan	436	0.36	0.16	0.07	2.25	5.45	0.20
Sinapore	11,152	0.95	1.37	0.72	0.69	1.33	0.33
Sri Lanka	538	0.27	0.16	0.09	1.69	3.03	n.a.
Latin America							
Argentina	4,039	0.21	0.11	0.08	1.91	2.51	0.16
Barbados	4,777	0.52	0.21	0.11	2.48	4.58	n.a.
Bolivia	755	0.37	n.a.	0.19	n.a.	1.91	0.29
Brazil	2,346	0.32	0.19	0.11	0.38	2.81	0.05
Chile	2,725	0.46	0.84	0.21	0.55	2.15	0.04
Colombia	1,432	0.18	0.13	0.08	1.38	2.22	0.15
Costa Rica	1,867	0.17	0.07	0.27	2.43	0.64	0.05
Ecuador	1,322	0.17	0.10	0.14	1.70	1.18	0.06
Honduras	751	0.25	0.05	0.11	5.00	2.22	0.19
Jamaica	1711	0.28	0.42	0.24	0.67	1.16	n.a.
Mexico	2,952	0.24	0.32	0.10	0.75	2.38	0.01
Panama	1,950	0.58	0.09	0.19	6.44	3.09	0.42
Peru	1,292	0.12	0.11	0.07	1.09	1.68	0.42
Trinidad and Tobago	3,685	0.37	0.12	0.47	3.08	0.79	n.a.
Uruguay	2,514	0.28	n.a.	0.10	n.a.	2.84	0.17
Venezuela	3,167	0.15	0.12	0.08	1.25	1.94	0.24
Middle East							
Cyprus	6,588	0.81	0.22	0.24	3.68	3.45	0.48
Egypt	1,042	0.63	0.10	0.21	6.30	3.06	n.a.
Iran	2,397	0.22	0.04	0.01	5.50	29.33	n.a.
Jordan	1,289	0.71	0.65	0.11	1.09	6.64	n.a.
Tunisia	1,534	0.55	0.10	0.19	5.50	2.86	0.24
Turkey	2,259	0.19	0.14	0.02	1.36	11.73	0.01
Africa							
Ghana	553	0.06	n.a.	0.09	n.a.	0.69	n.a.
Kenya	441	0.29	0.16	0.07	1.81	4.24	0.03
Mauritius	2,125	0.54	0.27	0.05	2.00	10.34	0.03
Nigeria	551	0.11	0.06	0.16	1.83	0.69	0.08
South Africa	2,379	0.66	1.66	0.14	0.40	4.63	0.01
Zimbabwe	804	0.21	0.23	0.04	0.91	5.83	0.62

FDI = foreign direct investment; n.a. = not available

a. Bank assets divided by GDP. The time span for the data ranges from 1960 to 1997.
b. Market capitalization divided by GDP. The time span for the data ranges from 1976 to 1997.
c. Inward FDI stock divided by GDP. The time span for the data rages from 1980 to 1997.
d. Ratio of (Bank assets/GDP) to (Market capitalization/GDP).
e. Ratio of (Bank assets/GDP) to (FDI stock/GDP).
f. Foreign bank assets divided by total bank assets. The time span for the data ranges from 1990 to 1997.

Sources: Demirguç-Kunt and Levine (1999); Beck, Demirguç-Kunt, and Levine (1999); UNCTAD; *World Investment Report,* 1999.

percent (the foreign share in 2000 would be higher than these historical averages). Likewise, extreme ratios are observed between foreign bank assets and FDI stocks. Within the Asian crisis group, for example, the ratio ranges from 1.83 for Indonesia to 22.36 for South Korea.

A cross-section analysis of 59 countries (including industrial countries not shown in table 1.12), shows a regression coefficient of 0.83 between stock market capitalization and bank assets (controlling for GDP per capita), which is consistent with the coefficient reported by Levine and Zervos (1998).[85] However, on the basis of the experience of the 40 emerging economies shown in table 1.12, the regression coefficient between FDI stocks and bank assets (controlling for GDP per capita) is only 0.21, with a standard error of 0.09. This is a much looser relationship.

Foreign Capital Sources as Complements

The data assembled in table 1.4 can be used to portray the correspondence between FDI stock and foreign debt stock in five emerging-economy regions. The results for 1980, 1990, and 1998 are featured in figure 1.1. Although there are only five observations for each year, it is evident that no strong positive or negative correspondence exists between the two forms of foreign asset ownership.

The annual capital flow experience of the five regions during the 1990s, depicted in table 1.3, shows a very mild positive correspondence between portfolio investment and bank activity.[86] Controlling for regional effects, portfolio flows increase $16 for every $100 increase in bank activity. However, FDI flows *decrease* $3 for every $100 increase in bank activity (the coefficient is not significant). Taken together, these coefficients suggest that different types of capital inflow do not strongly complement one another. Similarly, Lane and Milesi-Ferretti (2000) find that the correlation between the portfolio equity stock and the FDI stock in developing countries in 1997 was only 0.07.

Foreign Capital Sources as Substitutes

If the categories of capital identified in common statistical categories are not complements, are they substitutes? Empirical analysis by Hausmann and Fernandez-Arias (2000) and Lane and Milesi-Ferretti (2000) point to country characteristics that determine both the overall volume of external

---

85. Although the regression coefficient is significant (with a t-value of 3.78), its standard error is 0.22, indicating the distinction between "bank countries" and "capital-market countries."

86. Recall that bank loans and deposits in table 1.3 measure both loans *from* foreign banks and deposits *by* residents of emerging markets in foreign banks.

Figure 1.1 Relation between FDI stock and debt stock by region, 1980, 1990, 1998

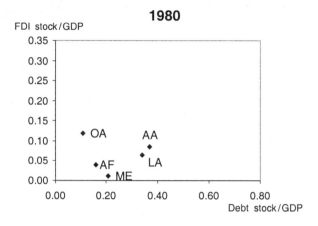

1980

FDI stock/GDP

Debt stock/GDP

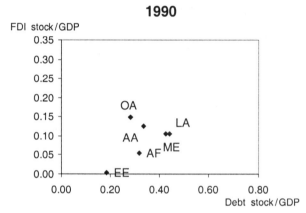

1990

FDI stock/GDP

Debt stock/GDP

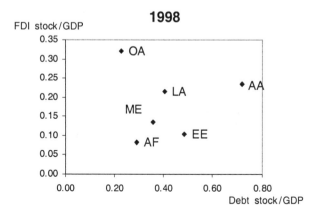

1998

FDI stock/GDP

Debt stock/GDP

AA = Five affected Asian countries; **OA** = Other Asia; **EE** = Emerging European economies; **LA** = Latin America; **ME** = Middle East; **AF** = Africa.

capital and the composition between bank loans, portfolio investment, and FDI. The nature of the characteristics suggests only a limited scope for substitution. Lane and Milesi-Ferreti find that trade openness stimulates all forms of external capital, but favors equity over debt. Trade openness particularly favors FDI. Trade openness, of course, depends on a country's long-term policy choices and its geographical position in the world economy. Hausmann and Fernandez-Arias emphasize, however, that FDI accounts for a particularly large share of external *private* liabilities in poor countries: The unconditional correlation between GDP per capita and the FDI share is –0.41.[87]

The available evidence does not persuasively demonstrate that FDI flows or portfolio investments are ready substitutes for bank finance. Policy measures that discourage bank loans might reduce the overall flow of capital to emerging markets. This could be particularly true in poorly governed, corrupt countries, where portfolio and foreign direct investors fear they will be taken to the cleaners (Smarzynska and Wei 2000; Wei 2000). But the available evidence also appears to suggest that, with appropriate incentives, financial institutions might shape capital flows in ways better suited to the long-term needs of emerging markets.

Two pieces of evidence can be cited for this suggestion. First, in their analysis of capital flows between the mid-1970s and 1992 to five industrial countries and five emerging markets, Claessens, Dooley, and Warner (1995) examined time series of different types of capital flows (bank loans, FDI, portfolio equity, long-term debt, and short-term debt). They concluded that the *share* of inflows corresponding to each type made no difference to the overall *level* of capital inflows reaching the destination country.

Second, there is the famous Chilean "policy experiment" with capital controls during the 1990s. Starting in 1990, Chile imposed an unremunerated reserve requirement (URR) on short-term capital inflows in hopes of dampening the total volume of foreign capital reaching the country. Chile's URR policy was not hugely successful in meeting its primary objective. However, De Gregorio, Edwards, and Valdes (2000), and Edwards (2000a) conclude that the URR shifted the structure of incoming capital toward longer-term lending—without affecting much the overall volume of foreign lending.

---

87. The share of FDI in *total* external liabilities (public and private) does not vary with the level of per capita GDP. Hausmann and Fernandez-Arias's (2000) analysis applies only to the share of FDI in *private* external liabilities. In their view, FDI should not be attributed with better characteristics than other kinds of capital inflows. It is just that poor countries must rely to a greater extent on FDI. Albuquerque (2000) makes the related argument that FDI will be a larger share of external private capital for countries with poor credit risk. Note that Lane and Milesi-Ferretti (2000) find that FDI is a smaller share of external *private* liabilities for larger countries. This suggests that larger countries (regardless of per capita GDP level) have an easier time attracting bank loans and portfolio investment.

Of course, loans with different maturity terms (short-term vs. long-term) are closer substitutes than, for example, bank loans and portfolio investment, or bank loans and FDI. The extent of substitution under *existing* institutional arrangements requires more investigation.[88] Additional research is needed to determine the extent of capital-market substitution that might emerge with *different* institutional features. Pending this research, we are "substitution optimists." We believe appropriate configurations of incentives in G-10 financial markets and emerging-market nations can shift the supply toward longer-term, less volatile flows.

Supply-side incentives within the G-10 countries can alter the terms of available capital flows from world financial centers. Such incentives, if put in place for a period of time can, we think, also alter institutional features in emerging markets. For example, proper incentives on the supply side can encourage destination countries to foster local stock exchanges and welcome foreign direct investment. Conversely, improper incentives on the supply side can make bank loans the cheapest, most accessible source of foreign capital—-and thereby lay the foundation for future financial turmoil.

---

88. As Michael Dooley points out (personal communication), if moral hazard provides a common impetus for two different categories of capital flow (e.g., interbank loans and syndicated loans), policy measures to curtail moral hazard will diminish flows in both categories.

2

The Players, Their Supervisors, and Moral Hazard

Our review of costs and benefits in the previous chapter highlighted short-term bank debt as a particularly troublesome component of international capital flows. In this chapter, our focus turns to the major suppliers of capital, concentrated in the G-10 countries. Much of the literature on international financial architecture implicitly assumes that the G-10 financial institutions and their supervisors have their monitoring and incentive systems "about right" and that crisis conditions lie on the demand side. Is this assumption correct? If not, more problems lie ahead —even if the IMF and emerging economies, working together, dramatically reform the demand side of international capital. As we argued, potential capital flows to and from emerging-market economies, already large, are likely to grow because of various strong incentives. Larger flows and stocks of international capital will bring benefits, but they also will create more worries about stability.

In this chapter, we examine the basis for the assumption that all is well on the supply side of world capital markets. We argue that distortions contribute to the instability of the cross-border bank lending demonstrated in table 1.2—and could in the future affect portfolio flows. The significant issue is the moral hazard that arises from the special status of banks in national financial systems. Although governments and supervisors have offset the safety nets they provide to banks—through legislative and institutional changes discussed below—constant innovation in financial markets creates opportunities to circumvent regulatory efforts. More can and should be done to achieve a better alignment between market forces and incentives for managers and shareholders of banks— and for their supervisors.

We argue in this chapter that the G-10 supervisors can improve the "plumbing" of the international financial architecture. In a coordinated way, the G-10 has a large role to play both in preventing and managing future crises. We first distill a few supervisory lessons from the Asian and Russian crises. Then we describe the private-market players, paying particular attention to the special role of banks in the international financial system and why moral hazard is such a persistent and subtle problem. We then analyze key issues in offsetting moral hazard through prudential supervision, beginning with national comparisons and ending with the G-10's international system through the Bank for International Settlements, the International Organization of Securities Commissions (IOSCO), and similar institutions in such related areas as insurance and accounting.

Lessons from Asia and Russia

The main features of the 1997-98 episodes are well known. Less understood, however, is the flavor of financial-institution involvement. The crisis in East Asia was distinct from the crisis in Russia. The Asian crisis was more gradual, beginning in mid-1997 with the collapse of the Thai baht, followed by banking and economic shocks that spread to Thailand's major regional trading partners and then to South Korea. As the crisis unfolded, Asians in the affected countries moved tens of billions of dollars offshore—using the facilities of G-10 banks. The bulk of the debt contracts that were at risk in Asia were short-term, nontraded, interbank loans.[1] Most of these loans originated with Japanese and European banks (table 1.7).

By contrast, the Russian crisis was a unilateral default ("restructuring") of sovereign debt—a tradable financial instrument. This instrument had been widely used as collateral to obtain credit from G-10 banks. Hence the default "immediately triggered the unwinding of leveraged positions by large, internationally active financial institutions."[2] Much of the financing for Russian and other emerging-market sovereign debt had been arranged and leveraged by US banks.

Although the shocks and financial institutions differed from crisis to crisis, the use of debt instruments was a common element. In the run-up to a crisis, financial houses extended credit to increasingly risky borrowers, and paid higher prices for emerging-market debt instruments. As knowledgeable players took more risks, less knowledgeable players followed them. Many firms borrowed heavily to leverage their bets. Leverage was easy, with hedge funds borrowing from banks and banks

---

1. See IMF (1998).

2. IMF (1998, 50).

borrowing from each other, using emerging-market debt instruments as collateral.

Russia became the poster country of high-risk finance. In 1996, Russian treasury bills (GKOs) were sensibly regarded as time bombs; no bank would accept them as collateral for a loan. But gradually the view took hold in Wall Street that, for political reasons, Russia had become too big to fail. Banks relented and began to accept GKOs as security, but at half their market value. By early 1998, some hedge funds were borrowing up to 95 percent of these assets as collateral.[3] Banks also lent to each other on similar terms.

When the IMF refused a bailout to prevent default on the GKOs, widespread surprise turned to panic. Everyone headed for the exits. Losses were huge because many firms had been doing the same thing, using the same risk-management models. All those positions could not be unwound simultaneously. Liquidity dried up. For a period, no one would lend, even to strong North American corporate accounts. The final chapter was the near-collapse of Long Term Capital Management, a huge hedge fund run by brilliant managers. The combination of unexpected events, LTCM's risk exposure, and high leverage contributed to its problems. The size, persistence, and pervasiveness of the widening spreads confounded its risk-management models, producing huge losses. After LTCM was refinanced by its major counterparties in September 1998, its weaknesses became clear. They included its risk-management systems, the inadequacy of its capital base, and most important the failure of market discipline. LTCM's counterparties did not understand the hedge fund's risk profile when they granted credit on generous terms, mainly on the basis of its managers' reputations (FSF 2000b).

The Asian and Russian episodes illustrate key issues on the supply side that deserve more attention: bias in the incentive systems of G-10 countries toward the use of debt, and the significant role played by the large international financial institutions, particularly banks. We do not dispute the importance of reforms (including better exchange rate systems) urged on the finance ministries, central banks, and borrowers in emerging economies. Some of the criticisms aimed at the IMF are also warranted. But we think the G-10 market players and financial supervisors deserve far more scrutiny.

The top financial players constantly innovate as new technologies make financial engineering possible. By the same token, they quickly respond to any shifts in the incentive structure imposed through official regulation. The activities of the top players are beyond the reach of the IMF. They must not, however, be beyond the reach of G-10 financial supervisors, particularly the bank and securities-market regulators.

---

3. See Risk Management: Too Clever by Half, *The Economist*, 14 November 1998, 82-85.

The Market Players

As the tables in chapter 1 illustrate, there are three main types of private-capital flows: bank loans and deposits, other portfolio investment, and foreign direct investment. Each type is associated with particular institutions—commercial banks, other financial institutions, and nonfinancial firms. In this section, we describe the size and nationality of the large players.

Commercial Banks

Table 2.1 lists the 50 largest commercial banks by market capitalization as of October 2000. Market capitalization, rather than sheer asset size, probably better measures a bank's ability to move funds from one country or sector to another.[4]

The large continental European banks (those in the euro zone plus Switzerland) in 1999 had market capital of about $524 billion and assets of approximately $6.4 trillion. When figures for UK commercial banks are added in, European market capitalization rises to about $850 billion and assets to about $8.6 trillion. Europe is a banking powerhouse. Indeed, the European role is so crucial that no approach to the regulation of international lending can survive without European support.

The Maastricht Treaty did not make Europe a single entity for banking supervision. The European Central Bank is finding its way in exchange rate and monetary policy. For the foreseeable future, national regulators will retain control over supervisory matters. Changes in the fabric of international understandings over bank supervision will require consensus among the European powers.

In market capitalization, at $850 billion the large US banks are about the same as their European counterparts; but in asset size, they are a distant second to the Europeans, at $3.8 trillion. The large Japanese commercial banks follow on market capitalization, at $300 billion, but are second to the Europeans with assets of $6.7 trillion.

Commercial-banking power is clearly concentrated in Europe, the United States, and Japan. Moreover, banks based in the G-10 plus Spain account for 90 percent of the market capitalization and assets of the top 50 commercial banks in the world. As table 2.2 shows, banks based in the G-10 countries plus Spain account for about 92 percent of the assets of all commercial banks located in BIS reporting countries, about 80 percent of the external assets of these banks, and about 72 percent of claims on

---

4. Several banks in China and Europe rank among the top 50 in terms of asset size, but poor-quality loans sharply diminish their market capitalization—and their ability to move money from country to country.

Table 2.1 World's largest 50 commercial banks by market capitalization, October 2000 (billions of dollars)

Global rank	Banks	Market capitalizaton[a] Sept. 1999	Oct. 2000	National rank[c]	Total assets, Dec. 1999	Net income, Dec. 1999	Shareholder equity,[b] Dec. 1999
Continental Europe							
8	ING Bank	46	66	1	351	1.7	14
12	UBS	58	55	2	614	3.9	22
13	Crédit Suisse Group	50	54	3	452	3.3	22
15	Deutsche Bank	36	48	4	843	2.6	23
17	Banco Santander Central Hispano	33	45	5	258	2.2	17
19	BNP Paribas		43	6	702	1.7	22
	Banque Nationale de Paris	26					
	Paribas	16					
21	ABN AMRO	29	34	7	460	2.6	13
25	Banco Bilbao Vizcaya Argentaria	25	28	8	240	2.2	18
26	UniCredito Italiano	21	26	9	170	1.3	10
30	Société Générale	19	22	10	408	2.4	12
29	HypoVereinsbank	20	22[d]	11	505	0.4	14
32	Dresdner Bank	21	21	12	398	1.1	12
43	San Paolo IMI	16	17[d]	13	141	1.1	8
45	Fortis Bank	34	16	14	330	1.2	9
49	Commerzbank	17	14	15	374	0.9	12
49	KBC Bank	13	14[d]	16	147	0.7	6
	Total for Continental Europe	482	524[d]		6,393	29.1	234
Japan							
3	Mizuho Holdings, Inc.		115	1			51[e]
3	Dai-Ichi Kangyo Bank[f]	39			463	−3.8	20
3	Industrial Bank of Japan[f]	32			390	−1.5	13
3	Fuji Bank[f]	42			489	−3.6	18
7	Sumitomo Sakura (tentative)		68	2	56[e]		
	Sumitomo Bank[g]	47			464	−4.8	15
	Sakura Bank[i]	31			414	−4.0	18
10	Bank of Tokyo Mitsubishi	72	56	3	664	−0.7	23
11	UFJ Holdings, Inc.		55[d]	4			36[e]
	Sanwa Bank[h]	39			425	−4.0	18
	Tokai Bank[h]	16			269	−2.4	13
	Toyo Trust & Banking[h]	n.a.			67	−1.3	5
40	Asahi Bank	20	18[d]	5	247	−2.1	12
49	Mitsubishi Trust & Banking[i]	16	14[d]	6	149	−1.4	7
50	Sumitomo Trust & Banking	11	10[d]	7	127	−1.2	6
	Total for Japan	364	336[e]		6,472	−48.1	260

(*table continues next page*)

Table 2.1 World's largest 50 commercial banks by market capitalization, October 2000 (billions of dollars) (*continued*)

Global rank	Banks	Market capitalizaton[a] Sept. 1999	Oct. 2000	National rank[c]	Total assets, Dec. 1999	Net income, Dec. 1999	Shareholder equity,[b] Dec. 1999
United Kingdom							
2	HSBC Holdings	97	122	1	569	5.4	37
9	Royal Bank of Scotland	19	58[d]	2	146	1.4	7
	NatWest[j]	39	n.a.	n.a.	292	n.a.	14
14	Lloyds TSB	68	52	3	285	4.1	14
18	Barclays	44	44	4	402	2.8	14
35	Abbey National	25	19	5	292	2.0	8
46	Standard Chartered	15	15[d]	6	88	0.6	6
46	Bank of Scotland	15	15[d]	7	116	1.0	6
	Total for United Kingdom	322	324[d]		2,191	17.3	106
United States							
1	Citigroup	149	237	1	717	9.9	50
4	J.P. Morgan Chase & Co.		83	2			35[e]
	Chase Manhattan[k]	63	n.a.	n.a.	406	5.4	24
	J.P. Morgan[k]	20	n.a.	n.a.	261	2.1	11
5	Bank of America	96	79	3	633	7.9	44
6	Wells Fargo & Company	65	78	4	218	3.7	22
16	Bank of New York Company	25	46	5	75	1.7	5
20	Bank One	41	42	6	269	3.5	20
22	Fleet Boston Financial	34	34	7	191	2.0	15
23	MBNA	18	30	8	31	1.0	4
24	First Union	34	30	9	253	3.2	17
27	Fifth Third Bancorp	17	24	10	42	0.7	4
27	Mellon Financial	17	24	11	48	1.0	4
33	State Street	n.a.	20	12	61	0.6	3
35	PNC Bank	16	19	13	75	1.3	6
35	Northern Trust	n.a.	19	14	29	0.4	2
35	Firstar	25	19	15	73	0.9	6
40	U.S. Bancorp	22	18	16	82	1.5	8
46	SunTrust Banks	21	15	17	95	1.3	8
50	National City	16	13	18	87	1.4	6
50	Wachovia	16	11	19	67	1.0	6
50	KeyCorp	12	11	20	83	1.1	6
	Total for United States	707	850		3,796	51.7	271
Other							
31	National Australia Bank	2	21	1	166	1.8	12
34	Hang Seng Bank Ltd	20	20[d]	2	n.a.	n.a.	n.a.
35	Royal Bank of Canada	13	19	3	184	1.2	9
40	Commonwealth Bank of Australia	14	18[d]	4	91	0.9	5
43	Toronto Dominion Bank	12	17	5	146	2.0	8
50	Westpac Banking Corp	12	13	6	92	1.0	6
50	Development Bank of Singapore	12	13[d]	7	64	0.6	6
	Total for other	105	121[d]		742	7.6	46

Table 2.1   (*continued*)

	Market capitalizaton[a]			Total assets, Dec.	Net income, Dec.	Shareholder equity,[b] Dec.
	Sept. 1999	Oct. 2000	National rank[c]	1999	1999	1999
Total for largest 50	1,980	2,155		19,594	58	917
Total for G-10	1,900	2,070		19,182	53	888

n.a. = not available/not applicable
G-10 = Group of Ten countries; see note to table 1.1.
a. Market capitalization is defined as the number of ordinary shares currently in circulation multiplied by the current share price. Market capitalization as of October 2000 is presented for the banks that had a market capitalization higher than $11 billion as of September 1999.
b. Shareholder equity is defined as the sum of issued common stock, capital surplus or premium, various reserves, and retained earnings. Shareholder equity includes group equity attributable to consolidated minority interests.
c. Rankings within the country or region.
d. Estimates based on the available rates of change from September 1999 to October 2000. The market capitalization and shareholder equity figures represent combined estimate for the merged banks.
e. Total for the merged banks.
f. Merged in September 2000
g. Merged in April 2001.
h. Will merge in April 2002.
i. Will merge with Nippon Trust and Tokyo Trust in October 2001.
j. NatWest Bank merged with the Royal Bank of Scotland in March 2000.
k. Announced a merger in September 2000.

Sources: Euromoney, *The Bank Atlas*, 2000, http://www.euromoney.com; American Banker, *The Top 100 World Financial Companies, Q3 1999*, http://www.americanbanker.com; Yahoo! Finance, *Company Profiles* finance.yahoo.com, Bloomberg Financials, http://www.bloomberg.com.

developing countries. In turn, the claims on developing countries represent about 4 percent of the assets of G-10 and Spanish commercial banks.

Portfolio Investors

Three groups of financial institutions dominate the flow of portfolio capital: investment banks, wealth managers, and insurance companies. Table 2.3 lists nine large investment banks, all based in New York with offices in London and other financial centers. In 1998, these nine firms had a combined market capitalization in excess of $130 billion, and controlled assets in excess of $1.8 trillion.

Investment banks act as guardians to the securities markets: Nearly all public and private shares, bonds, and asset-backed securities are brought to market by an investment bank. Fulfilling the same function, they are expanding the securities markets of emerging economies. They also act as the pilots of privatization, mergers, and takeovers—now a core feature of

Table 2.2 Total assets and external assets of all commercial banks, June 2000 (billions of dollars)

Country	Total assets[a]	External assets Amount	Share of total assets (percent)	Claims on developing countries[b] Amount	Share of total assets (percent)
Austria	423	91	22	33	8
Bahamas	316	244	77	61[c]	19
Bahrain	100	92	92	46[c]	46
Belgium	806	309	38	26	3
Canada	720	98	14	31	4
Denmark	244	58	24	6	2
Finland	121	31	25	4	3
France	2,486	607	24	135	5
Germany	4,535	901	20	240	5
Ireland	423	160	38	2	0
Italy	1,345	191	14	47	4
Japan	8,460	1,199	14	258	3
Luxembourg	821	495	60	124[c]	15
Netherlands	1,080	296	27	67	6
Norway	157	14	9	3	3
Singapore	574	405	70	202[c]	35
Spain	889	124	14	57	6
Sweden	348	67	19	12	2
Switzerland	1,632	709	43	177[c]	11
United Kingdom	5,802	1,990	34	138	2
United States	6,223	889	14	144	2
Total for all BIS reporting countries	37,506	8,968	24	1,813	5
Total for G-10	34,326	7,378	21	1,331	4

BIS = Bank for International Settlements.
G-10 = Group of Ten countries; see note to table 1.1.

a. Total assets are calculated as banking institutions (deposit institutions) reserve, claims on the public sector, claims on the private sector (lines 20, 21, 22 from IFS), plus external assets. Figures are converted into US dollars using the market exchange rate at the end of June 2000.
b. Developing countries are countries other than Andorra, Australia, Austria, Belgium, Canada, Cyprus, Denmark, Finland, France, Germany, Gibraltar, Greece, Iceland, Ireland, Italy, Japan, Liechtenstein, Luxembourg, Malta, Netherlands, New Zealand, Norway, Portugal, Spain, Sweden, Switzerland, Turkey, the United Kingdom, the United States, the Vatican City State, and the former Yugoslavia.
c. These countries do not disclose their claims on developing countries. Such claims are arbitrarily (and generously) estimated at half the external assets of commercial banks in Bahrain and Singapore and a quarter of the external assets of banks in the Bahamas, Luxembourg, and Switzerland.

Sources: IMF, *International Financial Statistics (IFS)*, November 2000; Bank for International Settlements; *BIS Quarterly Review*, November 2000, http://www.bis.org.

Table 2.3 Large investment banks, 1998 (billions of dollars)

	Revenue	Assets	Market capitalization[a]
Merrill Lynch[b] (United States)	36	300	25
Morgan Stanley Dean Witter[b] (United States)	31	318	50[c]
Goldman Sachs (United States)	22[d]	217[e]	29[c]
Lehman Brothers Holdings[b] (United States)	20	154	10[c]
Salomon Smith Barney[f] (United States)	8	211	n.a.
Credit Suisse First Boston[g] (United States/ Switzerland)	7	280	n.a.
Paine Webber[h] (United States)	7	54	6[i]
Bear Stearns[j] (United States)	8	154	5[i]
Donaldson, Lufkin, & Jenrette[k] (United States)	5	72	7[i]
Total	144	1,760	132 plus
Total for G-10	144	1,760	132 plus

n.a. = not available (subsidiaries of large holding companies: Citigroup and Crédit Suisse Group, respectively; individual market capitalization is not available).
G-10 = Group of Ten countries; see note to table 1.1.
a. Market capitalization is calculated by multiplying the total number of shares by the share price at the company's fiscal year-end.
b. *Source: Fortune* Global 500, 1999. Data shown are for the fiscal year ended on or before 31 March 1999. Assets shown are those at the company's fiscal year-end, http://www.pathfinder.com/fortune/global500/index.html.
c. Figures, as of September 1999, are from *American Banker*, http://www.americanbanker.com/BankRankings.
d. *Source:* 1998 *Goldman Sachs Annual Review.* Assets as of November 1998, http://www.gs.com/about/annual/1998/4_fs/index.html.
e. *Source: Financial Times Company Financials.* Revenue as of 27 November 1998, http://www.globalarchive.ft.com/cb/cb_search.htm.
f. *Source:* 1998 *Citigroup Annual Report,* 20. Revenue figures for year ending 31 December 1998. Asset figures as of 31 December 1998, http://www.citigroup.com/citigroup/fin/data/c1998ar2.pdf.
g. Source: 1998/1999 *Crédit Suisse Group Annual Report,* 23, http://www.csg.ch/csg_annual_report_98/download/csg_ar98_p1_en.pdf.
h. *Source:* 1998 *Paine Webber Annual Report,* 34-35, http://www.painewebber.com/annual98/graphics/fininfo/index.htm.
i. Individual figures are obtained from Yahoo! The time for valuations is as follows: Bear Stearns, December 1999; Lehman Brothers, November 1999; Paine Webber and Donaldson, Lufkin & Jenrette, September 1999.
j. *Source:* 1999 *Bear Stearns Annual Report,* 55-56. Figures are for fiscal year ending 30 June 1998, http://www.bearstearns.com/corporate/investor/index.htm.
k. *Source:* 1999 *Donaldson, Lufkin, and Jenrette Annual Report,* "Financial Highlights," http://www.dlj.com/pdf/DLJ98_1.pdf.

global capitalism. In addition to their underwriting role, investment banks earn substantial profits from trading securities.

Wealth-management firms are the second group of portfolio institutions. They typically deal with the public—individuals and companies that want a trusted firm to manage their pensions and other funds. Table 2.4 lists 10 large wealth managers, all based in the G-10. Together, these 10 firms control $6.4 trillion in assets, and their own market capitalization

Table 2.4   Large asset managers in 1998 (billions of dollars)

	Total assets under management[a]	Market capitalization[b]
UBS (Switzerland)	1,145	58[c]
Fidelity Investments (United States)	773	n.a.
Kampo (Japan)	698	n.a.
Credit Suisse Group (Switzerland)	680	50[c]
AXA Group (France)	647	39[c]
Barclay's Global Investors (United States)	616	44[c]
Merrill Lynch & Co. (United States)	501	25[c]
State Street Global Advisors (United States)	493	n.a.
Capital Group Cos. (United States)	424	n.a.
Zurich Financial Services (Switzerland)	415	45[c]
Total	6,392	261 plus
Total for G-10	6,392	261 plus

n.a. = not available (usually a nonpublic company).
G-10 = Group of Ten countries; see note to table 1.1.

a. Figures are assets under management at fiscal year-end 1998.
b. Market capitalization is calculated by multiplying the total number of shares by the share price at the company's fiscal year-end.
c. Figures from *American Banker*, http://www.americanbanker.com/BankRankings.

Sources: *Institutional Investor*, 1999, http://www.iimagazine.com/research/interface.html; US (II300), Asia (Asia200), and Europe (Euro100) Asset Management Rankings, *American Banker*, http://www.americanbanker.com/BankRankings.

exceeds $260 billion. For the most part, wealth managers are long-term portfolio investors.

Hedge funds represent a highly specialized investment vehicle that is not widely available to the public. Most hedge funds are leveraged; they employ dynamic (and sometimes opportunistic) trading strategies involving positions in several different markets; they adjust their investment portfolios frequently in anticipation of asset price movements or changes in yield differentials between related securities. Hedge funds are opaque to market monitoring: They are subject to little direct regulation and are under few obligations to disclose information. Hence, the size of the industry is difficult to measure.

If they are measured by capital under management or by assets, hedge funds are small relative to established wealth managers. As table 2.5 shows, the capital managed by 20 large hedge funds in late 1998 amounted to less than $50 billion. Estimates vary widely, but if all hedge funds are counted, their assets range from $100 to $300 billion. Even the highest number is less than 5 percent of the combined assets of investment banks and traditional asset managers.

The amount of leverage used by hedge funds depends on trading strategies that are in turn shaped by investor attitudes toward risk. Leverage

Table 2.5   Largest hedge funds according to capitalization, August 1998 (billions of dollars)

Fund	Capital under management
Domestic[a]	
Tiger	5.1
Moore Global Investment	4.0
Highbridge Capital Corp	1.4
Intercap	1.3
Rosenberg Market Neutral	1.2
Ellington Composite	1.1
Hedged Taxable-Equivalent	1.0
Quantitative Long/Short	0.9
Sr International Fund	0.9
Perry Partners	0.8
Offshore	
Jaguar Fund NV	10.0
Quantum Fund NV	6.0
Quantum Industrial Fund	2.4
Quota Fund NV	1.7
Omega Overseas Partners	1.7
Maverick Fund	1.7
Zweig Dimenna International	1.6
Quasar International Fund NV	1.5
SBC Currency Portfolio	1.5
Perry Partners International	1.3
Total[b]	47.1

a. Long Term Capital Management (LTCM) was in serious difficulty in August 1998, and is omitted from the list.
b. Estimates of hedge fund capital and the number of funds vary significantly. MAR/Hedge estimated 1,115 funds with $109 billion capital under management at the end of 1997; Van Hedge Fund estimated 5,500 funds with capital of $295 billions at the same date.

Source: Adapted from Eichengreen (1999a).

is achieved using such instruments as repos (repurchase agreements), futures and forward contracts, and other derivative products.[5] It is also very difficult to measure. A Financial Stability Forum (FSF 2000b) study of hedge funds noted that—although there are problems with the way data vendors report these positions—estimates suggest most hedge funds use modest amounts of leverage, averaging 2:1, but ranging to 4:1 in some. FSF (2000b) further notes difficulties with evaluating the risk-adjusted performance of hedge funds because of their dynamic trading strategies.

---

5. Positions are established by posting margins rather than the face value of the position.

The positive role of hedge funds—providing diversification to investors because their returns have low correlations with standard asset classes—is counterbalanced by some negative features. Hedge funds and other highly leveraged institutions (HLIs) may take concentrated positions and engage in aggressive market practices that amount to "ganging up" on a small economy (such as Hong Kong).[6] Under normal market conditions, HLI positions are not destabilizing, but some of the aggressive practices documented in 1998 are worrisome. The FSF study group participants agreed (2000b, 112) that such practices raise important issues for market integrity, but they could not agree that market manipulation was sufficiently widespread to be a serious concern for policymakers.

Insurance companies are the third group of portfolio institutions. These are divided into two categories: property and casualty companies, and life and health insurance companies. Ten large companies of each category are listed in table 2.6. In 1998, the 10 property and casualty insurance companies had $1.6 trillion in assets and more than $330 billion in market capitalization. The 10 life insurance companies had $2.8 trillion in assets.[7] Combining both categories, 100 percent of assets are controlled by insurance companies based in the G-10 and Spain. In portfolio management styles, life insurance companies tend to hold longer-term assets, whereas property and casualty companies tend to hold shorter-term instruments.

Nonfinancial Multinational Enterprises

The last players are the nonfinancial multinational enterprises (MNEs). The world's 100 largest corporations measured by 1998 revenue are recorded in tables 2.7 and 2.8. The 30 financial giants among the top 100 are separately shown in table 2.7. Most of the firms appeared in previous tables. Together these 30 financial giants had revenues of $1.3 trillion and controlled assets of $11.3 trillion.[8]

Table 2.8 lists the 70 top nonfinancial giants. Their revenues in 1998 were $4.0 trillion, and their assets (at book value) measured $4.5 trillion. Measured by revenue or assets, about 95 percent of the giants are based in the G-10. These firms are responsible for a large share of the world's

---

6. See IMF (1999c) for a description of the "double play" that hedge funds are accused of using in an attempt to destabilize Hong Kong in August 1998.

7. Many life insurance companies are owned by their policyholders, and therefore do not have a market capitalization.

8. By comparison, the larger set of 96 financial firms listed in previous tables controlled $32.2 trillion in assets. This is the total amount of assets recorded in tables 2.1 (50 commercial banks), 2.2 (9 investment banks), 2.4 (10 asset managers), and 2.6 (20 insurance companies). The largest hedge funds might add $300 billion to the total.

Table 2.6   20 large insurance companies in 1998
(billions of dollars)

Property and casualty insurance companies	Revenue[a]	Assets[b]	Market capitalization[c]
Allianz (Germany)	65	402	62[d]
Assicurazioni Generali (Italy)	48	178	30[d]
State Farm Insurance Cos. (United States)	45	111	n.a.
Zurich Financial Services (Switzerland)	39	215	45[d]
CGU (United Kingdom)	38	176	20[d]
Munich Re Group (Germany)	35	131	n.a.
American International Group (United States)	33	194	135[d]
Allstate (United States)	26	88	20[d]
Royal & Sun Alliance (United Kingdom)	25	76	11[d]
Loews (United States)	21	71	7[e]
Total	375	1,642	330 plus
Total for G-10	375	1,642	330 plus

Life and health insurance	Revenue[a]	Assets[b]	Market capitalization[c]
AXA (France)	79	452	39[d]
Nippon Life Insurance (Japan)	66	363	n.a.
ING Group (Netherlands)	56	464	46[d]
Dai-ichi Mutual Life Insurance (Japan)	44	253	n.a.
Sumitomo Life Insurance (Japan)	40	206	n.a.
TIAA-CREF (United States)	36	250	n.a.
Prudential Ins. Co. of America (United States)	34	279	n.a.
Prudential (United Kingdom)	34	197	30[d]
Meiji Life Insurance (Japan)	28	146	n.a.
Metropolitan Life Insurance (United States)	27	215	n.a.
Total	444	2,825	n.a.
Total for G-10	444	2,825	n.a.

n.a. = not available (usually an insurance company owned by its policyholders).
G-10 = Group of Ten countries; see note to table 1.1.

a. Data shown are for the fiscal year ended on or before 31 March 1999.
b. Assets shown are those at the company's fiscal year-end.
c. Market capitalization is calculated by multiplying the total number of shares by the share price at the company's fiscal year-end.
d. Market capitalization data as of September 1999, from *American Banker,* http://www.american banker.com.
e. Individual company's market capitalization as of September 1999, from Yahoo!, yahoo. marketguide.com.

Sources: Fortune Global 500, 1999, http://www.pathfinder.com/fortune/global500/index.html; *American Banker,* http://www.americanbanker.com/RankingBanks/1999; Yahoo! Marketguide, yahoo.marketguide.com.

Table 2.7   Financial firms in the 100 largest companies, by revenue, 1998 (billions of dollars)

Global rank	Company	Revenues[a]	Assets[b]	Type
Continental Europe				
15	AXA (France)	79	452	Insurance
23	Allianz (Germany)	65	402	Insurance
28	Ing Group (Netherlands)	56	464	Insurance
37	Credit Suisse (Switzerland)	49	475	Banks: commercial and savings
39	Assicurazioni Generali (Italy)	48	178	Insurance
42	Deutsche Bank (Germany)	45	736	Banks: commercial and savings
56	Zurich Financial Services (Switerland)	39	215	Insurance
68	Munich Re Group (Germany)	35	131	Insurance
72	ABN AMRO Holding (Netherlands)	34	507	Banks: commercial and savings
77	Credit Agricole (France)	33	459	Banks: commercial and savings
80	HypoVereinsbank (Germany)	32	541	Banks: commercial and savings
84	Fortis (Belgium)	31	397	Banks: commercial and savings
98	Société Générale (France)	30	450	Banks: commercial and savings
United Kingdom				
47	HSBC Holdings	43	485	Banks: commercial and savings
58	CGU	38	176	Insurance
74	Prudential	34	197	Insurance
United States				
16	Citigroup	76	669	Diversified financials
35	Bank of America Corp.	51	618	Banks: commercial and savings
44	State Farm Insurance Cos.	45	111	Insurance
64	TIAA-CREF	36	250	Insurance
67	Merrill Lynch	36	300	Securities
71	Prudential Ins. Co. of America	34	279	Insurance
76	American International Group	33	194	Insurance
79	Chase Manhattan Corp.	32	366	Banks: commercial and savings
83	Fannie Mae	31	485	Diversified financials
88	Morgan Stanley Dean Witter	31	318	Securities
Japan				
21	Nippon Life Insurance	66	363	Insurance
45	Dai-ichi Mutual Life Insurance	44	253	Insurance
54	Sumitomo Life Insurance	40	206	Insurance
91	Bank of Tokyo-Mitsubishi	31	664	Banks: commercial and savings
Total		1,279	11,341	
Total for G-10		1,279	11,341	

G-10 = Group of Ten countries; see note to table 1.1.

a. Data shown are for the fiscal year ended on or before 31 March 1999.

b. Assets shown are those at the company's fiscal year-end.

Source: Fortune Global 500, *1999*, http://www.pathfinder.com/fortune/global500/index.html.

Table 2.8 Nonfinancial firms in the 100 largest companies, by revenue, 1998 (billions of dollars)

Global rank	Company	Revenues[a]	Assets[b]	Transnationality index[c]	Type
Continental Europe					
2	DaimlerChrysler (Germany)	155	160	44.1	Motor vehicles and parts
11	Royal Dutch/Shell Group (Netherlands)	94	110	58.9	Petroleum refining
17	Volkswagon (Germany)	76	70	56.8	Motor vehicles and parts
22	Siemens (Germany)	66	67	52.1	Electronics, electrical equipment
32	Metro (Germany)	52	22	n.a.	Food and drug stores
34	Fiat (Italy)	51	76	40.8	Motor vehicles and parts
36	Nestle (Switzerland)	50	41	93.2	Food
46	Veba Group (Germany)	43	51	27.5	Trading
49	Renault (France)	41	45	45.7	Motor vehicles and parts
53	Deutsche Telekom (Germany)	40	93	n.a.	Telecommunications
57	Royal Philips Electronics (Netherlands)	38	33	86.4	Electronics, electrical equipment
59	Peugeot (France)	38	40	38.7	Motor vehicles and parts
62	Electricité de France (France)	37	113	n.a.	Utilities, gas and electric
63	Rwe Group (Germany)	37	47	n.a.	Utilities, gas and electric
65	BMW (Germany)	36	36	60.7	Motor vehicles and parts
66	Elf Aquitaine (France)	36	43	57.6	Petroleum refining
69	Vivendi (France)	35	58	n.a.	Engineering and construction
70	Suez Lyonnaise des Eaux (France)	35	85	n.a.	Energy
78	ENI (Italy)	32	49	31.7	Petroleum refining
86	Bayer (Germany)	31	34	82.7	Chemicals
92	ABB Asea Brown Boveri (Switzerland)	31	32	95.7	Electronics, electrical equipment
93	BASF (Germany)	31	31	59.5	Chemicals
95	Carrefour (France)	30	20	n.a.	Food and drug stores

(table continues next page)

Table 2.8 Nonfinancial firms in the 100 largest companies, by revenue, 1998 (billions of dollars) (*continued*)

Global rank	Company	Revenues[a]	Assets[b]	Transnationality index[c]	Type
United Kingdom					
19	BP Amoco	68	85	59.2	Petroleum refining
43	Unilever	45	36	92.4	Food
United States					
1	General Motors	161	257	29.3	Motor vehicles and parts
3	Ford Motor	144	238	35.2	Motor vehicles and parts
4	Wal-Mart Stores	139	49	n.a.	General merchandisers
8	Exxon	101	93	65.9	Petroleum refining
9	General Electric	100	356	33.1	Electronics, electrical equipment
14	Intl. Business Machines	82	86	53.7	Computers, office equipment
25	US Postal Service	60	55	n.a.	Mail, package, and freight delivery
27	Philip Morris	58	60	51.1	Tobacco
29	Boeing	56	37	n.a.	Aerospace
30	AT&T	54	60	21.9	Telecommunications
40	Mobil	48	43	59.7	Petroleum refining
41	Hewlett-Packard	47	34	51.1	Computers, office equipment
50	Sears Roebuck	41	38	n.a.	General merchandisers
55	E.I. du Pont de Nemours	39	40	n.a.	Chemicals
61	Proctor and Gamble	37	31	47.7	Soaps, cosmetics
75	Kmart	34	14	n.a.	General merchandisers
81	Texaco	32	29	45.3	Petroleum refining
82	Bell Atlantic	32	55	n.a.	Telecommunications
85	Enron	31	29	n.a.	Energy
87	Compaq Computer	31	23	n.a.	Computers, office equipment
89	Dayton Hudson	31	16	n.a.	General merchandisers
94	J.C. Penney	31	24	n.a.	General merchandisers
96	Home Depot	30	13	n.a.	Specialty retailers
97	Lucent Technologies	30	27	n.a.	Electronics, electrical equipment
100	Motorola	29	29	n.a.	Electronics, electrical equipment

Japan

5	Mitsui	109	56	35.8	Trading
6	Itochu	109	57	33.3	Trading
7	Mitsubishi	107	75	36.9	Trading
10	Toyota Motor	100	125	40.0	Motor vehicles and parts
12	Marubeni	94	55	30.0	Trading
13	Sumitomo	89	46	25.9	Trading
18	Nippon Telegraph & Telephone	76	147	n.a.	Telecommunications
20	Nissho Iwai	68	39	38.8	Trading
24	Hitachi	62	82	21.4	Electronics, electrical equipment
26	Matsushita Electric Industrial	60	67	33.2	Electronics, electrical equipment
31	Sony	53	53	62.8	Electronics, electrical equipment
33	Nissan Motor	51	58	51.1	Motor vehicles and parts
38	Honda Motor	49	43	64.1	Motor vehicles and parts
48	Toshiba	41	51	25.2	Electronics, electrical equipment
51	Fujitsu	41	43	32.6	Computers, office equipment
52	Tokyo Electric Power	40	122	n.a.	Utilities, gas and electric
60	NEC	37	42	n.a.	Electronics, electrical equipment
90	Tomen	31	18	n.a.	Trading
99	Mitsubishi Electric	30	35	n.a.	Electronics, electrical equipment

China

73	Sinopec	34	52	n.a.	Petroleum refining

Total (average for transnationality index)	3,988	4,479	49.0
Total for G-10 (average for the index)	3,954	4,427	49.0

n.a. = not available
G-10 = Group of Ten countries; see note to table 1.1.

a. Data shown are for the fiscal year ended on or before 31 March 1999.
b. Assets shown are those at the company's fiscal year-end.
c. The index of transnationality is calculated as the average of ratios of foreign assets to total assets, foreign sales to total sales, and foreign employment to total employment, as of 1997 (UNCTAD).

Sources: Fortune Global 500, *1999*, http://www.pathfinder.com/fortune/global500/index.html; UNCTAD (1999).

93

foreign direct investment. The "transnationality index" (table 2.8) shows that, on average, they conducted about half their business outside their home country.[9]

Overview of the Players

Our review of the major players points to two major features. First, a handful of big players—fewer than 200 firms, all told—control the action in international capital markets. Their dominance will doubtless erode, but for now financial power is strikingly concentrated with them. Second, the big players are overwhelmingly based in the G-10 countries plus Spain. The responsibility to supervise them rests not in the IMF, nor in Basel, but squarely in Washington, London, Tokyo, and the other G-10 capitals. At year-end 1999, the G-10 countries plus Spain accounted for 84 percent of world banking assets, 86 percent of world stock market capitalization, and 76 percent of international debt securities (BIS 2000a; World Bank 2000b).

International private capital flows are of three types: bank loans and deposits, portfolio investment, and foreign direct investment. In cumulative total flows to emerging markets, FDI was the biggest story in the 1990s, amounting to $954 billion (table 1.2). Portfolio flows were next, cumulatively amounting to somewhere between $612 billion (table 1.2) and $764 billion (table A.1). Bank loans and deposits are the most complicated story.

The Key Role of Banks

Banks are more important as an epicenter than as a wellspring. Banks generate waves in the flow of capital to emerging markets, rather than a continuous steady stream. According to data compiled by the Institute of International Finance (table A.1), net bank lending to emerging markets cumulated to $269 billion in the 1990s. However, deposits by emerging-market residents in G-10 banks more than offset G-10 bank lending to these countries during the decade. According to IMF data, cumulative bank loans net of deposits amounted to a negative $135 billion (table 1.2).

In other words, when loans and deposits are combined, net bank activity that moves financial resources to emerging markets is small in comparison with portfolio investment and FDI. But bank loans are the lubricant of any financial system. Depending on circumstances, banks can be shock absorbers or shock propagators. In recent decades, with

---

9. The transnationality index is calculated as a simple average of the share of assets, sales, and employees outside the home country.

respect to emerging markets, banks have more often been propagators than absorbers. The average annual swing in bank lending to emerging markets was nearly $50 billion—by far the largest source of year-to-year fluctuations in capital flows. Both interbank loans between Europe, Japan, and Asia, and sovereign Russian debt used as loan collateral, played a major role in the 1997-98 crises—not because banks are profligate players, but because of the incentives they face and the instruments they use. Accordingly, our story begins with banks.

Banks in the Modern Financial System

As we noted in the previous paragraph, the problem of financial volatility in emerging-market economies is associated with bank lending. If and when repayment problems arise, cross-border private bank loans and bond placements are such that private creditors have no plausible means of seizing assets from either private or sovereign borrowers. Thus, although international finance can nourish entrepreneurs and accelerate growth, a necessary complement may be a drastic creditor response in the event of nonpayment—to withhold fresh funds and force an economic crisis (Dooley 2000).

This argument is based on the characteristics of banks. They are not "bad" per se. They perform three essential functions in any financial system: pooling the resources of disparate savers, and channeling these resources into productive investment; improving resource allocation through their expertise in assessing and monitoring borrowers; and facilitating the division of risk among numerous creditors.[10] But by their very nature, banks are prone to two problems: asymmetric information (the borrower knows more about the potential risk and return of its projects than the bank); and adverse selection (riskier borrowers will pay higher interest rates and thus may constitute a disproportionate share of bank loan portfolios).[11]

Bank loans are illiquid fixed-price instruments. They cannot easily be converted to cash, although they can be bundled into securities (known as "securitization"). Once loan terms have been agreed on, the only way a bank can adjust for shifting market conditions is by changing the quantity of its exposure. When a borrower runs into trouble, the bank can mix

---

10. See Levine (2000) for a concise description of the role of banks in the financial system.

11. The asymmetric information problem helps to explain why banks dominate the immature financial systems of emerging-market economies. The general lack of information on borrowers and undeveloped legal systems to enforce contracts hamper suppliers of long-term financial instruments such as equities and bonds in evaluating risk and reward. Banks are best suited in these circumstances to solve the asymmetric information problem by evaluating and monitoring private loans. As more and better information becomes available, capital markets develop and financial systems mature.

and match from two unpleasant menus: It can roll over existing loans and extend new credit, or it can call some part of existing loans and attempt to recover the principal. It can also hedge by selling short other claims on the borrower. These choices entail either an unwelcome extension of the bank's exposure or credit rationing against the borrower. When trouble brews, all banks encounter the same conditions; in the aggregate, they prefer less exposure, and ensuing credit restrictions lead to volatile bank lending.

Innovation

Since the 1980s, national and international banking systems have been transformed by deregulation, intensified competition, and the information and communications-technology revolutions. The market environment is one of intense competition, particularly in traditional banking activities. The innovations point away from traditional activities of plain vanilla deposit taking and loan making. Three big themes are discernible. First, the walls separating commercial banks, investment banks, portfolio managers, and insurance firms are falling, even if they are still distinct. Second, large banks are shifting toward securitization—creating securities out of everything from credit card debt, to trade finance, to disaster insurance—and earning fees in the process. Third, all large banks are shifting toward trading activity, making markets and taking short-term stakes in bonds, shares, and derivatives.[12] These activities, when successful, satisfy the search for higher yields.[13]

Many of the new financial instruments that banks trade are "off balance sheet." This means that banks are not required to allocate capital against them. In swap contracts, for example, neither side pays cash at the outset, and therefore neither party has an asset in the traditional sense.[14] Futures and options contracts can be written with a relatively small initial

---

12. Derivatives have no value of their own. They "derive" their value from the value of the underlying asset. They include swaps, futures (contracts for future delivery at specified prices), and options (which give one party the right, but not the obligation, to buy from or sell to a counterparty at an agreed price).

13. Maxfield (1998) analyzed available evidence of emerging-market investor objectives, most of it before the crisis. Analysis of portfolio equity flows is sensitive to the choice of period, with year-over-year data indicating that investors respond to country "fundamentals." Other evidence suggests more ambiguity. Ranking by "investor impatience," i.e., the search for yield over value, Tesar and Werner (1995) find short-term bank flows to be the most yield driven, followed by portfolio investment, FDI, and long-term bank lending.

14. Because market risk, credit risk, and country risk interact in complex ways, new financial instruments have been created to help reduce negative interactions. One is the "total return swap," which has become an instrument of choice for hedge funds looking for high leverage. Banks also use the total return swap to cover risks without increasing their capital requirements.

margin relative to the potential risk. Credit derivatives limit credit risk by transferring the potential loss associated with corporate loans and bonds, sovereign debt, and other loan portfolios to counterparties.[15]

Deregulation and innovation, working in combination, seem to have pushed banks into trading activity and leveraged plays, but not into share ownership—even in jurisdictions that have no prohibition against equity stakes. Among the G-10 banking systems, the highest ratio of share ownership to assets was only 5 percent in 1996, reached in Germany and Japan (Berlin 2000).[16]

The wave of innovation in financial instruments, and the accompanying expansion of banking beyond its old boundaries, is a two-edged sword. On one side, it allows risk management far beyond what was traditionally possible. Risk can now be shifted from firms that can ill afford losses to those that can. Banks can profitably act as intermediaries in shifting risk. On the other side, the innovation wave creates huge opportunities for leveraged plays, fostering a speculative search, by banks themselves, for high returns that in turn magnify their own risks.[17]

Leverage

The potential for damage is illustrated in an extreme form by figure 2.1. To precisely measure a firm's leverage, all positions must be known and realistically valued—which may be impossible to do. Because many activities—such as repos[18] and derivatives—do not appear on the institution's

---

15. Credit derivatives include total return swaps, credit default swaps, credit-linked notes, and collateralized debt obligations. They are the fastest-growing sector of the global derivatives market.

16. Banks seem to specialize in lending even when they are allowed to mix finance and commerce, for reasons related both to how they are expected to behave with distressed firms and to other intricacies of lender liability (Berlin 2000). Yet a recent cross-country study found that restrictions on banking and commerce are associated with greater financial instability (Barth, Caprio, and Levine 2000).

17. Leverage is the magnification of the rate of return (positive or negative) on an investment, beyond the rate obtained by solely investing funds owned by the institution. It is often defined as the ratio of assets to equity. Leverage is achieved by increasing the size of an investment by borrowing or using derivative instruments such as futures or options. These allow investors to earn a return on the notional amount underlying the contract by committing a small portion of equity in the form of a margin deposit or option premium payment.

18. In a repo (repurchase agreement), one party (typically a trader) buys a bond and sells it to a dealer for cash with a promise to buy it back the next day at the same price plus the overnight interest rate. As long as the overnight interest rate is lower than the interest accruing on the bond, the trader earns some income on the bond. The extreme form of these kinds of transactions was discovered at LTCM, the failed US highly leveraged institution, which appears to have controlled more than $120 billion in assets from an investment of about $3 billion. This leveraging was accomplished mostly through the use of repos (Mayer 1999).

Figure 2.1   Hypothetical example of leverage

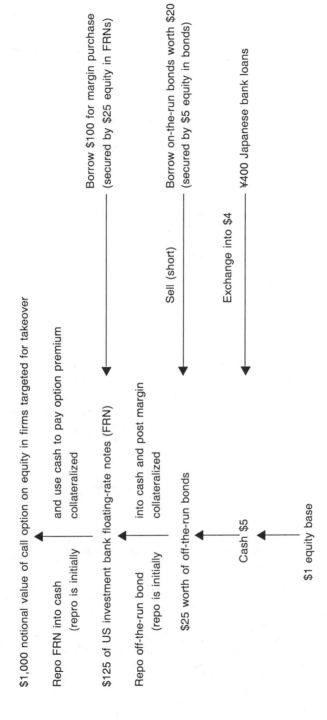

$1,000 notional value of call option on equity in firms targeted for takeover

Repo FRN into cash
(repro is initially   and use cash to pay option premium
collateralized

$125 of US investment bank floating-rate notes (FRN)

Borrow $100 for margin purchase
(secured by $25 equity in FRNs)

Repo off-the-run bond
(repo is initially   into cash and post margin
collateralized

$25 worth of off-the-run bonds

Sell (short)

Borrow on-the-run bonds worth $20
(secured by $5 equity in bonds)

Cash $5

Exchange into $4

¥400 Japanese bank loans

$1 equity base

FRN = floating rate notes
Repo = repurchase agreement
Source: IMF (1998).

balance sheet, and because balance sheets are published quarterly at best, outsiders have a difficult time assessing the extent of a firm's leverage.[19] Leveraging by a single firm enhances its risk of default; the widespread use of leverage in the financial system can magnify market adjustments, especially when they require "deleveraging"—unwinding prior positions. Rapid adjustments can cause credit to dry up and asset prices to plummet. In a mark-to-market environment, falling asset prices trigger calls for additional collateral that can ripple through markets.

Risk Management

Because it is confronted with the widespread use of leverage and proliferating kinds of risk, international finance is increasingly driven by risk evaluation and control.[20] Different institutions face various risk profiles and differing kinds of risk. The most common risks can be quickly ticked off. Banks, because of their traditional intermediary role of channeling the resources from savers to borrowers, face significant *credit risk*, the risk of default or delay in the payment of principal and interest. They must also manage *market risk*, the risk that the prices of their liabilities may change faster than their assets. Market risk devastated US savings and loan institutions in the late 1980s.

Closely associated with market risk are *interest-rate risk* (unexpected changes in market interest rates that slash margins, net income, and the economic value of a bank's equity) and *foreign exchange risk* (losses that arise when assets denominated in an appreciating foreign currency are less than liabilities denominated in that currency). Banks make numerous loans to other banks around the world; portfolio investors buy securities; direct investors acquire fixed assets; and all incur *country risk* (economic and political uncertainty in the host country). During the height of the Asian crisis, for example, interbank loans to Japanese banks reflected the credit risk of lending to these banks, the so-called Japan premium.

Substantial attention has been lavished on country risk analysis since the 1982 debt crisis in developing countries. Yet, in spite of this expertise, the Asian crisis occurred in part because of a sudden upward reappraisal of country risk after the Thai baht collapsed in April 1997. Banks and other financial institutions must also manage *liquidity risk*, the risk that market conditions will change, unexpectedly depressing demand and prices of assets at the time they want to sell these assets. And they must manage *operational risk*—failures in control systems or people that cause

---

19. Another example of asymmetric information: Both risk and leverage are difficult for outsiders to assess without full, timely disclosure.

20. A longer discussion of these issues can be found in Managing Global Finance in IMF (1999c).

financial loss or damage reputations. Operational risk devastated Barings Bank in 1995.

Financial institutions practice risk management to measure all these risks, the potential damage to their investment positions, and ultimately the chance of becoming insolvent. VAR (value at risk) risk models measure, subject to certain assumptions, the amount of the firm's capital that is exposed in each period. For example, the VAR model might say that, in a 3-standard-deviation worst case (a case that is not supposed to happen more than 1 percent of the time), the firm will loose 25 percent of its capital during the next year.

VAR models are widely used but like all models they have weaknesses. They rely on past values to estimate key variables; in financial markets, past values are not always good predictors of future risks. Moreover, rising volatility and higher loss correlation among different asset classes in a portfolio will cause all banks using these models to reduce their exposures at the same time by switching to less volatile and less correlated assets, such as US Treasury bills (Persaud 2000).

Newer risk models entail stress testing and scenario analysis. Scenario analysis envisages possible adverse changes, one at a time, that might affect the investment portfolio. Stress testing estimates potential losses when several individual risk factors simultaneously move against the firm, but it too uses historical probabilities.

Financial Volatility

The combination of trading activity and modern risk management lie at the root of financial volatility. When risks increase, banks must either raise more capital to cover the greater risk or reduce their exposure, by cutting loan exposure, by selling securities, or by undertaking new derivative trades. Raising more capital is time-consuming, and in a crisis very expensive because bank shares are depressed. So banks look to the other alternatives. If the bank can reduce lending, it need not book a loss. But most banks use the same VAR models, and, as indicated above, these models will encourage them to reduce their outstanding loans at the same time, actually magnifying loan volatility.

If banks attempt to reduce their exposure to risk by selling securities or undertaking new derivative trades, they may trigger large price shocks because of limited, and shrinking, market liquidity.[21] The liquidity problem is compounded when a small number of large institutions hold the same positions.[22] Take your pick: loan volatility or price

---

21. For example, derivative markets usually rely on underlying securities markets that produce continuous prices. When these markets are interrupted, financial shocks can trigger a cascade of margin calls and sell orders that move prices very sharply.

22. See IIF (1999a).

volatility. As two experts have observed (Folkerts-Landau and Garber 1998),

> [V]olatility even in one country will automatically generate an upward re-estimate of credit and market risk in a correlated country, triggering automatic margin calls and tightening of credit lines. . . . Thus, apparently bizarre operations that connect otherwise disconnected securities markets are not the responses of panicked green screen traders arbitrarily driving economies from a good to a bad equilibrium. Rather, they work with relentless predictability and under the seal of approval of supervisors in the main financial centers.

One of the lessons of the 1997-98 crisis must surely be that market participants and their regulatory supervisors relied too heavily on quantitative tools and insufficiently on judgment.[23]

The Anomaly of Modern Banking

These changes in the banking environment accentuate an existing anomaly. The anomaly is that banks, even as they grow larger and increasingly engage in more risky and complex transactions, are perceived to enjoy implicit and explicit public guarantees.

The guarantees grow out of an incentive problem inherent in banking: *asymmetric information*, which we mentioned above. Depositors know less about a bank's management and the quality of its balance sheet than do its managers and shareholders. Thus, in times of uncertainty or adversity, bank depositors—uncertain whether they will have access to their deposits—are prone to bank runs. This prospect has, in turn, compelled governments to treat banks differently than other firms, because a bank that fails can disrupt the rest of the economy.[24]

To prevent such crises, governments have entered into quid pro quo arrangements with banks. Governments provide them both with an implicit safety net, in the form of an unstated promise by the central bank to act as a lender of last resort in a liquidity crisis, and an explicit safety net, in the form of a public deposit insurance fund to reassure depositors. In return, the banks submit to closer government oversight and regulation of their activities than is usual for industries in the private sector.

The "insurance" provided by the public safety net contributes to another incentive problem, *moral hazard*. Banks acquire greater tastes for risk and face less market discipline than other firms. The explicit deposit insurance safety nets actually have, or are perceived to have, blanket coverage that extends beyond the retail depositors (households and small

---

23. See Ferguson (1999).

24. As Gerald Corrigan (1982) put the matter, "Banks are special." Corrigan (2000) reiterated this view, even after all the changes of the past two decades. Unlike other institutions, banks offer on-demand transactions, are a backup liquidity source for other institutions, and serve as a "transmission belt" for monetary policy.

businesses) for which they were originally intended. The implicit central bank safety nets extend, in a crisis, to nearly all depositors and banks. Thus banks are both viewed, and behave, as if they will be bailed out if they get into trouble.

The existence of a public safety net raises a perennial question: Do banks have an unfair advantage over other financial institutions because of the subsidy provided by the safety net? This question was at the heart of intensive study and debate in the United States leading up to the passage in November 1999 of the Financial Services Modernization Act (also known as the Gramm-Leach-Bliley Act). The size of the gross subsidy is difficult to estimate, despite determined research efforts. Some suggest it is well under 100 basis points and is at least partly offset by the direct costs of deposit insurance premiums, interest payments on bonds issued by the Financing Corporation,[25] reserve requirements, regulatory expenses, and operational costs associated with collecting deposits.[26] Conversely, Kwast and Passmore (2000) suggest that banks can expand their scope far beyond the levels that other financial institutions could reach with the same equity base but without the public safety net.

A related concern in the US debate is whether allowing banks to expand their activities into securities and insurance will ultimately extend the safety net and add to the subsidy. The Financial Services Modernization Act deals with this issue by maintaining a legal separation between banks and the rest of the banking organization, known as large complex banking organizations (LCBOs): They must engage in most securities activities and insurance underwriting through separately capitalized investment bank subsidiaries or holding company affiliates. This act can be said to have merely brought US banking laws closer to those of most other industrial countries (Barth, Brumbaugh, and Wilcox 2000; Barth, Nolle, and Rice 2000). If the fire wall is well-maintained and stoutly defended, the safety net will neither expand in practice nor become a source of comfort to noncommercial bank subsidiaries of LCBOs.

The quid pro quo exacted by governments to offset the subsidy is closer public-sector monitoring of banks' activities through prudential supervision. The effectiveness of this closer official scrutiny—and closer market monitoring—are the subjects of the next section.

Prudential Supervision

Are G-10 bank supervisors adequately responding? In this section we first assess the case for and compare the structures of prudential supervisory

---

25. The Financing Corporation was created by Congress in 1987 to sell bonds to raise funds to help resolve the savings and loan crisis.

26. See Levonian and Furlong (1995); Jones and Kolatch (1999); Shull and White (1998); and Whalen (1999a, 1999b).

systems, both within and among the G-10 economies plus Spain, and consider whether these offset the subsidy provided by the public safety net. Despite offsetting regulation and supervision, implicit and explicit guarantees by G-10 governments to their banks *are still* a source of banking instability in the emerging-market economies.

National Systems for Prudential Supervision

Governments use prudential supervision to reduce the moral hazard and adverse selection created by their own safety nets. Supervisors establish regulations and monitor compliance to limit risk taking and ensure the safety and soundness of the banking system. In a thoughtful analysis of the case for prudential supervision, Frederic Mishkin (2000) identifies the main forms that supervision can take, including the tasks of granting banking charters and licenses, establishing capital requirements, setting deposit insurance premiums and defining disclosure requirements, as well as carrying out bank examinations. Bank examiners gather information from banks and evaluate whether they are following the regulators' rules; in cases of weakness, they are empowered to change banks' behavior and close them if necessary.

Supervisors also may restrict competition, define the activities in which banks may engage and restrict their asset holdings, and separate banks and other financial (or nonfinancial) activities. During the past two decades, the barriers separating commercial banks, investment banks, insurance firms, and securities firms have been all but eliminated (table B.1). Deregulation has stimulated competitive forces that drive diversification and consolidation of the financial industry, nowhere faster than in the United States.

The Financial Services Modernization Act of 1999 confirmed this trend. It eliminated restrictions dating back to the Glass Steagall Act of 1933, which once prevented banking, insurance, and securities firms from entering each other's businesses (Barth, Brumbaugh, and Wilcox 2000). Cross-pillar mergers among banks, insurance, and securities firms are well under way to form giant financial holding companies. The 1999 merger between Citibank (banking) and Travelers (insurance) created the model for megafinance and confirmed new challenges for supervisors.

Mishkin (2000) notes the corresponding evolution in US supervision, from an emphasis on rules-based regulation (detailed rules for operational behavior and the quality of line items in the balance sheet) to an approach that stresses the soundness of bank management practices, especially risk management.

Appendix B outlines the systems of financial supervision now in the place in the G-10 countries plus Spain. Some systems, like the UK and Canadian approach, are models of simplicity—organized to keep pace with the spreading reach of financial conglomerates. Other systems, like the US and French approaches, show traces of the bureaucratic divisions that made sense in an era when banking, securities, and insurance were sharply separated.

The US Model

The US model of financial regulation, delineated in the Financial Services Modernization Act of 1999, blends functional and umbrella supervision. Bank and thrift regulators oversee depository institutions. New nonbank activities are subject to both functional regulation (e.g., by the Securities and Exchange Commission and state insurance examiners) and umbrella supervision (of financial holding companies) by the Federal Reserve.[27]

The UK Model

Another supervisory model exists in the United Kingdom, as well as in Australia, Canada, and Switzerland.[28] In this model, banking supervision is separated from the monetary policy function. The regulatory structure is considerably simplified by relying on a consolidated financial regulator, separate from the central bank, for both banking and nonbanking activities. The remaining question, answered differently depending on the country, is the extent to which the regulator relies on home-country surveillance of banks and conglomerates that have a local presence.

Regulatory Models Compared

Appendix B provides more detail on the differences in these models. German simplicity contrasts with French complexity. In France, the banking commission is chaired by the governor of the central bank and includes representatives from the Treasury. The commission supervises compliance with regulations, but the central bank inspects banks on behalf of the commission.[29] In countries such as the United States and France, with multiple supervisors and crossover functions, internal coordination is critical. At the same time, multiple agencies create regulatory competition. When each agency knows what the other is doing, transparency within government circles can help to limit principal-agent problems of regulation.[30]

The discussion as to where, in the public bureaucracy, financial super-

---

27. See Meyer (1999a).

28. Canada has a similar degree of simplification, with the exception that securities firms are still regulated by provincial authorities.

29. See Pratti and Schinasi (1999, 67).

30. The agents are the bank regulators, and the principals are the taxpayers. Agents may pursue their own interests, including bureaucratic survival and postgovernment employment opportunities, rather than the national interest in banking safety and soundness.

vision should be placed goes back many years. Peek, Rosengren, and Tootell (1999) argue that a synergy exists between monetary policy and prudential supervision because information gained in the course of supervision can increase the accuracy of macroeconomic forecasts. A twist to this argument is that the information on the state of financial institutions available to the central bank as supervisor can facilitate its role as lender of last resort. Conversely, there is the concern that a supervisory role will compromise the central bank's independence of action with respect to its core mandate—maintaining price stability. As these arguments have played out, financial supervision has generally been shared between central banks and other regulators, or placed entirely in the hands of an independent regulator. However, in Italy, the Netherlands, and Spain, central banks are the sole banking supervisor.

Goodhart (1995) examined the arguments and evidence for each model and concluded that there were no overwhelming arguments or evidence for one or the other.[31] Going forward, a key problem for any financial supervisory system is dealing with (and closing as necessary) weak banks. If both central banks and other regulators have this responsibility, close coordination between them is critical. Another problem is large conglomerate banks, LCBOs. Although they are less likely to fail because of the diversification of their assets and liabilities, they are more likely to be rescued. They are also more likely to be multinational enterprises with international implications. Goodhart observes that regulation of these entities might be put in the hands of the central bank because it is less amenable to political pressures. In any event, the complexity of LCBO operations suggests that greater supervisory rigor is necessary.

The US Congress was persuaded that broad oversight would help contain the moral hazard problem, and accordingly gave the Federal Reserve the role of umbrella supervisor, with the understanding that the Fed will scrutinize depository activity more intensely than nonbank financial activities. Under this approach, LCBOs such as Citigroup are subject to much closer monitoring than smaller and simpler institutions.[32] The US regulatory model requires enormous cooperation between the Fed, other bank supervisors, and the functional regulators for insurance and securities, but it also benefits from regulatory competition.

Public Safety Nets

One of prudential supervisors' biggest challenges is to reduce moral hazard. For many years, commercial banks engaged in communal self-insurance

---

31. National systems of supervision are path dependent; they are determined by the structure of financial institutions and history in each country. If Goodhart (1995) is right, outcomes are not materially better or worse with one model of supervision rather than another.

32. See Ferguson (1999).

to deal with crises. They formed voluntary groups that agreed to rescue troubled members. As financial markets evolved and competition intensified, banks were no longer willing to play this role. Private-sector insurance is one alternative, but moral hazard and adverse selection would appear to prevent it from happening. Public safety nets have developed because of the low probability and high cost of potential bank runs. A clear trade-off is involved. The effectiveness of insurance in preventing bank runs is greater the more comprehensive the coverage. But the more comprehensive the coverage, the greater the moral hazard—bank managers, bank directors, investors, and depositors all take on greater risks in the belief that the safety net will protect them against losses.

All G-10 countries have compulsory public safety nets for banks (table 2.9). Deposit insurance agencies are officially organized in Canada, the Netherlands, Sweden, Switzerland, and the United States; organized by the industry in France, Germany, Italy, and the United Kingdom; and jointly organized by the public and private sectors in Belgium, Japan, and Spain.

How well do G-10 governments offset the subsidy provided by the public safety net? This is a question on which there is substantial debate. As banking organizations have become more complex, the challenges that supervisors face have become more difficult. One challenge is to align the incentives facing bank managers and shareholders with those of depositors. Another is the principal-agent problem in supervision. We have discussed the incentive structures for financial institutions, but we have said little about the incentives for supervisors themselves and the distortions they can generate in the financial system.

In one of the many studies of the US savings and loan crisis of the 1980s, Kane (1989) documented both problems. He described managers using cosmetic approaches to disguise the magnitude of insolvency; regulators practicing forbearance even though they knew of the deteriorating risk profiles of the institutions for which they were responsible; and legislators increasing deposit insurance without regard for any offsetting changes in supervision. A subsequent overhaul of the legislative framework for the Federal Deposit Insurance Corporation (FDIC), known as the FDIC Improvement Act of 1991 (FDICIA), aimed to introduce a clearer incentive structure for both regulators and regulated institutions.

The changes introduced by this US legislation are worth discussion with respect to the other G-10 countries as well. First, FDICIA created a stronger signal to management and investors by targeting deposit insurance at small depositors only and by risk-weighting the deposit insurance premiums paid by banks to reflect their capital adequacy and bank examiner ratings. Among the G-10 countries rated in table 2.10, deposit insurance premiums vary considerably—but it is not clear that the differences have much to do with risk-weighting. Most G-10 countries employ funding formulas based, for example, on the total domestic deposit

Table 2.9 Deposit insurance schemes in the G-10 countries: Explicit safety net

Country	Date established	Membership, management[a]	Co-insurance[b]	Coverage limit (dollar equivalent at end of July 1998)[c]	Foreign currency deposit covered	Interbank deposit covered	Funding[d]	Source of funding	Bank's premium costs	Contingency funding from banks or governments
United Kingdom	1982	Compulsory, private	Yes	Larger of 90 percent co-insurance to 33,000	No	No	Unfunded	Banks only	Callable (subject to maximum 0.3 percent of total deposits)	Parliament may increase the maximum payable; £125 million advance facility with Bank of England
United States	1934	Compulsory, official	No	100,000	Yes	Yes	Funded	Banks and government	Up to 0.27 percent total domestic deposits	Borrowing up to $3 billion from US Treasury
Japan	1971	Compulsory, joint	No	71,000 but in full until year 2000	No	No	Funded	Banks and government	0.084 percent of insured deposits	Borrowing up to ¥500bn from Bank of Japan subject to Ministry of Finance approval
Canada	1967	Compulsory, official	No	40,800	No	Yes	Funded	Banks and government	0.33 percent of insured deposits (maximum)	Borrowing up to C$6 billion authorized; further borrowing subject to parliamentary approval
Germany	1966	Compulsory private	Yes	90 percent coinsurance to 22,000	Yes	No	Funded	Banks only	0.03 percent of deposits	Annual levy may be doubled
Italy	1987	Compulsory private	Yes	125,000	Yes	No	Unfunded	Banks and government	Callable (maximum of 1 percent of total deposits)	Two options: defer payment or diminish compensation to be paid

(table continues next page)

Table 2.9 Deposit insurance schemes in the G-10 countries: Explicit safety net (continued)

Country	Date established	Membership, management[e]	Co-insurance[b]	Coverage limit (dollar equivalent at end of July 1998)[c]	Foreign currency deposit covered	Interbank deposit covered	Funding[d]	Source of funding	Bank's premium costs	Contingency funding from banks or governments
Netherlands	1979	Compulsory, official	No	22,000	Yes	No	Unfunded	Banks and government	On demand, maximum of 5 percent of own funds	Government backing subject to parliamentary approval
France	1980	Compulsory, private	No	65,400	No	No	Unfunded	Banks only	Callable (on demand, calls up to FFr200 million)	Extra calls up to FFr1000 million can be made in a 5-year period
Switzerland	1984	Voluntary, official	No	19,700	No	No	Unfunded	Banks only	Callable (on demand)	Underwritten by member banks
Sweden	1996	Compulsory, official	No	31,400	Yes	No	Funded	Banks and government	0.5 percent of deposits	Full emergency coverage while replacing it with a limited system after the emergency
Belgium	1974	Compulsory, joint	No	16,600; 22,000 in year 2000	No	No	Funded	Banks and government	Callable 0.02 percent of deposits from clients	None, insurance limited to assets in fund
Spain	1977	Compulsory, joint	No	16,439	Yes	No	Funded	Banks and government	0.2 percent of deposits (maximum)	Government backing through the Banco de España, subject to approval by royal decree

a. Bank membership in the fund can be either compulsory or voluntary, and the management of the fund can be official and official and private joint, or private.
b. Coinsurance refers to the situation where depositors face a deductible against their insured funds.
c. Coverage limit refers to the explicit amount the authorities promise to insure.
d. Funded scheme means that it is funded ex ante, unfunded otherwise.

Sources: Goodhart (1995); Demirgüç-Kunt and Detragiache (2000); Demirgüç-Kunt and Sabaci (2000).

base. Explicit safety net protection also varies, but only Canada focuses on the protected class.[33] All G-10 countries specify a limit on depositor protection. Under FDICIA, the insurance fund is prohibited from protecting uninsured depositors or creditors at a failed bank, although a discretionary system-wide override is provided for exceptional circumstances—but with stringent requirements for consultation and accountability. Other G-10 countries allow for contingency funding from the public purse, alongside unwritten lender-of-last-resort support. Among large banks, a significant and growing portion of deposit liabilities, including foreign currency and interbank deposits, are uninsured—but depositors assume they will be protected in a crisis.

FDICIA also made some significant qualitative changes to address the principal-agent problem by penalizing weak banks and rewarding strong banks. For example, banks whose capital declined faced progressively tougher regulatory sanctions that, for example, required them to eliminate dividends, restrict their lending, and change their managements. Regulators have also been forced to take prompt corrective action (to reduce the practice of regulatory forbearance in hopes that a bank's fortunes might improve).[34] Unfortunately, comparative qualitative assessments across the G-10 are difficult to make due to lack of information.[35]

This discussion highlights the complexity of evaluating the extent to which prudential supervision and market discipline reduce the moral hazard associated with G-10 safety nets. Our argument is that public safety nets in the G-10 can be linked to banking instability in *other* countries, specifically in the emerging-market economies that have attracted G-10 cross-border bank lending. This lending is a leading source of volatility in capital flows; the large financial institutions, many of which are complex banking organizations, are based in and regulated by authorities in the G-10 economies. These two features of the international financial system are closely related, although it is not possible to test this relationship econometrically.

Two World Bank studies, however, indicate a basis for concern. One study is a cross-country econometric analysis of the relationship between bank stability and deposit insurance (Demirgüç-Kunt and Detragiache 2000), which found a negative relationship. Their estimated model for banking crises in a sample of 61 countries (both industrial and developing) suggests that explicit deposit insurance raises the probability of a crisis by at least 30 percent.[36] Crises are especially likely in countries

---

33. Japan's legislation says it does, but recent experience shows this is not the case.

34. See Goldstein (1997) for a summary of the changes.

35. See Barth, Nolle, and Rice (2000) for a beginning in this area.

36. Demirgüç-Kunt and and Detragiache (2000, table 1) report a logit coefficient of 0.696 with a standard error of 0.397 (the coefficient is significant at the 8 percent threshold). This suggests that the "true" coefficient could well be as small as 0.30 (the reported value minus the standard error).

with immature financial supervisory systems (and not in the G-10), but their analysis does underscore the view that deposit insurance weakens market discipline.[37]

An earlier World Bank analysis established similar results. One was that market discipline is undermined by deposit insurance schemes; another was that illiquid banks are forced to pay more for their funds unless a generous deposit insurance scheme is in place (Demirgüç-Kunt and Huizinga 1999). This econometric study also provides clear-cut evidence that depositor monitoring of banks declines with the existence of deposit insurance schemes. At the heart of the problem is the question of whether deposit insurance is accompanied by increased government monitoring.

This evidence, and the weight of other arguments, suggests that moral hazard is still an issue in the G-10 countries. Consider the ongoing debate about instilling greater market discipline on risk taking by banks. At one extreme is the perennial proposal to do away with safety nets, leaving markets to monitor the players and to force adjustments, but to protect small savers by creating "narrow banks," such as postal saving systems, that are allowed to invest these savings only in risk-free government securities. Whatever the merits of narrow banking, this solution is too extreme to be politically feasible.

A moderate alternative is to force more disclosure by financial institutions to facilitate market monitoring. But transparency has its own problems. Persaud (2000) argues that financial markets cannot reliably discern sustainable from unsustainable positions in the short term. This uncertainty causes banks to "herd" behind market leaders, to exploit their supposedly superior information: "The more herding investors and bankers know about what each other is up to, the [more] unstable markets may become." The implication is that greater transparency in the marketplace by itself will not solve the problem—and, in the short term, more information may exacerbate herding. Further supervisory steps (discussed in the next chapter) are required.

Yet another proposal is to promote private-sector involvement in bank monitoring through market-based alternatives such as Calomiris's subordinated debt proposal (Calomiris 1997; Federal Reserve Board 1999). Banks could be required to issue and maintain a minimum amount of

---

37. Other findings in the Demirgüç-Kunt and Detragiache (2000) study include these propositions: The impact of deposit insurance on bank stability tends to be stronger the more extensive is the coverage offered to depositors, when the scheme is funded, and where the scheme is run by the government rather than by the private sector. Conversely, deposit insurance is detrimental to bank stability where bank interest rates have been deregulated and where the institutional environment is weak. Additional findings on deposit insurance are reported from a recent World Bank conference (8-9 June 2000; http://www.worldbank.org/research/interest/confs/upcoming/deposit_insurance/home.htm). Also see Smalhout (2001).

subordinated debt (e.g., uninsured certificates of deposit) to finance a small fraction (such as 2 percent) of their total nonreserve assets. The subordinated debt would be allowed to earn a set yield *no more* than 50 basis points over the risk-free yield on government treasury bills. This rule would supposedly force banks to operate in a safe manner. Otherwise, subordinated debt holders would redeem their uninsured certificates of deposit, and equity investors would sell their bank shares. Despite its practical problems, the beauty of the subordinated debt requirement is that it enlists market incentives to push banks to avoid excessive portfolio risk.[38]

The thrust of these proposals is very relevant to the arguments in our study. Even in the G-10 countries, government monitoring by itself has not eliminated moral hazard among banks. More work is needed to introduce market monitoring and to improve the incentive structures both for financial institutions and their supervisors. We return to this issue with our recommendations in the next chapter.

Portfolio Institutions: Tomorrow's Problem?

Before proceeding to the issues of international supervision, we flag another potential problem for national regulators. The big asset managers profiled in tables 2.4 and 2.6 answer to diverse groups of pensioners, shareholders, and policyholders. They allocate funds across a number of countries to diversify their risks. They hold liquid assets that can be traded, and they have a higher proportion of long-term assets than banks. Economic shocks can be absorbed through price changes, and their effects spread across time and markets. Thus, when conditions change in a particular market, they are more likely to ride out the storm than to flee. In other words, they have less incentive than banks to pull their investments in the face of adversity. In the 1990s, most large asset managers established a record of "riding out the storm" rather than "running with the wind," although, as we saw in chapter 1, instances of running with the wind were detected in some portfolios. As we write, these institutions have a good record overall in the emerging markets, so why worry?

The Russian crisis and the near-collapse of LTCM previewed the dangers that may await future portfolio managers and G-10 financial ministers. We have presented evidence indicating a systemic bias toward bank

---

38. In late 1996, Argentina began requiring its banks to finance 2 percent of total deposits in the form of subordinated debt, but without a maximum yield provision. The Argentine authorities expect that market discipline will act in concert with the public safety net. One obvious problem with the subordinated debt proposal is that banks may encourage some of their customers to buy the subordinated debt.

lending and debt finance to emerging markets and we have argued for substitution toward equity finance and direct investment.[39]

That is not the end of the story. We noted in the previous chapter that institutional investors can become momentum investors, selling in a downturn. As more portfolio capital is invested in emerging markets, some players may adopt the high-risk, high-leverage strategies of the most aggressive hedge funds. Indeed, the data in box 1.1 show that G-10 portfolio investors held somewhat more long-term debt (more than $500 billion) than equity (less than $400 billion) in emerging markets at the end of 1997. Long-term debt is an ideal vehicle for high-risk, high-leverage strategies. These strategies, practiced on a large scale, could compound a future crisis, harming emerging markets. A big enough crisis could, in turn, pressure G-10 central banks and finance ministers to arrange bailout plans. Instead of shrinking as a systemic financial problem, moral hazard could increase.

National securities regulators are the first line of defense against this scenario. They play a critical role in the safe evolution of capital markets. But regulators today are mandated to approve the issuance of new securities and to monitor the continuing disclosure of material information by issuers. They are far less concerned with, or empowered to monitor, the behavior of the increasingly large wealth-management firms that are the major *purchasers* (and therefore resellers) of these securities.

Within their mandates, the goals of national securities regulators (table 2.10 and appendix B) are similar to the concerns of bank regulators with system safety and soundness. Their focus is also on the incentive systems for management and boards of directors and on disclosure by corporations that issue marketable securities, such as shares, bonds, and asset-backed securities.[40] Issuers of securities possess greater knowledge about the quality of these assets than do the purchasers; hence, investor protection is a key concern of regulators. Moreover, market discipline works best when markets know what is happening. Well-functioning corporations are key agents of wealth creation and social progress. Underperforming corporations waste resources. During recessions, bad corporations get into bad trouble, often with severe social consequences. Inadequate incentives for managers and inadequate accountability for boards and managers thus have negative externalities. Regulators play a vital role in exposing weakness, so that market disciplines come to bear sooner rather than later.

Regulatory emphasis is constantly shifting as financial markets evolve and as the macroeconomic environment changes. Regulators try to balance

---

39. See Rogoff (1999). Also see Berlin (2000) for a perspective on the limited role that banks play as share owners.

40. See Habib and Ljungqvist (2000) for recent empirical analysis showing that corporate share market values are higher when corporate executives have a larger ownership stake.

Table 2.10 Financial-sector regulation, G-10 countries, 2000

	Financial institutions and their supervisors			
Country and supervisory structure	Retail banking	Wholesale banking	Securities	Insurance
United Kingdom	*Financial conglomerates* Financial Services Authority (FSA) = umbrella supervisor			
	FSA	**FSA**	**FSA**	**FSA**
	• Commercial banks (Securities and Investments Board) • Building societies (Building Societies Commission) • Friendly societies (Friendly Societies Commission) • Pensions and life insurance, etc. (Personal Investment Authority)	• Investment funds • Unit trust groups • Pension funds • Merchant banks • Clearing houses • Venture capital	(Securities and Futures Authority) • Primary issuers of securities • Stock exchanges • Stockbrokers	(Insurance Directorate of the Treasury) • Insurance companies • Insurance brokers
United States	*Financial holding companies* Federal Reserve (FR) = umbrella supervisor			
		Federal Reserve	**Securities and Exchange Commission**	**Regulated by States**
	• National banks **(OCC)** • State banks: Members **(FR)** Nonmembers **(FDIC)** • Cooperative banks **(FDIC/FR)** • Insured industrial banks **(FDIC)** • Thrift holding companies **(OTS)** • Savings banks **(OTS/FDIC/FR)** • Savings and loan associations **(OTS)** • Edge Act corporations **(FR)**	• Investment banks • Finance companies	• Primary issuers of securities • Stock exchanges • Stockbrokers • Investment advisors • Mutual funds • Public utility holding companies	• Insurance companies • Insurance brokers

United Kingdom: Treasury — Bank of England — FSA

United States: Treasury — OCC, OTS, FDIC, SEC — FR

(table continues next page)

Table 2.10 Financial-sector regulation, G-10 countries, 2000 (continued)

Country and supervisory structure	Retail banking	Wholesale banking	Securities	Insurance
			Financial institutions and their supervisors	
Japan		*Financial holding companies* Financial Supervisory Authority (FSA) = umbrella supervisor		
	FSA	FSA	FSA (Securities and Exchange Surveillance Commission)	FSA
Prime minister's office — Ministry of Finance; Bureau of Financial Regulation; FRC; FSA; SESC	• City banks • Regional banks • Trust banks • Long-term credit banks	• Investment banks • Asset managers	• Primary issuers of securities • Stock exchanges • Stockbrokers • Pension funds	• Insurance companies • Insurance brokers
Canada		*Financial holding companies* Office of the Superintendent of Financial Institutions (OSFI) = umbrella supervisor		
	OSFI	OSFI	Regulated by provinces	OSFI
Department of Finance; Bank of Canada; OSFI; CDIC	• Banks (previously Office of the Inspector General of the Banks) • Trust and loan companies	• Cooperative credit associations • Fraternal benefit society • Pension funds (previously Department of Insurance)	• Primary issuers of securities • Stock exchanges • Stockbrokers • Asset managers	• Insurance companies (previously Department of Insurance) • Insurance brokers

Financial institutions and their supervisors

Country and supervisory structure	Retail banking	Wholesale banking	Securities	Insurance
Germany		*Financial holding groups* Federal Banking Supervisory Office (FBSO) = umbrella supervisor		
	**FBSO** • Universal banks • Savings banks • Securities banks	**BSO** • Other financial institutions (e.g., management, foreign currency dealings) • Financial enterprises (e.g., leasing, organizations, credit card companies, investment advisors)	**FSSO** • Primary issuers of securities • Stock exchanges • Stockbrokers • Asset managers • Pension funds	**FISO** • Insurance companies • Insurance brokers
Italy		*Bank foundations* Ministry of Finance = umbrella supervisor		
	Bank of Italy • Commerical banks • Savings bank • Securities banks	**Bank of Italy** • Asset managers • Open-end investment companies (SICAVs)	**Consob** • Primary issuers of securities • Stock exchanges • Stockbrokers	**ISVAP** • Insurance companies • Insurance brokers

(table continues next page)

Table 2.10　Financial-sector regulation, G-10 countries, 2000 (*continued*)

Country and supervisory structure	Retail banking	Wholesale banking	Securities	Insurance
		Financial institutions and their supervisors		
The Netherlands		*Financial conglomerates* Council of Financial Supervisors = umbrella supervisor		
	Netherlands Bank	**Netherlandsche Bank**	**Securities Board** **of the Netherlands**	**Insurance Board**
	• Credit institutions (universal banks, cooperative banks, security credit institutions, mortgage banks)	• Investment institutions (securities issuing and trading—primary and secondary markets)	• Stock exchanges • Stockbrokers	• Insurance companies • Insurance brokers
France	**Banking Commission** • Ensuring that credit institutions (and investment firms since the Financial Activity Modernization Act of 1996) comply with laws and regulations • Execute instructions regarding all off-site monitoring and on-site supervision **Banking and Financial Regulatory Committee** • Formulates general regulations for credit institutions and investment firms (capital adequacy requirements, accounting rules, etc.) **Credit Institutions and Investment Committee** • Authorizes and examines financial institutions, except for those within the competence of the Banking Commission		**Commission des Operations des Bourse** • Primary issuers of securities • Stock exchanges • Stockbrokers	**Commission de Contrôle des Assurances** • Insurance companies • Insurance brokers

The Netherlands supervisory structure: Securities Board, Insurance Board, Netherlandsche Bank, The Council of Financial Supervisors

France supervisory structure: Banking and Financial Regulatory Committee, Credit Institutions and Investment Committee, Banking Commission, Ministry for Economic Affairs and Finance, Bank of France

Financial institutions and their supervisors

Country and supervisory structure	Retail banking	Wholesale banking	Securities	Insurance
Switzerland				
Swiss National Bank	*Large banking group*			
	Swiss Federal Banking Commission (SFBC) = umbrella supervisor			
Swiss Federal Banking Commission		**SFBC**	**SFBC**	**Federal Office of Private Insurance**
Federal Office of Private Insurance		• Investment banks	• Primary issuers of securities	• Insurance companies
Private audit firms authorized by SFBC		• Asset management companies	• Stock exchanges	• Insurance brokers
		• Investment funds	• Stockbrokers	
			• Mortgage bond business	
	SFBC			
	• Universal banks			
	• Savings banks			
Sweden				
Ministry of Finance		*Financial holding company groups*		
		Financial Supervisory Authority = umbrella supervisor		
Financial Supervisory Authority		**Credit Market Department**	**Securities Market Department**	**Insurance Market Department**
Riksbank		• Investment funds	• Primary issuers of securities	• Insurance companies
			• Stock exchanges	• Insurance brokers
			• Stockbrokers	
	Credit Market Department			
	• Commercial banks			
	• Savings banks			
	• Friendly societies			

(table continues next page)

Table 2.10 Financial-sector regulation, G-10 countries, 2000 (continued)

Country and supervisory structure	Retail banking	Wholesale banking	Securities	Insurance
		Financial institutions and their supervisors		
Belgium		*Bank holding companies* Banking and Finance Commission = umbrella supervisor		
	Banking and Finance Commission • Commercial banks • Savings banks • Securities banks	**Banking and Finance Commission** • Asset management firms • Investment funds	**Banking and Finance Commission** • Primary issuers of securities • Stock exchanges • Stockbrokers	**Insurance Control Office** • Insurance companies • Insurance brokers • Mortgage companies • Pension funds
		Securities Regulation Fund • Other investment firms and credit institutions (institutions participating in regulated off-exchange market in strips and Treasury certificates)		

Bank of Belgium → Insurance Control Office; Banking and Finance Commission; Securities Regulation Fund

Country and supervisory structure	Retail banking	Wholesale banking	Securities	Insurance
Spain		*Bank holding companies* Banco de España = umbrella supervisor		
	Banco de España • All credit institutions (commercial banks, savings banks, credit cooperatives, official credit institutions, finance, factoring, and leasing companies, mortgage-loan companies, etc.) • Interbank, foreign exchange, and book-entry public debt markets		**Comision Nacional del Mercado de Valores (CNMV)** • Primary issuers of securities • Stock exchanges • Stockbrokers • Venture capital (companies and funds)	**Directorate General Insurance** (Ministry of Economy and Finance) • Insurance companies • Pension funds

Banco de España; Ministry of Economy and Finance → CNMV

Financial institutions and their supervisors

Country and supervisory structure	Banking	Securities	Insurance
Supranational (EU)	**Banking Advisory Committee (BAC)** • Formulates standards for prudential supervision **Banking Supervision Committee (BSC)** • Systemic risk monitoring	**High Level Securities Supervisors Committee (HLSS)** • Coordination of securities market supervision **Securities Contact Committee** • Regulation and implementation of securities admission	**Insurance Committee (IC)** • Formulates standards for prudential supervision
BAC/IC/HLSS Conglomerates: Regulation of prudential supervision			
International	**Basel Committee** • Supervision and regulation, best practices	**International Organization of Securities Commisison (IOSCO)** • Supervision and regulation, best practices	**International Association of Insurance Supervisors (IAIS)** • Supervision and regulation, best practices
Joint Forum Conglomerates: Supervision & regulation: Best practices			
FSF Coordination across supervisors of various functions			

Notes: See appendix B for more information. Boldface type indicates senior or oversight supervisor; normal type indicates adjunct or front-line supervisor; solid line indicates direct responsbility to the senior-ranking authority; dotted line indicates coordination in supervisory activities.

(table continues next page)

Table 2.10 Financial-sector regulation, G-10 countries, 2000 (*continued*)

Glossary of names: United Kingdom: FSA = Financial Services Authority. United States: FR = Federal Reserve; OCC = Office of the Comptroller of the Currency; FDIC = Federal Deposit Insurance Corporation; SEC = Securities and Exchange Commission; OTS = Office of Thrift Supervision. Japan: FRC = Financial Reconstruction Commission; FSA = Financial Services Agency; SESC = Securities and Exchange Surveillance Commission. Canada: OSFI = Office of the Superintendent of Financial Institutions; CDIC = Canada Deposit Insurance Corporation. Germany: FBSO = Federal Banking Supervisory Office; FSSO = Federal Securities Supervisory Office; FISO = Federal Insurance Supervisory Office; BSO = Banking Supervisory Office. Italy: Consob = Commissione Nazionale per le Societa e la Borsa; ISVAP = Instituto per la Vigilanza sulle assicurazioni private e di Interesse colletivo. Switzerland: SFBC = Swiss Federal Banking Commission. Spain: CNMV = The Comision Nacional del Mercado de Valores. Supranational: BAC = Banking Advisory Committee; BSC = Banking Supervision Committee; IC = Insurance Committee; HLSS = High Level Securities Supervisors Committee. International Dimension: FSF = Financial Stability Forum. IOSCO = International Organization of Securities Commission. IAIS = International Association of Insurance Supervisors.

Sources: United Kingdom, Bank of England, http://www.bankofengland.co.uk, Financial Services Authority, http://www.fsa.gov.uk; United States, Board of Governors of Federal Reserve System, http://www.federalreserve.gov; Japan, Bank of Japan, http://www.boj.or.jo, Financial Reconstruction Commission http://www.fsa.go.jp/frc/indexe.html, Financial Services Agency, http://www.fsa.go.jp; Canada, Bank of Canada, http://www.bank-banque-canada.ca, Office of the Superintendent of Financial Institutions, http://www.osfi-bsif.gc.ca/AndreE/index.html; Germany, Deutsche Bundesbank, http://www.bundesbank.de, Federal Banking Supervisory Office, http://www.bakred.de; Italy, Banca d'italia, http://www.bancaditalia.it, Commissione Nazionale per le Societa e la Borsa http://www.consob.it, Instituto per la Vigilanza sulle assicurazioni private e di Interesse colletivo, http://www.isvap.it; The Netherlands, De Nederlandsche Bank, http://www.dnb.nl; France, Banque de France, http://www.banque-france.fr; Switzerland, Schweizerische Nationalbank, http://www.snb.ch/index3.html; Sweden, Sveriges Riksbank, http://www.riksbank.se/default.asp; Belgium, National Bank of Belgium, http://www.bnb.be/sg/index.htm; Spain, Banco de España, http://www.bde.es, The Comision Nacional del Mercado de Valores, http://www.cnmv.es; Supranational (EU), *Institutional Arrangements for the Regulation and Supervision of the Financial Sector*, 2000; International Dimension, Bank for International Settlement, http://www.bis.org; International Organization of Securities Commissions, http://www.iosco.org; International Association of Insurance Supervisors, http://www.iais.org; Financial Stability Forum, http://www.fsforum.org.

the inflexibility of tight surveillance against the need to encourage innovation and growth. The US Securities and Exchange Commission is worried about aggressive accounting by firms and biased reports by securities analysts in an equity environment that prizes steadily higher quarterly earnings.[41] Japanese regulators are preoccupied with opaque interconnections between portfolio institutions, banks, and nonfinancial firms through the keiretsu system. Canadian regulators, reeling from high-profile scandals of managers intentionally misleading investors, are strengthening market discipline through legal penalties aimed at managers and directors of offending firms.

When panic strikes, a securities regulator cannot do much. As the 1987 stock market crash and the LTCM debacle in the fall of 1998 both demonstrated, steep stock and bond price declines can create systemic risks. If severe enough, the wealth effect of falling securities values, and the fear of widespread insolvency, can depress real activity. Flooding the system with liquidity is a central banker's solution—something a securities regulator cannot do.[42] But just as financial supervisors can change the incentive structure to discourage bankers from making risky loans in good times, so securities regulators can pay more attention to incentives on the *demand* side when capital markets are strong.

Prudential Supervision and Innovation—A Footnote

In concluding this discussion of prudential supervision in the G-10, an additional point is worth noting. National regulators face a persistent trade-off between emphasizing financial system safety and soundness while encouraging innovation—in spite of the added risks innovation brings to financial markets. Former US Treasury Secretary Lawrence Summers (2000, 3) has argued by analogy:

> The jet airplane made airplane air travel more comfortable, more efficient, and more safe, though the accidents were more spectacular and for a time more numerous after the jet was invented. In the same way, modern global financial markets carry with them enormous potential for benefit, even if some of the accidents are that much more spectacular. As the right public policy response

---

41. The problem is illustrated by the divergence since mid-1998 between reported earnings by the Standard & Poor's (S&P) 500 and the after-tax profits of all corporations in the national accounts. Generally, these two series move closely with one another. Between mid-1998 and mid-1999, S&P 500 reported that earnings increased by more than 20 percent while after-tax profits of all corporations increased by less than 5 percent (Chase Bank, US Economic and Policy Research: US Weekly Prospects, Chase Securities, Weekly Newsletter, 5 June 2000, 5).

42. For example, the US Securities and Exchange Commission had no direct role in calming markets in the 1987 or 1998 panics.

to the jet was longer runways, better air-traffic control, and better training for pilots, and not the discouragement of rapid travel, so the right public policy response to financial innovation is to assure a safe framework so that the benefits can be realized, not to stifle the change.

Accepting Summers's analogy for the international financial system, better-informed supervisors and investors are a necessary part of the financial system framework. Supervisors require more timely information on the risk profiles resulting from positions taken by financial institutions. They also need a better understanding of risk-management systems. Snapshots of an institution's risk profile and risk-management procedures are no longer adequate. In a world where huge bets are quickly made (and possibly lost—as with Barings Bank in 1995 and LTCM in 1998), supervisors must focus on the soundness of banking *systems* for evaluating and managing risk on a daily basis. Some progress has been made in addressing these issues. US banking examiners are extending their information requirements in banking examinations and increasing their involvement in large, complex, institutions.[43] More awareness is also required of the fact that they are national organizations in a world of cross-border capital flows. To a much greater extent, they need a multinational reach. International supervision and coordination among supervisors are the subject of the next section.

International Supervision: A Decentralized Framework

Our analysis suggests that G-10 supervisors have unfinished business. Bank supervisors need to start yesterday; securities regulators can wait until tomorrow. One G-10 member acting alone cannot correct the bias. In good times, the lending business will simply migrate to other G-10 banks. In bad times, financial problems will not stop at the national border. A way has to be found to establish common international standards for the key financial players in order to prevent crises, and to agree on approaches for managing them. The path has already been laid out. In the wake of the bank failures of the past 25 years, bank supervisors have tried to establish such standards. They have done this without creating a new global institution.

The essence of the international framework is decentralization—global rules and design standards without global institutions that are perceived to intrude on national sovereignty. The awkward jargon for this framework is vertical subsidiarity—"think internationally, act nationally." The international thinking is done by a committee of regulators that meets

---

43. These issues are discussed in Ferguson (1999) and Meyer (2000a).

regularly at the Bank for International Settlements in Basel. The committee establishes principles and standards that are interpreted, implemented, and enforced by national authorities.[44] In this section, we describe these supervisory efforts and their weaknesses. We present our recommendations for addressing these weaknesses in the next chapter.

Basel I

The Basel Capital Accord of 1988 (Basel I)[45] drew the lesson from the financial crises of the mid-1970s that more adequate capital levels in international banks would help reduce the systemic risk of bank failure. The primary goal of Basel I was capital adequacy; other standards were put in place not so much for their own virtue as to defend the primary goal.

Capital adequacy requirements were designed to ensure that individual institutions have the ability to absorb losses, particularly credit losses. Accordingly, a backup system of scoring credit risk was devised that required large amounts of bank capital for some types of loans, smaller amounts for others, and zero for a select list of preferred assets. Reporting requirements were designed to disclose problems and ensure that a troubled bank would take timely steps to restore its capital base in the wake of a loss. The Basel I framework worked tolerably well in limiting the call on the public purse in the G-10 countries—with the notable exceptions of France and Japan. The framework failed to moderate risky bank lending to emerging markets, however.

Basel I was not developed with emerging markets in mind. The original idea behind it was to develop a common supervisory approach to cross-border banking operations. It grew out of political pressure from US lawmakers, who were determined to require international banks operating in the United States to meet US banking standards. Toward this goal, in 1983, Congress passed the International Lending Supervisory Act. US and British banking authorities subsequently agreed on a common target: the adoption of strict common capital-adequacy standards. In 1988, other G-10 governments agreed to go along; voluntary acceptance of the standards throughout much of the rest of the world followed.[46] The rationale for the capital targets was two-fold. The first was to require banks to hold sufficient amounts of capital (8 percent of risk-adjusted

---

44. The international committee of financial authorities agreed on a common definition of banks' tier-one, or "core," capital; national authorities defined tier-two capital in their own manner, which permitted greater variations in national working definitions and practices.

45. International Convergence of Capital Measurement and Capital Standards (BIS 1988) was prepared by the Basel Committee on Banking Supervision.

46. See Reineke (1998).

assets) to cushion losses on those assets. The second was to dull their appetites for risk; banks with large capital bases would have more to lose if they failed and therefore would take fewer risks.

Rapid change in financial markets soon revealed flaws in the Basel I Accord. In a complex world with numerous sources of risk, it focused heavily on credit risk but overlooked other risks in a bank's portfolio and the correlation between returns on different asset classes. The Basel formula required banks to maintain a fixed amount of capital against each of its asset classes. But the formula did not distinguish the riskiness of the borrower within each class. As a result, one large loan to a low-risk corporate borrower, such as General Electric, would require the same amount of capital as 10 smaller transactions with high-risk borrowers.

The system was also biased toward short-term loans. Loans maturing in less than a year required a 20 percent risk weight, whereas those maturing after more than a year required a 100 percent risk weight. Interbank lending was particularly favored. For example, loans to banks in OECD countries required less capital than loans to private firms in the same countries, creating the anomaly that interbank loans to South Korean banks required less capital than loans to General Electric.[47] This anomaly encouraged banks to shed high-quality assets if the Basel rules required the allocation of more capital than banks thought they needed.

Another weakness was that financial innovators quickly circumvented the Accord. Because short-term loans required less provisioning than long-term loans, banks responded by securitizing their long-term debt portfolios, and lending short-term against the collateral of the newly created asset. This allowed banks to circumvent the capital requirements geared to the terms of the underlying debt. At the same time, the Basel I Accord failed to encourage risk mitigation techniques such as credit derivatives, collateral, guarantees, and on-balance-sheet netting, the flip side of financial innovation. Because off-balance-sheet products were not covered by the Accord, another anomaly appeared when Barings Bank collapsed in 1995. Barings met capital adequacy standards, but collapsed because its systems for managing risk failed; traders were allowed to speculate in futures contracts that did not appear on the balance sheet.

Basel II

Work to overhaul Basel I began in 1995 and produced consultative papers issued in June 1999 and January 2001.[48] These papers have been

---

47. South Korean banks have had notoriously weak balance sheets because the practice of "directed lending" left them with many poor loans (in making these loans, the banks were expected to follow government objectives rather than creditworthiness criteria).

48. Basel Committee on Banking Supervision (1999, 2001).

the subject of extensive consultation and revision; as a result, the new Accord is expected to be introduced in 2004.[49] The Basel II framework has three parts (pillars): revisions to Basel I minimum-capital requirements; supervisory review criteria; and greater emphasis on market discipline. Broadly, Basel II aims to maintain the level of capital in the system, but achieve better alignment of banks' capital with their risk profiles, and keep up with financial innovation.

To align capital requirements with market realities (the first pillar), Basel II concentrates on the 100 or so largest banks—the type of players listed in table 2.1—and on the holding-company parents of banking groups.[50] Capital requirements will differentiate between an increased number of credit groups or "risk buckets," including claims on governments, other banks, corporations, mortgage-backed securities, and other asset-backed securities.

Basel II originally proposed to use external ratings to set capital charges for a number of these credit risks. Many banks objected, arguing that they assess credit risk better than Standard & Poor's, Moody's, or Fitch/ IBCA.[51] Basel II thus proposes two approaches to rating: a standard approach using external ratings, and an "advanced" approach that allows selected banks to use their own internal rating systems. To encourage the development of rigorous internal control systems based on these internal rating systems, Basel II also proposes to levy capital charges for operational risk (the risk of direct or indirect loss resulting from inadequate or failed internal processes, people, and systems, or from external events).

Some critics of this proposal dismiss it as an abrogation of the principle of external, independent monitoring and as "dangerously naïve."[52] But regulators argue that the new capital charge on operational risk should offset this concern. It is also far from clear how cross-national comparisons of rating and internal risk-assessment systems will be made (Engelen 2000). The development by the European Union of its own capital rules could well complicate the international resolution of these issues. Public assurances by EU officials in January 2001, however, indicated that their main concerns are to create a level playing field and avoid regulatory arbitrage (Hargreaves 2001). There is also the significant problem of the procyclical character of risk weights: When a crisis hits, losses are

---

49. See Berry (2000) for an update in an interview with William J. McDonough, chair of the Basel Committee on Banking Supervision.

50. For obvious reasons, these proposals are addressed to large banks, and simpler capital standards are allowed for small banks that focus on their domestic credit markets.

51. See Ammer and Packer (2000) for an empirical critique of the success of rating agencies in distinguishing risk by sector and region.

52. See Auerback (2001).

incurred or accrued, capital is lost, and loan exposure must be reduced or securities sold to restore the requisite capital-adequacy ratios. A more risk-sensitive framework could amplify volatility.

As the second pillar of Basel II, supervisory review criteria are being beefed up to encourage supervisors to intervene earlier in potential problem situations and to compel banks to align their capital positions with their risk profiles. Bank supervisors will be authorized to require banks to hold capital in excess of minimum requirements if they have concerns about general management, overall strategy, risk-management performance, or the macroeconomic environment. Of course, if one G-10 supervisor imposes higher capital requirements in isolation, the same disparity will emerge that presaged Basel I: Some banks will be disadvantaged in the international marketplace and will loudly complain that excessive supervision is driving business to their competitors. Hence, close international cooperation among supervisors is critical.

To implement the third pillar, market discipline, banks will be required to make fuller, more timely disclosure of capital adequacy and the risks to which that capital is exposed. A number of measures are being studied that might help supervisors evaluate bank performance, such as comparisons of uninsured deposit interest rates, subordinated debt yields, and equity prices. The idea is that these yields and prices might alert supervisors to market perceptions of risk. Of course, market perceptions are only as good as market information. More direct and controversial ways to reinforce market discipline would dramatically increase public disclosure of bank positions and risk management systems.

Many questions are still outstanding about how to resolve the technical details of capital requirements and whether the requirements will achieve their intended goal of better assessment and mitigation of the risks in banks' portfolios. There is no substitute for skilled supervisors. The intricacies of effective design and implementation suggest that supervisors need to be highly competent technically, knowledgeable about banking, portfolio characteristics, and the factors that influence bank exposure to credit risk (Mishkin 2000). And they must be aided by vigilant shareholders, market forces, and transparency of information.[53]

Standard setting at the global level is desirable, but ultimately, the effectiveness of these efforts will be tested at the national level, especially in times of systemic financial distress. Here the record of Basel I was not a bright, shining success. Japanese banking regulators have traditionally allowed banks to include real estate and securities in their capital base. When the value of these assets plummeted in the early 1990s, regulators allowed banks to continue valuing these depreciated (and often bankrupt) assets at their old, inflated levels. Japanese authorities

---

53. Benedict Roth, Complacency Towards Catastrophe, *Financial Times*, 23 January 2001.

insisted, until the mid-1990s, that eroded capital bases could be rebuilt in a market-driven fashion. They rightly foresaw that huge loan losses would undermine public support for the ruling party and require a politically unpopular bailout.

Japanese foot dragging on Basel I was the worst,[54] but not unique. Other examples can be found of "politically mandated forbearance." The Federal Reserve Bank of New York held important hands during the LTCM crisis of 1998. Mexico is still resolving the banking crisis that erupted in 1995; South Korea has not yet closed the insolvent banks that behaved so badly before the crisis of 1998. In the aftermath of a crisis, national regulators cannot always be relied upon to discipline politically powerful bankers.[55] One of the little-noticed consequences of these differing approaches is that those banks with strong regulatory systems received an implicit "export subsidy" for their services. US banks, which had not engaged extensively in emerging-market lending in the 1990s, were better positioned than their German and Japanese counterparts to expand their international assets in the wake of the crises.

Other Financial Forums

The Basel model of vertical subsidiarity has already been extended to other financial regulatory bodies. In 1993-94, the BIS established a Tripartite Group of Banking, Insurance, and Securities Regulators. In 1994-95, the BIS increased its cooperation with the International Organization of Securities Commissions, when the two organizations issued parallel papers on guidelines for national regulators concerning risk management and disclosure of derivative trades. In 1996, a permanent Joint Forum on Financial Conglomerates was established to examine supervisory issues and develop working arrangements among the different functional supervisors of conglomerate institutions that offer combinations of banking, securities, and insurance products. Draft papers on the supervision of conglomerates were released for comment in 1998, applying capital-adequacy principles to these groups, and providing guidelines both for assessing the integrity and competence of top managers and for sharing assessments between regulators.

In 1997, the Basel Committee on Banking Supervision extended its reach beyond capital standards to broader aspects of banking supervision with the publication of the Core Principles for Effective Banking Supervision. In 1999, a wide range of regulatory and standard-setting bodies were gathered under the umbrella of the Financial Stability

---

54. See Japanese Banks: Fiddling while Marunouchi Burns, *The Economist*, 27 January 2001, 67-69.

55. See Calomiris (1997).

Forum (FSF), itself established under BIS aegis.[56] The FSF has already issued recommendations for stepped-up supervision and transparency, as well as guidelines for best practices in a number of areas, including offshore financial centers and highly leveraged institutions, or hedge funds.[57]

Conclusion

Although the structural weaknesses in emerging-market economies are widely acknowledged to have been causal factors in international capital-market volatility, this chapter points to the role of large G-10 banking organizations as major suppliers of the most volatile instrument: short-term debt. We have examined evidence of the impact of public safety nets in the G-10 economies—the deposit insurance systems, the prudential supervisory systems, and the lender-of-last-resort functions of central banks—on the incentive structures of these organizations.

Although supervisors in most countries, working nationally and together in the BIS, have made significant efforts to mimic market forces in their prudential supervision, the most sophisticated financial institutions find innovative ways to circumvent the rules. New global regulatory bodies are not about to be created. G-10 national bank regulators should themselves address the short-term debt bias in the international financial system by changing incentive systems. G-10 securities regulators should also take steps to get ahead of the curve, paying close attention to large portfolio swings by institutional investors, particularly in times of crisis. In short, more needs to be done at national and international levels to change the rules of the game. That is the subject of the next chapter.

---

56. The Financial Stability Forum includes banking, securities, insurance, and accounting regulatory bodies; the OECD on taxation, corruption, and corporate governance; and the IMF.

57. See Martin (2000).

3

The Group of Ten and Financial Architecture: Changing the Rules of the Game

There is a "hole" in the debate about reforming the international financial architecture. For every bad borrower, and for every failed project, there is also a culpable lender or investor. G-10 institutions bear more responsibility for financial crises in emerging-market economies than the tone of criticism might suggest. Although the appetite for financial risk is currently more subdued than in the late 1990s, a renewed flow of capital—in line with our projections in chapter 1, but in the absence of fundamental reform—could set the stage for a future crisis. We question whether the adjustments driven both by the market and the G-10 regulators have been sufficient to correct forces on the supply side of international finance that contribute to crises.

Yet the main debate in the G-10 is whether private-sector players should bear more of the costs of managing crises when they do occur. This approach is too relaxed. As we argued in the previous chapter, the special role of banks in finance and the associated public safety net distort financial markets. Despite significant efforts by G-10 governments to reduce moral hazard through prudential supervision and greater reliance on market discipline, empirical evidence and theoretical debate persuade us that moral hazard is still a pernicious influence on cross-border capital flows.[1]

Changing the rules of the game in the industrial countries is at least as important as strengthening the regulators and financial institutions in the emerging markets. The basic unresolved issue is the differing

---

1. Claessens and Klingebiel (1999) and Kaufman (1999), among others, are in accord with our diagnosis of endemic moral hazard.

emphasis reformers put on the dangers of moral hazard among the suppliers of capital, and the contribution that lending behavior makes to systemic liquidity crises. Liquidity crises impose severe economic, social, and political costs on borrowers. These costs, in turn, build pressure for international safety nets anchored by the IMF. Reformers who argue for stronger safety nets have not resolved the moral hazard consequences.

In this chapter, we begin with a discussion of moral hazard and the debt bias and then explore two routes to address moral hazard. One route is to change the incentives to influence the taste for and management of risk by banks and the financial institutions to which they lend. The three pillars of Basel II are a start in the right direction, but more attention on the mandates, resources, and incentives structures for supervisors is desirable. Other measures also make sense, such as tax changes to promote forward provisioning, trade policy changes, and improvements in public disclosure. The second route is to change the way liquidity crises are resolved by creating ex ante a clear framework for withdrawing the assurance of full and timely repayment when problems arise. These two approaches are not necessarily substitutes—they may even be complements—in their effects on incentive structures.

The Debt Bias

The dangers associated with debt denominated in foreign currency are well documented. Many of these dangers are associated with sovereign debt. But the first half of the 1990s was a period of booming international bank credit for private borrowers, particularly in Asia.[2] If the dangers associated with cross-border, cross-currency debt, especially short-term debt, are so well known, why does it persist?

Most studies that aim to answer this question have focused on the borrower's perspective. This analysis emphasizes that short-term foreign currency debt is "cheaper" to the borrower than the alternatives. After a period of bad economic management, for example, the only foreign capital flows on offer may be short-term bank loans. This may also be true for countries plagued by corruption and bad governance. Even when other alternatives are available, short-term debt will usually carry a lower interest rate than long-term debt, and short-term debt will not compel controlling shareholders to surrender their ownership privileges. In other words, debt maturity "solves" an incentives problem on the part of the borrower.

Governments with deteriorating credit ratings see short-term debt as less expensive and more accessible than long-term debt. Private corporations see short-term debt as less expensive than bonds and less

---

2. In Mexico (1994), Brazil (1999), and Russia (1998)—in contrast to Asia (1997/98)—the debt was sovereign.

intrusive than equity stakes. Another consideration is that countries and companies with poor disclosure records engender less trust, limiting their ability to borrow long term and forcing greater reliance on short-term debt (Diamond and Rajan 2000).

Not all the incentives are on the borrower's side. Banks engage in short-term international lending because the capital requirements are lower and the aura of liquidity is greater. Lending to governments and private-sector borrowers may be a "loss leader" that promotes the sale of other financial products that will generate fee income rather than interest payments. In the 1990s, banks exploited significant yield differentials across international borders through the "carry trade"—which involved borrowing at relatively lower home-market interest rates and investing at higher interest rates offered in emerging-market securities, such as treasury bills and bank deposits. Such transactions were especially popular in Thailand, where domestic securities, before the events of 1997, were regarded as relatively safe bets from the standpoint of both credit and exchange risk (Blustein 2001).

Although the analysis of private-sector lending and borrowing is complex, at least three features are evident to us. One is unintentional regulatory bias on the supply side. As chapter 2 indicated, Basel I unintentionally encouraged a short-term debt bias, most notably through the conduit of interbank lending. A second feature, also discussed in chapter 2, is the moral hazard associated with the customary national safety nets for banks and the more recent international safety nets created by the international financial institutions through their roles in crisis resolution. Most (but not all) analysts agree that moral hazard plays a role. They argue that it is difficult for the IMF (and for national governments) to stand aside when financial crises, contagion, and panic erupt. Indeed, anecdotes in Blustein (2001) describe the intense pressures for an official rescue package for Russia directed by private-sector players at IMF staff in 1998. In July 2000, G-7 finance ministers enunciated a key reform principle for the IMF: "IMF lending should not distort the assessment of risk and return in international investment" (Group of Seven 2000). The G-7 agreed to introduce a system of penalty interest rates to discourage countries from turning to the IMF for crisis lending.

By contrast, the Institute of International Finance maintains that moral hazard is overblown as a concern. The IIF (1999b) points to the wrenching adjustments that officials had to make in emerging-market economies and the large losses sustained by private creditors. They estimate that provisions made by European banks during the Asian crisis amounted to 10 percent of total claims of these banks on East Asian economies. Others argue that cross-border lending decisions were not influenced by the expectation of IMF "bailouts."[3]

---

3. See IMF (2000b) for an analysis of these views.

We agree that the expectation of future IMF intervention per se is not an explicit decision criterion in lending decisions. No bank would make a loan to an emerging economy if it thought the probabilities argued for a crisis during the life of the loan. All banks with loan exposure suffered in the crises. Nevertheless, we do see the IMF as an implicit factor, just like national safety nets. Safety nets of all kinds are an integral part of the decision-making framework in banks—in the sense that safety nets reduce the extent of loss in extreme adversity. In technical terms, a portion of the extreme "bad" tail of probability outcomes is sliced off by public safety nets, both national and international. Strong growth performance in the borrowing countries during the early 1990s, combined with a herding tendency among financial institutions, prompted many banks to believe they had to participate in the emerging markets. They assumed a safety net would be there if needed. Our own informal discussions with market participants, and Blustein's extensive interviews, both support this view.

A third feature in the supply-side bias relates to the characteristics of lenders. Many international banks have admitted they underestimated the risks of lending to emerging markets. Informal inquiries have revealed that credit risk-assessment procedures were found wanting and that management sometimes pushed the risk envelope (Hawkins and Turner 2000). The amounts involved were small relative to the total assets of the "big players" profiled in the previous chapter. Indeed, for some institutions, the size of cross-border loans and security holdings were so small that it was not cost-effective to acquire detailed knowledge of country fundamentals. Such institutions became susceptible to country-specific rumors. Some call this behavior the "Calvo-Mendoza problem," after the researchers who documented it (Calvo and Mendoza 1999).[4] But the totality of mistakes and misjudgments, and the subsequent rebalancing of loan and investment portfolios, badly hurt the small emerging markets.

There were some exceptions to this picture. Those banks that had penetrated local markets and had specialized local knowledge of borrowers actually *increased* their lending in the crisis countries after the local banking systems encountered insolvency problems in 1997 (Diamond and Rajan 2000).

Theoretical analysis that emphasizes the benefits of short-term debt for government and private-sector borrowers rests on the assumption that short-term debt, long-term debt, and portfolio equity are not close substitutes (Jeanne 2000). This assumption may have been valid in the past and may have continuing validity in some markets. But the growing number of giant financial institutions, and the erosion of the so-called

---

4. Calvo and Mendoza (1999) demonstrated that contagion can be an outcome of optimal portfolio diversification as securities markets grow in size and complexity.

equity premium in several G-10 stock markets, suggests that there may be more room for substitution in the future.[5] On this crucial question, we are "substitution optimists." Even if substitution is limited, it must be recognized that, whereas the benefits of short-term loans are largely private, the costs of crises are both private and public. When creditors call their loans, depositors withdraw their funds from banks, or fund managers reallocate their investment portfolios, the ensuing liquidity crises can have high costs in output and employment.

In sum, we think the dangers of excessive short-term debt require more policy attention to reduce moral hazard and the systemic risks associated with liquidity crises. Markets, left to their own devices, will continue to experience market failures because of involvement by cross-border players. There is a role for the public sector to correct these market failures on the lender side.

Changing the Rules for Bank Risk

The first route to reducing moral hazard and the contribution that banks make to liquidity crises involves public supervision of banks' risk taking. For several years, national regulators have discussed a three-pillar approach, which we call Basel II: refining the capital adequacy requirements, stronger supervision, and more use of market discipline. In this section, we recommend some refinements in the Basel II reforms. On the basis of the analysis in the previous chapter, we also suggest that the G-10 governments should tighten their public safety nets and reevaluate the incentive structures facing national regulators. Supervisors should move quickly and in a coordinated way to head off the buildup of concentrated lending and correlated risk taking. Allied measures, such as forward loss provisioning and changes to taxation and trade arrangements, are also suggested.

Bank Capital Reform at Basel

Basel II aims to raise the capital that banks must hold to cushion against credit losses resulting from such internal factors as bad lending decisions, and from such external factors as economic downturns and crisis contagion. Banks that engage in risky transactions will have to set aside more capital than those that do not. Under Basel I, the smaller risk weight on short-term loans relative to long-term claims might have seemed rational (short-term claims are less likely to get into trouble), but the bias encouraged short-term lending to non-OECD countries at the

---

5. See Claessens and Klingebiel (1999).

expense of longer-term lending. When all banks engage in such lending, the borrower becomes vulnerable to sudden changes in lender sentiment.

Basel II reforms are designed to reduce this bias by introducing a more risk-sensitive framework that measures both credit and operational risk (Basel Committee on Banking Supervision 2001). Minimum capital requirements for credit risk may be addressed in two ways. The first is a standardized approach in which credit exposures are assigned risk weights on the basis of assessments by external credit institutions. The second, or "advanced," approach allows banks to use their own internal risk models to assess the various credit risks. This change is closely linked to the inclusion of new risk weights for operational risk. The sophisticated banks, relying on internal ratings, will be able to reduce capital requirements associated with credit risk, thereby gaining a competitive advantage. But the capital requirements associated with operational risk will largely offset these savings unless a bank has very rigorous internal controls. The other two pillars—stronger supervisory review and more market discipline—will also be employed to increase discipline on banks. These pillars are discussed below.

In theory, higher capital requirements—imposed by regulators—can be expressed as a tax on capital. The reason is that capital requirements, when binding, limit the bank from exploiting to the full its own perceived ability to borrow cheap (from depositors) and lend dear (e.g., to corporations). The argument for *not* letting banks individually decide what level of capital is appropriate for their operations is that, on an individual basis, they will not properly "internalize" the marginal contribution they make to systemic liquidity risk.

There are reasons to ask whether the proposed Basel II capital-adequacy refinements will achieve their intended effects. First, if the cost of short-term debt for emerging-economy borrowers is indeed increased, will there be sufficiently close (and less risky) substitutes available to those borrowers? Second, will the reforms be circumvented, as have other reforms preceding them, by financial innovation?

Raising the cost of short-term debt will, to some extent, reduce global welfare by raising the cost, and reducing the quantity, of the product.[6] The reduction in global welfare will be greater if long-term debt (loans or bonds) and portfolio equity are not available as substitutes.[7] Empirical

---

6. Basel II will not unambiguously raise the cost of short-term lending. Although the overall effect of the revised risk buckets will be to reduce risky short-term credits, two features of the new rules suggest that lending to emerging markets will still be potentially profitable. One is that the reforms still allow a lower risk weight on interbank loans of less than 3 months, as long as they are local-currency loans. The other is that 100 percent risk weight on non-OECD corporate lending has been reduced, making this form of financing more attractive than in the past.

7. See Jeanne (2000) for a welfare analysis of such measures.

research suggests that banks will reduce their loan portfolios in response to higher capital requirements. A simulation of the impact of higher capital requirements on US bank balance sheets in the early 1990s estimates that a 1-percentage-point increase in the risk-based capital requirements on loans reduced their growth rate by 5 percent (Furfine 2000). Moreover, the same simulation model predicts that higher risk-based capital requirements on loans will prompt banks to sharply increase their holdings of risk-free securities (e.g., T-bills).

In chapter 1, we examined the literature on substitution among different sources of capital. We noted the Claessens, Dooley, and Warner (1995) study, which was based on analysis of quarterly data between the mid-1970s and 1992, and which concluded that the extent of substitution is very high between different types of capital flows to destination countries. Their method of analysis was to ask whether adding, as an independent variable, the contemporaneous *share* of total capital inflows accounted for by a particular type (FDI, portfolio equity, long- and short-term loans) improved the forecasting power of a simple time-series prediction model for total capital inflows. For a sample of five industrial countries and five emerging markets, adding the share variable barely improved the model's forecasting power. If particular types of capital flow were truly independent of one another, one would expect that country conditions (such as good governance or low tax rates) that—for example—attracted FDI would add to the total level of capital inflows otherwise predicted by the time-series model. This did not happen. Claessens and his colleagues draw the inference that, when conditions favor one type of capital inflow, it displaces other types.[8]

The Chilean experiment with unremunerated reserves between 1990 and 1996 also suggests a fairly high degree of substitution between short-term loans and longer-term flows (Edwards 2000b). Before the 30 percent unremunerated reserve requirement was imposed on short-term loans in 1990, long-term capital inflows were about 10 percent of total capital inflows. By 1995, long-term flows had risen to 90 percent. This was much higher than in other developing countries and, according to tests performed by Edwards, the larger role of long-term capital did not come at the expense of a reduction in total capital flows to Chile.

On the basis of this kind of evidence, we are, as noted above, "substitution optimists." We think it is reasonable to dampen bank lending with an expectation that bond, equity finance, and FDI (outside the public safety net) will expand—if not one-for-one, then to a substantial degree. Broadly, this is the direction of Basel II.

---

8. To quote Claessens, Dooley, and Warner (1995, 171) on the rationale for their analysis: "We reasoned that if the total capital account is independent of a particular flow, then adding the contemporaneous share of the flow should not affect our forecasting ability. Conversely, if a flow helps determine the total capital account, then adding the contemporaneous share should help the forecast."

Still, we have concerns with Basel II. One that persists from Basel I is that the Basel II capital proposals may likewise change the behavior of banks in undesirable ways. Banks distinguish between "regulatory capital," the amount of capital mandated by the regulator (calculated by applying standardized weights to asset classes), and their own assessment of "economic capital." Economic capital is the reserve against unexpected losses that the bank regards as adequate—given its expected loss experience—to achieve a target credit rating for interbank loans.

Large banks complain that regulatory rules often require them to hold too much regulatory capital relative to their own assessment of economic capital. Regulatory capital then becomes a constraint that banks circumvent, using financial innovations such as securitization or credit derivatives, rather than raise more capital in the equity market. The consequence is a counterintuitive outcome: To get around regulatory capital requirements, banks remove the strongest, rather than the weakest, assets from their balance sheets.

The new Basel risk-weighting system could, moreover, amplify the cyclical character of bank lending. Uniform requirements imposed on the largest market players may encourage them both to enlarge and reduce their exposures at the same time (as, e.g., the link—made by Persaud 2000—between VAR models and bank herding, referred to in chapter 2). The Basel Committee argues that the benefits of the more risk-sensitive capital framework should outweigh this concern by reducing the incentives for banks to make high-risk investments at the top of the cycle. But the committee leaves the door open to further reforms. One is forward provisioning, discussed below, where banks would be expected to reflect in their credit ratings assessments of how well borrowers withstand the stresses of the business cycle (Basel Committee on Banking Supervision 2001, paragraphs 40-45).

These unintended consequences of the current approach to ensuring that banks better match their capital and their risk profiles are cause for concern. They help to explain why so much effort and debate has gone into refining the application of the existing capital requirements. We support the direction of Basel II, but we think several modifications are desirable. We start with the question of risk weights on short-term borrowing:

■ *Risk weights should raise the cost of short-term borrowing in those emerging-market economies with weak financial systems. Loans to those borrowers, whether corporate or sovereign, should carry higher risk weights.*[9]

---

9. A distinction should be made, however, between secured credits, such as trade finance, and unsecured credits, such as interbank lending. The former should be subjected to risk weighting on an ad hoc basis.

■ *Risk weights should relate the cost of borrowing by hedge funds (highly leveraged institutions, or HLIs) to the extent of their underlying leverage.*[10]

Our next recommendation addresses the Basel II proposal for credit scoring. Basel II discussions began with the suggestion that independent rating agencies, such as Moody's, Standard & Poor's, and Fitch/IBCA, should be used to judge the credit characteristics of bank loans. Responding to criticism of this proposal, the Basel Committee decided to allow large banks to use their own risk weights, thereby determining their own capital-adequacy standards. The internal-ratings approach, as it is known, has its own dangers. Among large banks, the internal-ratings model is susceptible both to banks misunderstanding their risks and making mistakes in measuring them. It is also prone to moral hazard—banks, faced with the consequences of mistakes or misunderstandings, attempting to deal with the resulting balance-sheet weakness by intentionally underestimating their risks and capital requirements.

National supervisors must decide which banks will be allowed to use internal ratings. Under political pressure, national supervisors may push permission too far down into the system, thereby spreading the risks of errors or misunderstanding to medium-sized banks.

Supervisors also face a dilemma in dealing with mistakes or abuse. They could threaten to publish their own adverse bank ratings, but that would undermine a core regulatory role, which is to maintain the confidence of both financial institutions and the public. In principle, regulators should impose stiff financial penalties on misbehaving banks. In practice, Basel II addresses the issue by imposing capital requirements for operational risk. This requirement signals the importance of rigorous control systems in the large banks.

The move toward internal ratings makes sense for large international banks with sophisticated control systems, but only when it is supported by stepped-up supervision and market monitoring. The potential for moral hazard should be explicitly addressed:

■ *When a bank is allowed to use this model, regulators should agree (again at the international level) on a schedule of severe fines that will be imposed when risks are underrated.*

As we have indicated, the Basel II approach to capital adequacy is flawed but worth supporting, for the inescapable reason that banks should be required to hold capital equal to the marginal contribution they make

---

10. The Financial Stability Forum Working Group on HLIs (FSF 2000b) considered such a measure but settled instead for improved supervision of HLI credit providers and increased HLI disclosure. This is similar to the recommendation of the Council on Foreign Relations (1999). We agree with the dissenters (Council on Foreign Relations 1999, 129).

to systemic liquidity risk. Basel II has two other pillars—stronger supervision and more market discipline—that have received less public attention, yet are essential adjuncts in reducing moral hazard.

Stronger Supervision: Aligning the Incentives of the Supervisors

Basel II's more risk-sensitive capital-requirements framework relies heavily on both market and regulatory discipline. Both have flaws. But they can act as complements. Banks can be monitored by market participants as well as by their supervisors. Supervisors can be monitored by their governments—and by markets. We see at least two dimensions of supervisory monitoring that governments should evaluate. One is the way they address the principal-agent problem: The interests of supervisors may diverge from the interests of taxpayers, leading to regulatory forbearance—slow or no action to head off problems. Governments need to ensure that supervisors are accountable for the costs of bank failures. This can be accomplished by mandating published reports on costs borne by the deposit insurance fund as a result of failures, which is now required in the United States under FDICIA (Kane 2000).

■ *Supervisors should be held publicly accountable for the costs of bank failures through mandated reports on costs imposed on the national deposit insurance fund.*

The second dimension of supervisors' incentives relates to the mandates they receive from their governments. Most national supervisors are expected to worry primarily about their own jurisdictions and whether the risk exposure of domestic financial institutions will damage the institutions, their investors, and their customers. As G-10 financial institutions and markets become more complex, regulators rely more and more on market discipline to guard against risk exposure. But market discipline is not always adequate. Mistakes by a few banks can disturb the financial system, especially if herding occurs.

If governments in emerging markets conclude that the benefits of financial openness are outweighed by the costs of financial vulnerability and fickle creditors, these governments are likely to seek their own solutions, such as capital controls or restricted foreign entry. Over time, these reactions will reduce efficiency and retard financial innovation. Thus, regulators in the G-10 countries have a common interest in fostering the international public good of financial stability.

G-10 governments could do more to promote their common interest in global stability if national regulators were also mandated to enhance the stability of the international financial system by greater information exchange and preventive cooperation.[11] The most sophisticated financial institutions in the G-10 countries constantly look for correlated cross-border exposures as part of their risk-management operations. Similarly, if officials see short-term exposure building in a certain market among lenders in several countries (evidence of herding), they should move pre-emptively, and in a coordinated fashion, to tighten capital requirements on "strategic" grounds.[12]

■ *National supervisors should take more responsibility for the systemic consequences of risk taking by the institutions they oversee, share information with their G-10 counterparts, and coordinate corrective action on a confidential basis.*

Market Discipline

Basel II relies on market discipline in two ways: through external ratings, and through better, more plentiful information disclosed to bank shareholders and other market participants. We believe Basel II should have gone further in bringing market discipline to bear on banks by encouraging the issuance of subordinated debt and allowing banks to include these securities in required capital. As we saw in chapter 2, subordinated debt proposals have been around a long time, and yet are still in limited use.

The subordinated debt proposal has several weaknesses. It would be onerous for small banks; market evaluations of the subordinated debt would require far better disclosure of bank portfolio risks than these institutions customarily provide; and bankers may create side inducements for other financial institutions, or even borrowers, to buy their debt, thus defeating the market test.[13] But limited experience with subordinated debt suggests it is a useful complement to supervisory discipline. For example, reports on Argentina, which has experimented with subordinated debt issues, observe that this instrument helps in market monitoring of bank supervisors (Mishkin 2000). We recommend that:

■ *Instruments that encourage market discipline—such as subordinated debt—should be introduced, and banks should be allowed to use them to meet part of their capital requirements. Accompanying regulation should ensure appropriate disclosure and prevent market rigging.*

---

11. Stiglitz (1999) made this suggestion.

12. See Persaud's (2000) arguments along these lines.

13. Another objection is less severe. The Basel approach to capital standards discriminates against subordinated debt by limiting the extent to which tier-two capital components (which would include the new subordinated debt) can satisfy total capital requirements. Presumably the Basel approach could be modified if the Calomiris model were adopted.

Recommendations for better disclosure and greater transparency are on all lists of proposals to improve international financial architecture. They aim to improve market conditions and strengthen the players rather than change the rules of the game. In theory, an efficient financial system has perfect information. The reality is different—with respect to both private-sector financial institutions and national balance sheets.

As financial systems in the G-10 countries have become more sophisticated and transactions grown more complex, even top managers have not known the risk profile of their institutions. Worse, other players can only guess at the real-time position of their counterparts. Dangerous structures can create the conditions for a crash—the financial equivalent of the ill-fated Texas A&M log pile. One avenue of prevention—many would argue the best one—is better disclosure or "increased transparency,"[14] to use the popular jargon. By alerting policymakers to problems at an earlier stage, the frequency and severity of financial crises can be reduced.

Not all agree. Persaud's (2000) analysis of herding argues that transparency, prudential standards, and risk management are necessary and desirable in the long term, but are counterproductive in the short term *because markets are not yet able to distinguish sustainable from unsustainable positions.* They herd in order to exploit available information and because risk-reward systems penalize them from straying from the pack—especially if they are wrong.[15] The chances of herding are also exacerbated (as noted above) if all banks use the same risk-management models, as Persaud argues they do. Indeed, Basel II is moving away from discretionary judgment on risk (what many call "horse sense") and toward quantitative models.

The implications of such changes are important: Greater transparency in the marketplace carries risks. "The more herding investors and bankers know about what each other are up to, the [more] unstable markets may become" (Persaud 2000). Persaud points out the paradox that with all banks using the same (static quantitative) approach, and with portfolio managers acting strategically—that is, keeping an eye on what other managers are doing—banks follow each other into and out of markets, contributing to systemic risk. As he observes, there is a role for financial institutions—ones that would look very much like hedge funds—in offsetting volatility by buying in market downturns when everyone else is selling assets.

Persaud may be right that more transparency will augment volatility in bank lending to emerging markets. This does not seem to be the experience in US stock and bond markets, however, where more timely disclosure of material information is associated with lesser volatility.

---

14. See King (1999).

15. Persaud (2000) defines "herding" to mean that banks and investors buy what others are buying, sell what others are selling, and own what others own.

After all, if bad news (or good news) is disclosed in small lumps, then markets can adjust step by step, instead of in one big leap. Moreover, financial analysts are highly paid to distinguish significant from insignificant information.

Even if there can be such a thing as too much transparency to other market players, as Persaud argues, confidential disclosure to regulators is quite another matter. More is good. Financial supervisors barely know what is happening in the off-balance-sheet, cross-border transactions of the institutions for which they are responsible. One reason is that, with the emergence of "universal" financial institutions, the big players cross the jurisdictional boundaries of both nations and old-line supervisory institutions. Another reason is innovative financial instruments.

For example, the US Securities and Exchange Commission (SEC) has authority over securities firms, but not over their holding companies or offshore activities. Yet Merrill Lynch in London is under the supervision of the new UK Financial Services Agency, which—unless it visits the US authorities and Merrill Lynch corporate headquarters—has no knowledge of what Merrill Lynch does in the United States. When Merrill does derivative transactions through its separately capitalized AAA derivatives subsidiary, does anyone supervise it? No. Because derivatives are not legally securities, so they are not within the regulatory reach of the SEC. The recognized derivatives regulator, the Commodity Futures Trading Commission, exempts over-the-counter financial derivatives from supervision.[16]

One response to the Merrill Lynch saga might be, "Why worry?" After all, GE or Itochu might well engage in the same range of off-balance-sheet transactions as Merrill Lynch, and although adverse results will upset shareholders, they are of no concern to regulators. There are two differences. First, although Merrill Lynch is not a bank, if it collapses there will be enormous pressure on both the Federal Reserve and the Bank of England to orchestrate a bailout. Second, it is far more likely that Merrill Lynch, rather than GE or Itochu, will execute rapid changes in its exposure profile as it affects banks.

Evidence of information imperfections such as that presented by Persaud suggests that initiatives, such as Basel II, to encourage more public disclosure by banks of their asset positions and risk-management systems should proceed, but with caution. National authorities need to follow through in two ways: by insisting on more disclosure, particularly of the international activities of LCBOs to regulators on a confidential basis, and by improving corporate governance incentives to increase the responsibilities of bank directors and managers for disclosure and risk management.[17]

---

16. See Mayer (1999).

17. Stiglitz (1999) makes an argument for incentive schemes for managers.

- *Incentives—such as personal liability obligations for officers and directors— would improve the governance, management, and regulatory compliance of all financial conglomerates.*

- *The largest banks and financial institutions should be required to publicly disclose both their balance-sheet and off-balance-sheet activities in emerging markets in a standard reporting format, in a moderately timely fashion—for example, at the end of each quarter but with a one-quarter lag.*

- *Securities regulators need to get advance information on large portfolio investments in emerging markets. In particular, they need to consider imposing the same sort of disclosure requirements that routinely apply to insider trading by companies listed on stock exchanges, and to tender offers in mergers and acquisitions.*

Persaud's caution about transparency is based on the short-term behavior of financial institutions. His prescription, however, reinforces our arguments. Because market discipline by itself has flaws, supervision and rules on bank capital are its necessary complements. He suggests that, if regulators notice herding, they also should impose additional "strategic" capital requirements on banks. Alternatively, supervisors could require banks to purchase "liquidity options" from central banks.[18]

Offsetting the Subsidy in the Public Safety Net

A significant influence on short-term debt is the subsidy that banks throughout the G-10 countries receive from the national safety net—that is, from deposit insurance systems, bank access to central bank liquidity, and bank access to payments and clearing systems. An empirical analysis by Kwast and Passmore (2000) indicates that US bank holding companies operate on much smaller equity-asset ratios than a large range of other financial institutions (investment banks, life insurance companies, property-casualty companies, "personal credit" companies, captive finance companies, etc.) Typically, the bank equity-asset ratios are about half the levels in other institutions. Moreover, Kwast and Passmore detected a tendency for holding companies to move activities that could be performed either by a bank or a nonbank subsidiary into their bank subsidiaries. In a critique of this paper, Kaufman (2000) argues that low capital-asset ratios in banks reflect the rapid processes that exist to resolve bank failures (both before and after FDICIA) rather than an actual subsidy.

As noted in chapter 2, the rationale for the public safety net is to protect small depositors against the threat of bank insolvency. Small depositors,

---

18. The liquidity option would entitle a bank to borrow a certain amount from the central bank within a specified time period at a specified interest rate, against acceptable collateral.

unlike large investors or other financial institutions, are unable to effectively monitor what is done with their deposits; hence the quid pro quo for the subsidy is regulation by the public sector (or, in some cases, by their peers). Studies of the size of the gross subsidy in the United States and measures to offset it indicate that regulators had some success in the late 1990s. But World Bank studies, as was pointed out, find a negative relationship between bank stability and deposit insurance. These studies imply that moral hazard is still a problem in many countries.

The compelling implication of these studies is that more needs to be done to instill market discipline and bring regulatory rigor to bank supervision and the resolution of bank failures. US studies arguing that a subsidy still exists imply that offsets should be increased—by increasing the direct costs of deposit insurance premiums, raising interest rates on bonds issued by the Financing Corporation, raising reserve requirements, and stronger supervision. The results of the World Bank studies also suggest that the generosity of deposit insurance schemes should be limited, and that private-sector monitoring should be enhanced.

Unfortunately, once most deposit insurance schemes are in place, they tend to be reevaluated only in the wake of a crisis. Tables 2.9 and 2.10 indicate the variation in G-10 arrangements. The European Union in 1994 established the outlines of compulsory deposit insurance schemes among its members to be adopted by 1995 (coverage of at least 20,000 euros and coinsurance of up to 10 percent). Design features were left to national regulators to work out, and their designs show wide variation (Barth, Nolle, and Rice 2000; Beck 2000).

Compare Germany's program with those in the United States or Japan. All private banks (many are public, owned by counties, cities, or *Lander*) that are members of the German Banking Association are also members of a deposit insurance fund that is financed and run by its members. Premiums are risk-adjusted. There is no public funding for the scheme, and the institutional environment—bank supervision, contract enforcement, and the rule of law—is robust. Weak incentives for depositors to monitor banks are offset by strong peer monitoring: The banks monitor each other, in part because it is they who must bear the costs of distressed members (Beck 2000).

In contrast, Japan still offers depositors a blanket guarantee but has prospectively changed its policy on limiting depositor insurance several times, most recently in January 2001.[19] Design options are thus a matter of debate, even in the G-10. These options include stricter definitions of retail banking, more reliance on coinsurance (thereby requiring depositors to bear part of the losses themselves), and risk-rated deposit

---

19. Upon his appointment to head the newly formed Financial Services Agency, Hakuo Yanagisawa stated his intention to eliminate blanket protection (see FRC's Demise Leaves Much to Be Done, *Nikkei Weekly*, 8 January 2001, 13).

insurance that ties the premium for the insurance to the rate a bank pays for subordinated debt (thereby relying on a market evaluation of risk).[20]

In summary, the latest cross-national studies imply that more can be done to offset the erosion of banking standards as a consequence of deposit insurance, not only in emerging-market economies, but also in the G-10. Surely it is possible for the G-10 economies to fully offset the impact of the public safety net. It is certainly desirable. We recommend:

- *In all G-10 economies, more emphasis should be placed on incentives to encourage private-sector monitoring of banks—wherever it is not an already established practice.*

- *Banks can be encouraged to adopt incentive systems such as the German peer-review model, in which banks bear some financial responsibility for the failure of one of their peer group.*

Forward Loss Provisioning

Another innovation that would encourage evaluation and monitoring of risk is forward loss provisioning. Banks are often reluctant to make adequate provision for their loan losses, and bank regulators are often hesitant about pushing banks to recognize losses before it becomes plain that borrowers are in trouble. No bank loan officer wants to admit she made a mistake, and few supervisors want to cry "fire" when there is only smoke. As a consequence, published loan-loss provisions usually lag the eruption of a financial crisis (Gavin and Hausmann 1998). Hence, when crisis strikes, banks typically have inadequate cushions of equity plus reserves to absorb the loss.[21]

Many large G-10 banks recognize this problem and are exploring approaches to loan-loss provisioning that rely on modeling techniques

---

20. The Financial Stability Forum convened a study group on deposit insurance that reported in mid-2000 (FSF 2000a). This group's work has been aimed mainly at emerging-market economies that are considering the adoption of limited safety nets in the wake of the 1997-98 crises (when they provided blanket guarantees to all depositors). The study group agreed on the common features of an effective system: an explicit, well-publicized framework; mandatory participation; limited coverage; ability of the insurer to access necessary resources; and robust information exchange among all participants in the safety net. More recently, in June 2000, the World Bank hosted a conference on deposit insurance—Deposit Insurance: Design and Implementation. The papers presented at the conference find many common, highly robust, features in effective systems, as well as relationships within and between various components of existing schemes and financial development. See the conference papers at http://www.worldbank.org/research/interest/confs/upcoming/deposit_insurance/home.htm.

21. See Claessens and Klingebiel (1999) for a table of loss provisioning rules in selected G-10 countries and emerging markets.

similar to those used in credit risk management and pricing models. The models attempt to measure exposure to credit risk for a long-term horizon, and make allowances for bad outcomes earlier than has been normal practice.

We believe banks should be encouraged to provision proactively. In some countries, this will require a change in tax laws so that loan-loss deductions can be taken in excess of historical experience. Current practice tends to permit deductions only for recognized problem loans. In this regard, we recommend that

■ *Tax authorities should automatically accept loan-loss provisions endorsed by bank regulators.*

■ *Regulators should link their endorsement of higher loan-loss provisions to the bank's own implementation of higher capital requirements.*

Implementation of these recommendations would have to be carefully coordinated across countries to avoid disadvantaging banks in one country relative to their international competitors.

WTO Liberalization of Foreign Entry

The research of Diamond and Rajan (2000) implies that local affiliates and subsidiaries of international banks can help ameliorate crises in emerging markets. Their actions can reduce the problem of asymmetric information faced by cross-border lenders and, more significantly, restore stability by maintaining or increasing credit access for local borrowers in times of stress. This suggests that G-10 governments should renew their efforts at the World Trade Organization (WTO) and in regional trade agreements to enhance entry opportunities in emerging markets for foreign financial institutions.

Few of the crisis countries allow much foreign bank activity, despite their potential to help with restructuring and recapitalization. By December 1999, for example, banks in South Korea with 40 percent foreign ownership accounted for only 16 percent of total bank assets; in Malaysia, 12 percent; and in Thailand, a mere 6 percent (IMF 2000b). The presence of foreign banks stimulates competition and greater efficiency, transfers technology and know-how, provides workforce training, and diversifies the sources of finance available to the local market.[22]

The IMF (2000b) cautions against very high concentrations of foreign bank ownership, such as is now the case in Argentina and Poland. The IMF cites potential problems with cross-border supervision and regulation, the "too big to fail" dilemma, and an additional channel of shock

---

22. See Dobson and Jacquet (1998) and Levine (1997).

transmission (from parent to subsidiaries or branches). Name-brand foreign banks can also skim off the low-risk business in an emerging market and raise the portfolio risks of their domestic bank competitors.[23] These considerations lead us to recommend that

■ *The goal of the World Trade Organization and regional trade arrangements should be to create the opportunity for sufficient foreign presence to promote, rather than inhibit, local competition and efficiency, and to enhance financial-system stability in domestic markets.*

In summary, the preceding discussion accepts the value of capital-adequacy rules but highlights the central value of more intense monitoring by G-10 supervisors, more emphasis on international coordination among the supervisors, and greater recognition of the complementarity between supervisory and market discipline.

In the next section, we address the second route to reduce moral hazard: Change the way liquidity crises are resolved. We advocate clear ex ante arrangements that would suspend payments ex post if borrowers' balance of payments profiles become unsustainable in exceptional circumstances. In other words, we want to change the payoffs in a liquidity crisis.[24]

Crisis Management: Changing the Payoffs

Proposals for managing liquidity crises that reduce the need for an international safety net in the form of a lender of last resort usually base their arguments on the assumption that making a loan to such a lender would involve a significant, undesirable degree of moral hazard. Proponents of these reforms, known as private-sector involvement (or "bailing in" private banks and investors, rather than bailing them out), search for ways to change the payoffs from crisis resolution in order to influence the strategies of the players ex ante. Many private-sector participants find the official debate about their involvement in crisis resolution worrisome. This contributes to uncertainty, which is then priced into new transactions, increasing their cost.

Before turning to the issues, it is worth noting an important conceptual debate explored by Roubini (2000). Is there a stable "middle ground" between two "corner solutions": the full bail-out practiced in Mexico in 1995 (when official lenders were the only ones to provide liquidity) and the full bail-in advocated by the Meltzer Commission majority (let private banks and investors take their lumps)? Those who claim there is no middle

---

23. Pointed out in a personal communication from Barry Eichengreen.

24. We resist the temptation to debate the fine points of standstill design.

ground argue that a partial bail-in, or a partial bail-out, will trigger a rush to the exit among asset holders that are either not yet fenced in by official controls, or not yet financed out by official support.

Corner solutions work to prevent creditor runs under certain conditions. Bail-outs work if a country is systemically important and illiquid (Mexico in 1995 is an example of a success), but one of the significant consequences is an increase in moral hazard. Bail-ins work because all those involved know standstills or capital controls will be imposed if there is trouble, so the incentive to rush for the exits disappears. But bail-ins are a fragile solution if a country's problem is bad policy or bad fundamentals rather than bad luck. In these cases, uncertainty can precipitate the rush to the front of the line and cause real costs and financial losses.

Although the logic of the corner-solution argument is clear, in practice middle-ground packages have often worked when the external financing gap was too large for official money to fill: Brazil and South Korea are the latest major examples. We concur with Roubini (2000): Middle-ground solutions, by combining official support with coerced private forbearance, are both the most likely and most desirable approach to future crises.

Standstills

A standstill is a temporary halt in external debt servicing when the cause of the financial crisis is a panic among foreign lenders and bondholders. Other capital account outflows may be caught up in the same freeze. When a liquidity crisis is brewing, foreign short-term creditors may rush to get paid with available foreign exchange. Other foreign investors may try to sell their local assets before prices plummet and the exchange rate crashes. Most likely of all, influential local investors will get wind of trouble early, and convert some of their local assets into foreign bank accounts.

The standstill concept was first addressed officially by the G-10 finance and central bank deputies in 1996 as they searched for alternatives to larger and larger official financial assistance packages and ad hoc crisis measures. Further work was done by the Group of Twenty-Two (G-22) working groups in 1998. Both groups suggested that, in exceptional cases where debt profiles become unsustainable, countries should be able to halt payments temporarily while they restructure their obligations. The G-22 working group also emphasized the desirability of cooperative rather than unilateral action. Cooperative restructuring might head off damage to a country's reputation and might forestall anticipatory runs against similar countries.

A number of arguments have been put forward against the standstill concept. One concern is that a potentially coercive rule would come to supercede the current regime of discretion and voluntary creditor action

(IIF 1999a). Fearing that standstills are in the offing, domestic and for-eign investors will run for the exits at the first whiff of trouble. Instead of adding stability, standstills in the toolkit would add fragility. Moral hazard on the part of debtor countries is also high on the list of argu-ments against standstills. By officially recognizing standstills, it is argued, the international community implicitly mandates "potential default." Thus, borrowers could come to view standstills as normal practice rather than as truly exceptional. The result would be a higher debt and equity pre-mium paid by all emerging-market countries, whether standstill candi-dates or not.

Concerns about both issues, it is argued, will cause capital markets to respond negatively, drying up private capital flows or making them more expensive, and slowing growth in developing countries (Council on For-eign Relations 1999). Some cite the Mexican crisis of 1982, when a debt moratorium triggered severe contagion in the rest of Latin America and closed access to capital markets for several years (De Gregorio et al. 1999).

Another objection is that widely held debt obligations are so messy to restructure that herding and contagion cannot be prevented. As former US Treasury Secretary Robert Rubin put it: "You used to be able to or-ganize a relatively small number of banks in order to develop some kind of temporary relief so the banking system could work through its prob-lems. [But with hundreds of institutional portfolio investors,] there's no way to organize a standstill that might prevent things from cratering."[25]

Implications

Involving the private sector in crisis resolution is a necessary innovation in a world dominated by private-capital flows. Ad hoc solutions do not hold adequate promise of changing the rules of the game. The Southeast Asian experience, particularly that of Indonesia, illustrates how difficult and socially costly ad hoc solutions can be. Voluntary crisis resolution worked in South Korea (1998) and Brazil (1999),[26] but we think these cases will not prove to be the future model.

The game is changing. Private creditors have been compelled, more by IMF and G-10 suasion than by voluntary action, to contribute to debt restructuring in Ukraine (1999), Pakistan (2000), and Ecuador (2000). In-formal discussions with market participants in late 2000 indicated an implicit acceptance of joint public-private efforts to resolve crises. What is missing is a clear framework—but one flexible enough to respond to the differing characteristics of successive crises.

---

25. *Wall Street Journal*, 1 February 1999, A6.

26. Brazil's crisis involved official debt, whereas South Korea's was centered on private debt. Korea provided public guarantees for the private debt and adopted very stringent macroeconomic policies to restore market confidence.

The press reports US, European Union, and Canadian convergence toward an agreement, under IMF auspices, on a few key points.[27] The private sector would be required to participate in crisis resolution involving large emerging markets when circumstances indicate that the borrowing country's financial problems will not be quickly resolved and the financial disturbance is deemed to be temporary. However, the private sector would not be required to participate in resolutions involving smaller emerging markets. Still being debated is whether standstills should somehow be "cooperative" or imposed on reluctant creditors, especially on bondholders who have no connection with each other.

Measures along these lines are required to change incentive structures and improve ex ante risk assessment and monitoring. They should be "on the shelf" for application if needed. One way to ensure that such measures will stay on the shelf is to promote mechanisms for better information sharing between public and private sectors. Committees of lenders and representatives of borrowers, working through the auspices of private institutions such as the Institute of International Finance, could provide a forum for interaction between private financial institutions and the public sector.

A critical unsolved issue is whether better information and agreed-on principles of joint crisis resolution will accelerate or retard the rush for the exits. The prospect of a standstill creates its own hazards. Creditors may rush early when trouble strikes, rather than take a patient stance. When a standstill is imposed on one country, creditors may get nervous about its neighbors and withdraw funds.

But, in our view, the growth of IMF resources during the next three decades will simply not permit it to cope with crises in the traditional way. Table 3.1 sketches two alternative growth paths for IMF resources. Path A maintains the historical relation between emerging-market imports and IMF resources. Path B maintains the historical relation between IMF resources and GDP growth of the G-10 countries. We think path B is far more likely than path A. This implies a declining IMF capacity to cope with growing private flows to emerging markets.[28] The full bail-out solution, exemplified by Mexico in 1995, will no longer be an option for large emerging markets. Perforce, other mechanisms must be found to supplement the IMF's traditional role of supplying hard currency in a crisis.

It is far from perfect, but the strongest idea to emerge from the debate so far is the comprehensive payments standstill—to be imposed rarely—by debtor countries with an IMF endorsement, in times of severe

27. *Wall Street Journal*, 28 September 2000, A2.

28. IMF Managing Director Horst Kohler harbors similar reservations: "It seems to me that we have to think about limits to the scale of crisis-lending that the IMF can be expected to undertake" (*IMF Morning Press*, 30 May 2000; http://www.mpress.com).

Table 3.1 IMF resources relative to financial magnitudes in emerging markets

	1970	1980	1990	1999	2010	2020	2030
	(billions of dollars at current prices)				(billions of dollars at 2000 prices)		
IMF quotas							
Path A (emerging-market import growth path)	28	76	130	289	600[a]	1,300[a]	2,800[a]
Path B (G-10 GDP growth path)	28	76	130	289	400[b]	520[b]	660[b]
Fund credit extended[c]	3	14	33	79			
Net IMF resources[d]	25	62	96	210			
Aggregate imports of emerging markets	82	606	918	1,728	4,000[e]	8700[e]	18,800[e]
Total reserves of emerging markets	21	179	350	1,044	3,000[f]	6000[f]	11,000[f]
GDP of emerging markets	797	2,927	4,747	6,521	10,000[g]	15,000[g]	22,000[g]
GDP of G-10	1,999	7,093	14,997	20,187	26,000[h]	35,000[h]	44,000[h]
Long- and medium-term debt and FDI stock in emerging markets	116	563	1,559	3,202	6,300[i]	11,900[i]	21,900[i]
				(percent)			
IMF quotas under path A as percent of:							
Aggregate imports of emerging markets	34.7	12.5	14.1	16.7	15.0[a]	15.0[a]	15.0[a]
Total reserves of emerging markets	137.7	42.5	37.0	27.6	20.0	21.7	25.5
GDP of emerging markets	3.6	2.6	2.7	4.9	6.0	8.7	12.7
GDP of G-10	1.4	1.1	0.9	1.4	2.3	3.7	6.4
Long- and medium-term debt and FDI stock in emerging markets	24.5	13.5	8.3	9.0	9.5	10.9	12.8

IMF quotas under path B as percent of:

(percent)

Aggregate imports of emerging markets	34.7	12.5	14.1	16.7	10.0	6.0	3.5
Total reserves of emerging markets	137.7	42.5	37.0	27.6	13.3	8.7	6.0
GDP of emerging markets	3.6	2.6	2.7	4.9	4.0	3.5	3.0
GDP of G-10	1.4	1.1	0.9	1.4	1.5[b]	1.5[b]	1.5[b]
Long- and medium-term debt and FDI stock in emerging markets	24.5	13.5	8.3	9.0	6.3	4.4	3.0

FDI = foreign direct investment
G-10 = Group of Ten countries; see note to table 1.1.

a. On path A, the IMF quotas are assumed to expand so that they bear a constant relation of 15 percent of the aggregate imports of emerging markets through 2030 (see note d).
b. On path B, the IMF quotas are assumed to expand so that they bear a constant relation of 1.5 percent of the GDP of the G-10.
c. Total fund credit and loans outstanding (calculated as outstanding purchases of local currencies plus outstanding loans).
d. Available resources of the IMF (calculated as IMF quotas less IMF credit extended).
e. The annual growth rate in the 1990s (about 8 percent in real terms) was applied to calculate the figures.
f. Total reserves are assumed to increase from about 20 percent of real GDP in 2000 to 30 percent in 2010, 40 percent in 2020, and 50 percent in 2030.
g. GDP in emerging markets is projected to grow at 4.0 percent per year in real terms.
h. GDP in the G-10 countries is projected to grow at 2.5 percent per year in real terms.
i. The sum of long- and medium-term debt and FDI stock is from table 1.4.

Note: Emerging markets represent the rest of the world other than the 23 industrial countries: Australia, Austria, Belgium, Canada, Denmark, Finland, France, Germany, Greece, Iceland, Ireland, Italy, Japan, Luxembourg, the Netherlands, New Zealand, Norway, Portugal, Spain, Sweden, Switzerland, the United Kingdom, and the United States.

Sources: IMF, *International Financial Statistics, Yearbook*, 1998; IMF, *International Financial Statistics*, February 2000; IMF, *World Economic Outlook*, October 2000; World Bank, *Global Development Finance*, 1998, 1999; United Nations, *World Investment Report*, 1995, 1997.

distress in large emerging markets.[29] When a standstill is invoked, domestic investors in the emerging market should not be allowed to reach the exit door before foreign creditors. Even with these qualifications, we do not list standstills among our frontline recommendations.

Will They Work?

Part of the logic of standstills is that they change the incentive structure for market participants ex ante. But there are significant problems in making them workable. To work, standstills probably have to be universal: They have to apply to all classes of investors. Partial standstills would invite investors to alter the legal form of their holdings so as to avoid emergency controls on repatriation of capital. Short-term loans might be "dressed up," for example, as hybrid equity, if standstill controls did not apply to portfolio equity investors.

But universal standstills have their own problems. They would have to restrict capital flight by residents (which is of considerable magnitude, as pointed out in chapter 1). Stopping residents from acquiring external assets could be very unpopular. Moreover, the list of potential creditors is very long, including various private nonresidents, official lenders, and domestic holders of wealth. Getting these diverse groups to agree on a fair distribution of delayed payment, and even losses, is a logistical nightmare.

Other problems with the standstill concept come to rest at the IMF's door. The Fund is the logical institution to declare a standstill. It would have to quickly identify the cause of a crisis and declare a standstill if warranted. Some debtor countries would be tempted to request a standstill, even if they did not need one. If the IMF denied a "confidential" request, that might produce its own mini-crisis.

In addition, the IMF is an important creditor in its own right. There will not be much political support for the standstill concept if the Fund tries to ensure preferential repayment for itself. Eichengreen (2000) concludes that if standstills are to be officially triggered by the IMF, its Article VIII.2(b) would first have to be changed, and creditor countries would have to recognize in their contract law the IMF's authority to trigger such standstills. Amendment of the IMF Articles is a major step. This or any other mechanism for invoking standstills will be unworkable as long as the United States opposes the concept.

---

29. The case for a payments standstill has been advanced by Miller and Zhang (1999), among others. Differing scholars, such as Eichengreen and Ruehl (2000), have argued for collective-action clauses in loan agreements. Cline (cited in Harwood, Litan, and Pomerleano 1999, chap. 1) thinks such clauses are a bad idea and would diminish bond issues by developing countries. Cline's objections were pointedly underscored by Mexico, which initially refused to insert a collective-action clause in its sovereign bond issues, arguing that such a clause would taint its standing in the capital markets.

Collective-Action Clauses

An alternative mechanism with the same motivating logic, to change the incentives ex ante, is the collective-action clause (CAC). The CAC concept mainly applies to bond contracts and syndicated bank loans; the idea is to facilitate the orderly restructuring of problem debts.[30] CACs are usually activated when the economic fundamentals in an economy or a sector deteriorate. Sweeping panic and a rush for the exits are not the problem. Bond and loan contracts that include a CAC allow the majority of creditors to negotiate settlements collectively without being obstructed by a minority of creditors who may be pushing for more radical measures, such as legal action to seize assets. UK bonds often include such clauses, and these bonds are traded in London. US bonds typically do not have CAC features.

A comparison of the borrowing costs of UK and US-style bonds indicates that CAC provisions reduce the cost of borrowing for the more creditworthy issuers, but less creditworthy ones face higher spreads.[31] This means that lenders penalize borrowers considered most likely to default, leading to pricing for risk. Eichengreen (2000) points out that more than half of sovereign bonds and two-thirds of all emerging-market bond issues do not yet include CACs. Nor are CACs yet used in syndicated loan contracts. On the basis of recent bond restructuring agreements in Pakistan and Ukraine, where CACs were in place, Roubini (2000) concludes that "CACs have had a very marginal role." But the incentive structure is gradually changing to encourage the wider use of CACs, while recognizing that they are no silver bullets. For example, qualification criteria for the IMF's Contingent Credit Line now include the use of CACs.

Collective-action clauses may gradually gain acceptance. But even if they become a customary part of syndicated loan and bond contracts, CACs cannot deal with the problem of panic. In a panic, many creditors besides holders of bonds and syndicated loans will rush for the exit.

When a panic threatens, and the problem is temporary liquidity in a country that intends to honor its commitments, in a truly voluntary fashion *all* the large G-10 financial institutions should organize an orderly rescheduling that allows for continued access to international capital markets. Voluntary debt rollovers will reduce the pressure on the IMF to

---

30. Buiter and Sibert (1999) suggest a different kind of clause for debt contracts. They suggest that all foreign currency lending be required to include a universal debt rollover option with a penalty. Such a clause would put a great deal of power in the hands of the borrower, who could choose to lengthen the maturity of debt and pay a predetermined penalty to do so. Such a mechanism could be triggered quickly, but like the CAC, it would have to be recognized by all lenders and their governments to become operational.

31. See Eichengreen and Mody (2000).

act as unlimited lender of last resort. Instead, they will distribute the pressure across public- and private-sector participants to restore sustainable debt profiles. In turn, this pressure will ex ante increase the market discipline facing G-10 financial institutions when they extend credit. The outcome should be more realistic pricing of risk.

Over the long haul, the prospects of universal standstills, CACs, and voluntary debt rollovers should change the structure of capital flows to emerging markets. These measures should both lengthen debt-maturity terms and promote the substitution of portfolio equity and FDI as alternative forms of capital flow. Why? Because the various techniques of delaying payment in a crisis have far less impact on the anticipated cash-flow profile for longer-term investment than for short-term debt.

Even so, it is not at all clear that private-sector measures alone provide an adequate answer to financial crises. Hence the case for the middle ground that blends private and official support in handling liquidity crises. For the foreseeable future, we expect to see ad hoc solutions, combining official support, such as IMF lending into arrears, with coerced and voluntary private-sector involvement in restoring payments structures to sustainable profiles.

Disclosure and Transparency

Before drawing our conclusions, there is an additional transparency issue that merits consideration. If international financial-market participants are expected to improve their evaluation of risk, more timely public information on borrowers is required, such as information on national balance sheets and on the strength of domestic financial sectors. Widespread concerns about disclosure and oversight, first identified in 1998 by G-22 working groups, have led the IMF to create standards for information dissemination, and the BIS and the Financial Stability Forum to create guidelines for strengthening financial systems (boxes 3.1 and 3.2). Setting standards is one thing. Implementation and monitoring are also necessary. The IMF and World Bank have taken on these tasks in the joint Bank-Fund Financial Sector Assessment Program (FSAP), and they are making this information public through *Reports on Observance of Standards and Codes* (ROSCs) and Financial Sector Stability Assessments (FSSAs).

The purpose of ROSCs is to monitor the implementation by national authorities of internationally recognized standards. The IMF is incorporating ROSCs into its Article IV surveillance missions, which draw upon the expertise of selected national supervisors who join the missions for this purpose. ROSC coverage is extensive (table 3.2). It includes assessments of "core" standards (for data, fiscal and monetary policy, and the banking sector) and "noncore" standards (for securities and insurance, payment systems, audit, accounting, and deposit insurance).

Box 3.1 The Status of IMF Reforms

Crisis Prevention

Macroeconomic Surveillance,
Early Warning, and Prequalification

The International Monetary Fund's traditional macroeconomic surveillance exercises—in the form of once-secret Article IV consultations—are now carried out in a more open manner. Public Information Notices (PINs), summarizing the outcome, are released for about 80 percent of Article IV consultations (the remaining 20 percent probably concern the most questionable countries). By March 2000, 58 IMF members had volunteered to participate in an 18-month pilot program for the release of Article IV staff reports.

A further step is that, upon a member's Use of Fund Resources (UFR), the chairman's statement following the Executive Board discussion, as well as the Letter of Intent (LOI), will be publicly released. By March 2000, 54 sets of program documents had been issued. In addition, an external evaluation of IMF surveillance methods was published in July 1999 and subsequently reviewed by the Executive Board, http://www.imf.org/external/pubs/ft/extev/surv/index.htm. In April 2000, the IMF Executive Board decided to establish an independent evaluation office within the Fund. Specifics on the new office were thrashed out in the Annual Meetings in September 2000.

The IMF recognizes the case for creating an early-warning system to help predict balance of payments crises, and prototype models are being tried within the IMF. However, cautious voices are still raised against excessive reliance on models and any publication of results.

In March 2000, the Executive Board endorsed the proposal that an important principle of the strengthened two-stage safeguards framework (an assessment process, followed by an on-site review) should become a standard requirement for Fund financial support.

Surveillance of Financial Supervisory Systems
in Emerging-Market Economies

More attention has been given to the analysis of each IMF member's financial-sector soundness, its capital account position, and its vulnerability to financial crises. A joint IMF-World Bank Financial Sector Assessment Program has been established, operating on a 1-year pilot basis since 1999, to help countries reduce their financial vulnerability and to enhance their long-term financial development. On the basis of FSAP reports on 12 countries, the IMF prepared Financial Sector Stability Assessments in 1999. The Fund is still working out the balance between confidentiality and candor in publishing the results.

Promote Disclosure and Transparency

The Special Data Dissemination Standard (SDDS), in place since 1996, seeks to report more timely data on reserves, foreign currency liquidity positions, and external debt. By July 2000, 29 of the 47 subscribers met SDDS data

(Box 3.1 continues next page)

Box 3.1 The Status of IMF Reforms (*continued*)

specifications, http://dsbb.imf.org/country.htm. By the end of 1999, most potential members in the General Data Dissemination Standard (GDDS) system had participated in seminars. Broad economic aggregates have been prepared for fourteen countries.

The SDDS guides countries that have, or that might seek, access to international capital market, http://dsbb.imf.org/sddsindex.htm. The GDDS, conversely, was established in 1997 for countries not in a position to subscribe to the SDDS, but seeking to improve their statistical systems, http://dsbb.imf.org/gddsindex.htm. In addition to providing more timely economic and financial data, the GDDS and the SDDS serve as templates for measuring key economic variables across countries (See box 3.2).

Crisis Management

Declaring a Crisis and Triggering a Standstill

The scope of private-sector burdens in resolving financial crises has been at the center of the debate. Many proposals have been suggested, but no consensus has emerged. The proposals range from collective-action clauses on bond covenants to market-based standstill arrangements. In practice, flexible case-by-case approaches have prevailed. The IMF has gradually shifted its role from dominant provider of assistance to one of several providers, and coordinator of most creditors.

Crisis Lending

IMF facilities are under close scrutiny. As of January 1999, a 45 percent quota increase was agreed on, bringing total quotas to about $300 billion (table 3.1). In September 1999, the Interim Committee, the highest decision-making body of the Fund, was transformed into the International Monetary and Financial Committee (IMFC), reflecting renewed focus on the *financial* nature of the Fund's operations. The first meeting of the IMFC took place in April 2000. Several principles for managing Fund lending in times of crisis emerged: streamlining and consolidating existing facilities; shortening the maturity of loans; and charging progressively higher rates of interest, in the event either of weak implementation of IMF conditions or repeated use of IMF resources.

Until recently, the Fund operated six assistance facilities (Williamson 2000): (1) traditional standbys; (2) the high-interest Supplementary Reserve Facility (SRF) introduced in 1998; (3) the Contingency Credit Line (CCL) announced in 1998, but so far unutilized; (4) the Extended Fund Facility (EFF), introduced in 1975 for longer-term loans to developing countries; (5) the Poverty Reduction and Growth Facility (PRGF); and (6) the Compensatory and Contingency Financing Facility (CCFF), which makes low-interest loans to countries experiencing exogenous shocks. Four facilities—the contingency element of the CCFF, the Currency Stabilization Fund, the Buffer Stock Financing Facility, and support for commercial bank debt reduction (i.e., the Brady Plan)—were eliminated at the April 2000 meetings of the IMFC, and the design of CCL is being reconsidered.

Box 3.2   Standard-setting Bodies

A clear outcome of the financial architecture debate is more transparency, which in turn means benchmarking more features of national economies against recognized standards. As a result, various standard-setting bodies have gained prominence in each pillar of the international economy.

The IMF remains at the center of the picture, because the work of other bodies comes together in the context of IMF surveillance. Together with the World Bank, the IMF summarizes the results in its *Reports on the Observance of Standards and Codes*. Three rounds of experimental case studies are scheduled to be reported to the 2000 Annual Meetings of the IMF and the World Bank, http://www.imf.org/external/np/rosc/2000/stand.htm. Here is a rundown of activity by various standard-setting bodies:

- *International Monetary Fund.* In the April 2000 meeting of the International Monetary and Financial Committee, governors of the IMF (24 ministers and central bank governors representing the 182 members of the IMF) encouraged the development of standards in areas of direct concern to the IMF—data dissemination; transparency of fiscal, monetary, and financial policies; and banking supervision. The IMF has spearheaded the *Code of Good Practices on Fiscal Transparency*, the *Code of Good Practices on Transparency in Monetary and Financial Policies*, the *Special Data Dissemination Standard*, and the *General Data Dissemination Standard*. Together, the IMF and the Basel Committee on Banking Supervision created *the Basel Core Principles*.
- *Basel Committee on Banking Supervision (BCBS).* The BCBS, established in 1974 by the G-10 central banks, formulates broad supervisory standards and guidelines, and recommends statements of best practices in banking. In addition to the G-10 countries, nine central banks in Asia, Latin America, the Middle East, and Europe were admitted to membership in 1996-97, http://www.bis.org/publ/index.htm.
- *International Organization of Securities Commissions.* IOSCO develops and promotes standards of securities regulation. It draws on more than 90 international members to establish standards for effective surveillance, http://www.iosco.org.
- *The World Bank.* The Bank cooperates with other international bodies in developing and promoting standards and best practices in corporate governance, insolvency regimes, and social policies.
- *Committee on Payment and Settlement Systems (CPSS).* The CPSS is established by the G-10 central banks to provide a forum for issues related to payment and settlement systems. It sets out core principles for the design and operation of systemically important payment systems. http://www.bis.org/publ/index.htm.
- *International Association of Insurance Supervisors (IAIS).* The IAIS, which was founded in 1994, establishes internationally endorsed principles and standards that are essential for effective insurance supervision. Its members includes insurance supervisors from more than 100 countries, http://www.iaisweb.org.
- *International Accounting Standards Committee (IASC).* The IASC, a private body formed in 1973, aims to harmonize accounting principles around the world. It has 153 member bodies from 122 countries, http://www.iasc.org.uk.

(Box 3.2 continues next page)

Box 3.2 Standard-setting Bodies (continued)

- *International Federation of Accountants (IFAC).* Through its International Auditing Practices Committee (IPAC), IFAC, a private organization, has formulated the International Standards on Auditing (ISA) and Audit Practice Statements. It has 153 member bodies from 113 countries, representing 2 million accountants, http://www.ifac.org.
- *Organization for Economic Cooperation and Development (OECD).* The OECD's Financial Action Task Force on Money Laundering (FATF) was established by the G-7 summit in Paris in 1989. It has set out a program of 40 recommendations to combat money laundering. With 26 members, FATF monitors progress against money laundering through a two-fold process of annual self-assessment and a more detailed mutual evaluation. Recently, the OECD published a document "naming names" of countries that facilitate tax evasion or are operating as harmful tax havens, http://www.oecd.org/fatf.
- *Financial Stability Forum.* The FSF was established in April 1999 following the proposal by Hans Tietmeyer, former president of the German Bundesbank. It has 40 members. It brings together 25 national regulatory authorities from 11 countries and 15 members from the above-mentioned international organizations. The FSF seeks to coordinate the efforts of these various countries and bodies to promote international financial stability, and reduce systemic risk. In its *Compendium of Standards*, the FSF provides a common reference for accepted economic and financial standards. The *Compendium* highlights 12 key standards for sound financial systems and lists another 54. The FSF has set up working groups on highly leveraged institutions, offshore financial centers, and capital flows. The activities of the working groups and their recommendations were reported onto the IMFC in April 2000, http://www.fsforum.org/standards/.

Since early 1999, ROSCs have been published on an experimental basis for 15 economies that agreed to participate.[32] The noncore reports are adapted from joint Bank-Fund FSAPs; wherever possible, national authorities are encouraged to do self-assessments, the rationale being that implementation is more likely to improve where countries feel they "own" the process. Technical assistance is available, and external assessment is used as a source of discipline. After review by the IMF Executive Board, the Fund makes the reports public.

Our summary of these assessments, in table 3.3, provides a rough checklist. It indicates which macroeconomic and financial systems are sufficiently complete and transparent to be rated. Our ratings indicate what one would expect: Immature financial systems, and countries with problematic macroeconomic fundamentals, need the most improvement.

---

32. These include Albania, Argentina, Australia, Bulgaria, Cameroon, Canada, Czech Republic, Estonia, Greece, Hong Kong Special Administrative Region, Tunisia, Turkey, Uganda, Ukraine, and the United Kingdom.

Table 3.2 IMF *Reports on Observation of Standards and Codes*

| | Coverage[a] | | | | | | | |
| | Core standards | | | | | Noncore standards | | |
Results published	Data	Fiscal	MFP	Banking	Other[c]	Descriptive	Substantive	Style of report[b]
First round (3)								
Argentina	x	x	x	x	SM, IM, AC	x		Staff assessment
Australia	x	x	x	x				Self-assessment
United Kingdom	x	x	x	x	SM, IM, AC, AP	x		Staff assessment
Second round (8)								
Bulgaria (reissued in March 2000)	x	x	x	x	SM, IM, DI		x	Staff assessment
Cameroon (reissued in May 2000)		x	o	o	IM, PS		o	Staff assessment (along with FSSA)
Czech Republic (reissued in June 2000)	x	x	x	x	SM		x	Staff assessment
Greece		x						Staff assessment
Hong Kong SAR	x	x	x	x	SM, IM, AC, AP	x		Staff assessment
Tunisia	x	x	x	x	SM		x	Staff assessment
Uganda	x	x	x	x	SM, IM	x		Staff assessment
Ukraine		x						Staff assessment

(*table continues next page*)

Table 3.2 IMF *Reports on Observation of Standards and Codes* (continued)

| Results published | Coverage[a] | | | | | | | Style of report[b] |
| | Core standards | | | | Other[c] | Noncore standards | | |
	Data	Fiscal	MFP	Banking		Descriptive	Substantive	
Third round (4)								
Albania	x							Staff assessment
Canada			o	o	SM, IM, PS		o	FSSA
Estonia			o	o	SM, IM, PS		o	FSSA
Turkey		x						Staff assessment

MFP = Monetary and Financial Policies.
FSSA = Financial Sector Stability Assessment.
SAR = Special Administrative Region.
x = IMF assessment, based on questionnaires answered by national authorities.
o = FSAP (Financial Sector Assessment Program) assessment.

a. Core standards cover data, fiscal code, monetary and financial code, and Basel core principle on banking. Noncore standards cover securities market regulation (SM); insurance market regulation (IM), payment system (PS), deposit insurance system (DI), accounting (AC), auditing (AD), etc.
b. Staff assessment: IMF assessment, based on questionnaires answered by national authorities. Self-assessment: prepared by national officials from the treasury. IMF played a role in assisting at review panel stage. However, the IMF does not, in its own words, share responsibility for the content of the report. This format has been used only in the case of Australia to date.
c. SM (securities market regulation), IM (insurance market regulation), PS (payment system), and DI (deposit insurance system).

Sources: IMF, *Experimental Reports on Observance of Standards and Codes*, September 2000, http://www.imf.org/external/np/rosc/; *Reports on Observance of Standards and Codes: An Update*, 20 March 2000; *International Standards and Fund Surveillance: Progress and Issues*, 16 August 1999; *Progress Report: Developing International Standards*, March 1999; Country Practices; IMF, *Progress Report on the World Bank-IMF Financial Sector Liaison Committee*, December 1999, http://www.imf.org/external/np/mae/fslc/121599.htm.

Our summary also indicates several problems with the assessments. First, one of the most obvious problems is that none of the major crisis countries has volunteered for inclusion in these early rounds (Argentina and Turkey volunteered before they became a crisis country in late 2000). A second problem—one of the most serious—is the impact of the assessments on IMF resources—at staff, management, and board levels. Missions expanded into the noncore areas because they found their understanding of core areas to be limited without added information. Thus the missions became thinly spread. The IMF has commented (IMF 1999f):

> Even if reports were phased in across the membership over a period of 3-4 years, for example, staff would still need to prepare around 50 reports per year. . . . If reports were confined only to the four previously identified core areas, Statistics Department and Fiscal Affairs Department would need to prepare around 50 modules annually, Monetary and Exchange Affairs Department . . . 100 modules, while area departments . . . 200 modules annually. The resource implications of this work program for departments would be enormous and would require substantial increases in staffing levels. Even more resources would be required if staff assessments were to cover non-core standards as well.

A third problem is determining the quality of the disclosed data. Most of the staff appraisals depend on questionnaires completed by national authorities; few are yet prepared by joint World Bank-IMF assessments. And a fourth problem is implementing best practices. When persistent weaknesses in national financial systems are disclosed through this monitoring process, how will countries be encouraged to correct these weaknesses? The best source of potential pressure is market discipline; and this could be triggered by full, timely disclosure of IMF reports. The worst offenders will, however, resist disclosure.

These are serious issues, but the clear benefit of the assessments is that they create a process and a system for gathering key information on a comparable cross-national basis where there was none, and they provide a new sources of information for markets.

Conclusion

Our analysis has focused on two approaches to change the rules of the game. We have identified a number of reforms that the governments of the G-10, and also Spain, should adopt. We have also examined related IMF reforms to create a framework for private-sector involvement in the resolution of liquidity crises. As we have indicated, undertaking both sets of reforms—beefing up G-10 financial-sector supervision and market discipline and amending the IMF Articles of Agreement—will require huge efforts, probably more effort and resources than these governments are willing to expend.

We conclude, therefore, that political and economic resources would be spent most productively carrying forward the Basel II framework,

Table 3.3 Assessment of the IMF *Reports on Observation of Standards and Codes*

Results published	Coverage[a]					
	Core standards					
	Laudatory[c]	Corrective, general[d]	Corrective, specific[e]	Critical[f]	Other[g]	Substantive (total)[h]
First round (3)						
Argentina	6	4	2	0	3	2 (15)
Australia	0	0	0	0	0	0 (0)
United Kingdom	3	2	3	2	0	5 (10)
Subtotal	9	6	5	2	3	7 (25)
Second round (8)						
Bulgaria	4	19	19	2	0	21 (44)
(reissued in March 2000)						
Cameroon	7	19	5	6	5	11 (42)
(reissued in May 2000)						
Czech Republic	7	8	9	9	1	18 (34)
(reissued in June 2000)						
Greece	1	6	3	0	0	3 (10)
Hong Kong SAR	8	2	3	1	1	4 (15)
Tunisia	4	7	15	0	0	15 (26)
Uganda	1	11	11	2	0	13 (25)
Ukraine	0	4	7	2	0	9 (13)
Subtotal	32	76	72	22	7	94 (209)
Third round (4)						
Albania	1	1	0	1	0	1 (3)
Canada	1	1	2	1	7	3 (12)
Estonia	0	9	8	4	4	12 (25)
Turkey	0	2	17	3	1	20 (23)
Subtotal	2	13	27	9	12	36 (63)

FSSA = Financial Sector Stability Assessment.
SAR = Special Administrative Region.

a. Core standards cover data, fiscal code, monetary and financial code, and Basel core principle on banking. Noncore standards cover securities market regulation (SM); insurance market regulation (IM); payment system (PS); deposit insurance system (DI); accounting (AC); auditing (AD); bankruptcy code (BC), etc.
b. Noncore areas covered in ROSCs to date are as follows: Argentina: SM, IM, AC; Australia: none; United Kingdom: SM, IM, AC, AD; Bulgaria: SM, IM, DI; Cameroon: IM, PS; Czech Republic: SM; Greece: none; Hong Kong SAR: SM, IM, AC, AD; Tunisia: SM; Uganda: SM, IM; Ukraine: none; Albania: none; Canada: SM, IM, PS; Estonia: SM, IM, PS; Turkey: none. Special attention should be given to what "0" stands for in noncore areas. In many cases, descriptions of current practices were given in these areas; this was especially true before FSSA reports were incorporated into ROSCs. For example, the UK report covers noncore areas such as securities market, insurance market, accounting, and auditing practices, as noted above. However, these are descriptive information based on questionnaires answered by the UK authorities without the IMF assessment. This kind of coverage items were treated as "0," as those without any coverage.
c. Praising the past development and potential for the future.
d. Mostly "anodyne," i.e., the direction is shown, but is not specific enough and does not say "how."

		Coverage[a]				
		Noncore standards[b]				
Laudatory	Corrective, general	Corrective, specific	Critical	Other	Substantive (total)[h]	Style of report[i]
0	0	0	0	0	0 (0)	Staff assessment
0	0	0	0	0	0 (0)	Staff assessment
0	0	0	0	0	0 (0)	Staff assessment
0	0	0	0	0	0 (0)	
3	7	8	2	0	10 (20)	Staff assessment
2	2	0	9	0	9 (13)	Staff assessment (along with FSSA)
0	2	1	2	0	3 (5)	Staff assessment
0	0	0	0	0	0 (0)	Staff assessment
0	0	0	0	0	0 (0)	Staff assessment
0	1	1	2	0	3 (4)	Staff assessment
0	0	0	0	0	0 (0)	Staff assessment
0	0	0	0	0	0 (0)	Staff assessment
5	12	10	15	0	25 (42)	
0	0	0	0	0	0 (0)	Staff assessment
2	3	2	3	3	5 (13)	FSSA
0	4	1	3	7	4 (15)	FSSA
0	0	0	0	0	0 (0)	Staff assessment
2	7	3	6	10	9 (28)	

e. Pinpointing the objects for reform, showing "how" to reform "what."

f. Pointing out an inconsistency or incompatibility of existing practices, or those that fall short of internationally recognized standards.

g. Scheduled planning ahead for implementation, areas of potential conflict, etc.

h. Substantive assessments here refer to the sum of the numbers for corrective, specific and critical.

i. Staff assessment: IMF assessment, based on questionnaires answered by national authorities. Self-assessment: prepared by national officials from the treasury. IMF played a role in assisting at review panel stage. However, the IMF does not, in its own words, share responsibility for the content of the report. This format has been used only in the case of Australia to date.

Sources: IMF, Experimental Reports on Observance of Standards and Codes, September 2000, http://www.imf.org/external/np/rosc/; Reports on Observance of Standards and Codes: An Update, 20 March 2000; International Standards and Fund Surveillance: Progress and Issues, 16 August 1999; Progress Report: Developing International Standards, March 1999; Country Practices; IMF, Progress Report on the World Bank-IMF Financial Sector Liaison Committee, December 1999, http://www.imf.org/external/np/mae/fslc/121599.htm.

but further than regulators themselves can be expected to do. By contrast, the consensus agenda concentrates on two features of the financial architecture: demand-side reforms in the emerging markets and bailing-in the private sector through coerced standstills. These features entail fundamental and contentious reforms, both in emerging markets and the IMF. Overcoming the necessary political hurdles (reflecting strong entrenched interests) will take enormous effort. If this effort is expended at the cost of neglecting the G-10 reforms we have suggested, we are skeptical that the fundamental moral hazard problem will soon be overcome, or that the volatility of financial flows to emerging markets will be reduced in the near term.

Instead, we would like to see a larger slice of the available political energy expended on G-10 supervisory reforms and middle-ground measures to involve the private sector, such as voluntary debt rollovers and CACs. These goals are likely to be achieved much more quickly than demand-side reform in the emerging markets (a long, step-by-step, country-by-country process), and they are likely to have a more continuous and beneficial influence than draconian universal standstills that either are seldom implemented, or are implemented much too often.

The rationale for more effort on G-10 reforms and middle-ground measures is to ensure that appropriate evaluation and pricing of risk soon become a permanent feature of world capital markets. We have argued that several measures are necessary:

- *Introduce, through the new Basel Capital Accord, incentives to ensure better calibration of capital requirements for the range of risks banks take.*

- *Reexamine the incentive structures for national supervisors. They should put more weight on systemic risks; they should coordinate more closely—beyond current initiatives—to include proactive information sharing and joint corrective action where they see concentrated, correlated risks in the cross-border positions of their financial institutions. Supervisors should also become publicly accountable for spotting and resolving problems.*

- *Encourage the use of instruments, such as subordinated debt, to increase market monitoring, and require greater disclosure by LCBOs of their risks and risk management systems.*

- *Tighten the G-10 frameworks governing deposit insurance systems, including incentive systems for the supervisors themselves, to offset the public subsidy and encourage greater market discipline. The US framework was carefully examined in the debate over the Financial Services Modernization Act of 1999. Has a similar careful assessment of public safety net subsidies been undertaken in the other G-10 countries? What about the large European state-owned financial institutions? What about Japan's blanket guarantee?*

- *Start a forward-looking review of the demand side of large portfolio investors. The goal is to design disclosure rules and other incentives that would forestall large portfolio swings from becoming a future financial problem.*

- *Create ex ante a clear framework for private-sector involvement in managing future crises through voluntary debt rollovers and collective-action clauses.*

These recommendations will require stepped up international cooperation among supervisors. But the changes are likely to have a lasting effect on incentive structures. How much change is needed? Informal evidence indicates that market-driven adjustment in the G-10 institutions has occurred since the latest crises. Some of the largest firms have completely overhauled their risk-monitoring and -management systems since 1997. Too much intervention by the public sector could amount to overkill, creating new distortions and inefficiencies in international capital markets.

One illustration of how this can happen comes from informal evidence that the appetite of hedge funds, not only for aggressive risk taking but also for more sedate arbitrage, has declined since the 1997-98 crises.[33] Another illustration is the IMF (2000c) report that market players predict that disfavor toward short-term debt instruments will encourage *even shorter* maturity terms, in the form of overnight interbank loans.

Two central questions arise from these conclusions. First, what would be the effect of implementing *all* the measures discussed here—stronger (not heavier) supervisory oversight and international coordination; better incentive structures for supervisors; higher risk weights on short-term loans to high-risk lenders; and tighter, more accountable deposit insurance arrangements? Second, what would be the sensitivity of cross-border capital flows to different combinations of these measures? Would some flows dry up entirely—for example, debt flows to high-risk borrowers? Would debt maturities lengthen? Would the measures create more serious distortions than the hedge fund example? Or would this combination encourage better pricing for risk by lenders—an objective well worth achieving?

These are crucial questions. Our answers are far from definitive, because experience with the policy measures we propose is limited. The limited evidence in related contexts suggests that, to some extent, various forms of capital are substitutes for one another. We are optimists, but the evidence is not conclusive.

---

33. Hedge funds now face more severe disclosure requirements by their bank creditors, as well as substantial official scrutiny. Like other financial institutions, they are avoiding exposure to the erstwhile crisis countries, fearing that the possible disclosure of such transactions will "spook" their investors.

With due regard for these uncertainties, we believe the rules of the game should be changed so that the incentive structures and the strategies of the players are altered. Because the effects of each reform are difficult to measure, they should be introduced gradually and in experimental ways, and financial institutions and regulators must be willing to learn as they go. But the arsenal should be prepared.

APPENDICES

Appendix A
Data on Capital Flows:
Sources and Comparisons

Definitional Issues

Tables 1.1 through 1.4 in the main text present various types of capital flows, private and official. Tables 1.1 and 1.4 highlight past and projected future private capital flows to emerging markets. Figures on both flows and stocks of international capital in these two tables come from various issues of the World Bank's *Global Development Finance* (*World Debt Tables* before 1997). Tables 1.2 and 1.3 summarize IMF data on net capital flows to emerging markets in the 1990s. The figures from IMF sources in tables 1.2 and 1.3 (referred to as *IMF tables*) are based upon standard balance of payments classification categories (as specified in the *Balance of Payment Manual*, 5th edition; IMF 1993).

In this appendix, we provide another set of net capital-flow data from a different source, the Institute of International Finance, *Capital Flows to Emerging Market Economies*. Tables A.1, A.2, and A.3 (referred to as *IIF tables*) lay out a summary for the decade of the 1990s, and regional tables for the second half of the 1990s. For the sake of handy comparison and more detailed data on private flows, the World Bank capital flow figures from *Global Development Finance* for the 1990s are provided in tables A.4, A.5, and A.6 (referred to as *WB tables*).

As might be expected, different sources give somewhat different pictures of capital flows and stocks in emerging markets. We have tried to conform the data in all three sets to the categories used by the IMF (as shown in tables 1.2 and 1.3). Forcing the other two sets into the IMF classification categories creates compatibility problems. However, the juxtaposition of the different data sets, classified in roughly the same way, reveals useful insights.

Table A.1 Net capital flows to emerging markets, 1990-2000
(Institute of International Finance estimates)

Flows	1990	1991	1992	1993	1994	1995
	(billions of dollars at current prices)					
Emerging Markets						
Total private capital inflows (net)	42.2	72.9	121.6	185.2	164.5	231.1
Bank loans and other debt (net)[d]	12.4	17.7	33.7	22.7	40.3	100.9
Portfolio investment (net)[d]	14.0	31.8	56.8	118.2	59.1	53.3
Foreign direct investment (net)[e]	13.8	23.4	31.1	44.3	65.2	76.8
Net official flows	39.3	37	36.8	27.1	28.8	37.9
Change in reserve assets	29.2	45.8	48.4	64.7	44.1	95.2
Current account balance	(15.7)	(21.1)	(50.8)	(80.1)	(72.3)	(88.2)
	(percent)					
As share of GDP of G-10[f]						
Total private capital inflows (net)	0.3	0.5	0.7	1.1	0.9	1.1
Bank loans and other debt (net)[d]	0.1	0.1	0.2	0.1	0.2	0.5
Portfolio investment (net)[d]	0.1	0.2	0.3	0.7	0.3	0.3
Foreign direct investment (net)[e]	0.1	0.1	0.2	0.3	0.3	0.4
Net official flows	0.3	0.2	0.2	0.2	0.2	0.2
As share of GDP of all emerging markets[g]						
Total private capital inflows (net)	0.9	1.5	2.5	3.7	3.1	4.3
Bank loans and other debt (net)[d]	0.3	0.4	0.7	0.5	0.8	1.9
Portfolio investment (net)[d]	0.3	0.7	1.2	2.4	1.1	1.0
Foreign direct investment (net)[e]	0.3	0.5	0.6	0.9	1.2	1.4
Net official flows	0.8	0.8	0.8	0.5	0.5	0.7

a. Estimated.
b. Absolute value of year-to-year changes.
c. The ratio of absolute deviation (note b) to the average flows for 1990-2000. The "own" figure relates the absolute deviation to average annual capital flows of the same type. The "total" figure relates the absolute deviation to the absolute deviation of total private capital flows. Negative signs are ignored in calculating relative deviations.
d. The IIF classification of debt securities (bonds, notes, etc.) depends on the holder. If a bank is a holder, they are classified under "bank loans and other debt (net);" if a nonbank financial institution is the holder, they are classified under "portfolio investment (net)." By contrast, the IMF (as in table 1.2) puts both equity and debt securities under "portfolio investment (net)" regardless of the holder. Accordingly, "bank loans and other debt (net)" in table 1.2 includes trade credits and loans; currency and deposits, and kindred assets and liabilities held by financial institutions.

1996	1997	1998	1999[a]	2000[a]	Flows, 1990-2000 Total	Flows, 1990-2000 Average	Absolute deviation[b]	Relative deviations (percent)[c] Own	Relative deviations (percent)[c] Total
(billions of dollars at current prices)									
327.9	265.7	147.8	148.7	193.1	1,900.7	172.8	55.3	32	
116.4	35.6	(58.8)	(40.5)	(11.1)	269.3	24.5	34.9	>100	63
121.8	114.7	77.1	45.6	71.1	763.5	69.4	33.9	49	61
91.7	115.3	117.9	138.8	119.8	838.1	76.2	14.4	19	26
7.6	38.9	52.8	11.9	9.1	327.2	29.7	14.2		
84.5	42.3	42.2	52.0	74.5	622.9	56.6	19.3		
(96.2)	(80.6)	(10.1)	8.3	(15.7)	(522.5)	(47.5)	22.5		
(percent)									
1.6	1.3	0.7	0.7	0.9			0.9		
0.6	0.2	(0.3)	(0.2)	(0.1)			0.1		
0.6	0.6	0.4	0.2	0.3			0.4		
0.5	0.6	0.6	0.7	0.6			0.4		
0.0	0.2	0.3	0.1	0.0			0.2		
5.6	4.3	2.3	2.3	2.8			3.0		
2.0	0.6	(0.9)	(0.6)	(0.2)			0.5		
2.1	1.9	1.2	0.7	1.0			1.2		
1.6	1.9	1.9	2.1	1.8			1.3		
0.1	0.6	0.8	0.2	0.1			0.6		

e. The IIF "foreign direct investment (net)" figures exclude intercompany loans, contrary to the IMF data in table 1.2.

f. The G-10 countries (actually 11 countries) supply most, but not all, of private and capital flows. The G-10 countries are Belgium, Canada, France, Germany, Italy, Japan, the Netherlands, Sweden, Switzerland, the United Kingdom, and the United States.

g. Emerging markets represent the rest of the world other than industrial countries. Industrial countries here include the G-10, Western Europe, Australia, and New Zealand.

Note: The discrepancy between the figures in table 1.2 and table A.1 stems from different classification methods used. Most important, the figures for "bank loans and other debt (net)" in table A.1 deal only with liabilities of residents of emerging economies, which equate to assets of industrial countries. Thus, when residents of emerging economies move their assets abroad, no entry appears in private capital flows. This largely explains the differences between tables 1.2 and A.1.

Source: Institute of International Finance data.

Table A.2 Net capital flows to emerging markets, by region, 1996-2000 (billions of dollars at current prices)

Flows	1996	1997	1998	1999[a]	2000[a]	Flows, 1996-2000 Total	Flows, 1996-2000 Average	Absolute deviation[b]	Relative deviations (percent)[c] Own	Relative deviations (percent)[c] Total
Asia Pacific										
Total private capital inflows (net)	176.3	67.9	5.8	39.3	59.4	348.7	69.7	56.0	80	82
Bank loans and other debt (net)	80.2	(13.3)	(58.5)	(30.7)	(14.2)	(36.5)	(7.3)	45.8	>100	23
Portfolio investment (net)	50.6	29.4	9.1	15.4	20.0	124.5	24.9	13.1	53	5
Foreign direct investment (net)	45.4	51.9	55.2	54.6	53.6	260.7	52.1	2.9	5	
Net official flows	5.0	36.7	31.2	4.3	8.3	85.5	17.1	17.0		
Change in reserve assets	54.6	8.9	51.5	54.7	48.7	218.4	43.7	24.4		
Current account balance	(51.8)	(2.8)	95.2	64.7	51.2	156.5	31.3	47.8		
Five affected countries[d]										
Total private capital inflows (net)	108.1	(0.2)	(36.4)	(3.7)	7.8	75.6	15.1	47.2	>100	
Net official flows	(1.6)	29.9	26.9	1.4	6.3	62.9	12.6	16.2		
Other Asia										
Total private capital inflows (net)	68.2	68.1	42.2	43.0	51.6	273.1	54.6	8.9	16	
Net official flows	6.6	6.8	4.3	2.9	2.0	22.6	4.5	1.3		
Latin America										
Total private capital inflows (net)	97.3	107.7	97.5	68.8	89.6	460.9	92.2	17.5	19	70
Bank loans and other debt (net)	15.9	18.1	5.8	(11.2)	6.4	35.0	7.0	12.3	>100	83
Portfolio investment (net)	45.7	40.8	42.8	13.5	35.7	178.5	35.7	14.6	41	71
Foreign direct investment (net)	35.8	48.8	48.9	66.5	47.6	247.6	49.5	12.4	25	
Net official flows	(10.5)	(2.6)	15.7	5.5	(1.9)	6.2	1.2	11.0		
Change in reserve assets	25.4	12.0	(9.4)	(12.0)	18.0	34.0	6.8	16.9		
Current account balance	(36.3)	(62.3)	(83.0)	(51.4)	(56.8)	(289.8)	(58.0)	20.9		

Africa/Middle East

Total private capital inflows (net)	3.8	15.7	9.4	8.7	11.6	49.2	9.8	5.5	55	58
Bank loans and other debt (net)	1.8	5.4	1.7	(1.7)	0.2	7.4	1.5	3.2	>100	5
Portfolio investment (net)	1.6	2.1	2.2	2.3	2.7	10.9	2.2	0.3	13	32
Foreign direct investment (net)	0.7	3.8	1.4	2.9	2.9	11.7	2.3	1.8	75	
Net official flows	1.8	(1.3)	(2.2)	(1.0)	(1.7)	(4.4)	(0.9)	1.5		
Change in reserve assets[c]	1.6	10.5	1.8	0.1	0.0	10.4	2.1	5.8		
Current account balance	(1.2)	0.7	(6.4)	(3.5)	(3.2)	(13.6)	(2.7)	3.1		

Europe

Total private capital inflows (net)	50.4	74.5	35.1	31.9	32.5	224.4	44.9	16.8	37	42
Bank loans and other debt (net)	18.9	23.3	2.1	4.5	4.4	53.2	10.6	7.0	66	69
Portfolio investment (net)	21.8	40.3	20.6	12.6	12.2	107.5	21.5	11.7	54	9
Foreign direct investment (net)	9.8	10.9	12.3	14.7	15.9	63.6	12.7	1.5	12	
Net official flows	11.2	6.1	8.1	3.0	4.4	32.8	6.6	3.4		
Change in reserve assets	2.8	10.8	1.9	9.3	7.7	32.5	6.5	6.5		
Current account balance	(6.8)	(16.2)	(16.0)	(1.6)	(6.9)	(47.5)	(9.5)	7.3		

a. Estimated.
b. Absolute value of year-to-year changes.
c. The ratio of absolute deviation (note b) to the average flows for 1996-2000. The "own" figure relates the absolute deviation to average annual capital flows of the same type. The "total" figure relates the absolute deviation to the absolute deviation of total private capital flows. Negative signs are ignored in calculating relative deviations.
d. Indonesia, Malaysia, South Korea, the Philippines, and Thailand.

Note: The discrepancy between the figures in table 1.2 and table A.1 stems from different classification methods used. Most important, the figures for "bank loans and other debt (net)" in table A.1 deal only with liabilities of residents of emerging economies, which equate to assets of industrial countries. Thus, when residents of emerging economies move their assets abroad, no entry appears in private capital flows. This largely explains the differences between tables 1.2 and A.1.

Source: Institute of International Finance, 24 January 2000, *Capital Flows to Emerging Market Economies*.

Table A.3 Net capital flows to emerging markets by region, 1996-2000 (percent of GDP)

	1996	1997	1998	1999	2000	Average percentage
Asia Pacific						
Total private capital inflows (net)	8.7	3.3	0.3	1.8	2.5	3.3
Bank loans and other debt (net)	3.9	(0.7)	(2.8)	(1.4)	(0.6)	(0.3)
Portfolio investment (net)	2.5	1.4	0.4	0.7	0.9	1.2
Foreign direct investment (net)	2.2	2.5	2.6	2.5	2.3	2.4
Net official flows	0.2	1.8	1.5	0.2	0.4	0.8
Five affected countries[a]						
Total private capital inflows (net)	10.0	(0.0)	(5.4)	(0.5)	1.1	1.0
Net official flows	(0.1)	3.0	4.0	0.2	0.8	1.6
Other Asia						
Total private capital inflows (net)	7.1	6.5	2.9	2.8	3.2	4.5
Net official flows	0.7	0.6	0.3	0.2	0.1	0.4
Latin America						
Total private capital inflows (net)	5.2	5.2	4.6	3.2	4.0	4.4
Bank loans and other debt (net)	0.8	0.9	0.3	(0.5)	0.3	0.3
Portfolio investment (net)	2.4	2.0	2.0	0.6	1.6	1.7
Foreign direct investment (net)	1.9	2.3	2.3	3.1	2.1	2.4
Net official flows	(0.6)	(0.1)	0.7	0.3	(0.1)	0.0
Africa/Middle East						
Total private capital inflows (net)	0.4	1.7	1.0	0.9	1.2	1.0
Bank loans and other debt (net)	0.2	0.6	0.2	(0.2)	0.0	0.2
Portfolio investment (net)	0.2	0.2	0.2	0.2	0.3	0.2
Foreign direct investment (net)	0.1	0.4	0.1	0.3	0.3	0.2
Net official flows	0.2	(0.1)	(0.2)	(0.1)	(0.2)	(0.1)
Europe						
Total private capital inflows (net)	4.5	6.5	3.0	2.7	2.6	3.9
Bank loans and other debt (net)	1.7	2.0	0.2	0.4	0.4	0.9
Portfolio investment (net)	1.9	3.5	1.8	1.1	1.0	1.9
Foreign direct investment (net)	0.9	1.0	1.0	1.2	1.3	1.1
Net official flows	1.0	0.5	0.7	0.3	0.4	0.6

a. Indonesia, Malaysia, South Korea, the Philippines, and Thailand.

Note: World GDP is expressed in dollars at market exchange rates (current prices).

Sources: Institute of International Finance, 24 January 2000, *Capital Flows to Emerging Market Economies;* IMF, *World Economic Outlook,* various issues; World Bank, *World Tables,* various issues.

There are three main differences between the data sources: first, how they treat net capital outflows by residents of the emerging market economies; second, the scope of the category, "bank loans and other debt (net);" and third, the treatment of interest payments (on "bank loans and other debt [net]") and profit remittances (on "foreign direct investment [net]").

Treatment of Resident Outflows

The WB tables (panel 1 in table A.4) do not reflect capital outflows, such as net lending or acquisition of assets abroad, by emerging-market residents. Neither do the IIF tables. Only in the IMF tables are net capital outflows by resi-dents of emerging markets offset against inflows from industrial countries.

The differing treatment of resident outflows between data sources creates a startling difference in the apparent magnitude of "total private capital inflows (net)" over the 1990s (total flows from 1990 to 1999). The decadal totals (10 years, eliminating 2000 estimates from the IMF tables and IIF tables for the sake of consistency) differ by between $400 billion and $760 billion (table 1.2 versus table A.1 versus table A.4, panel 1). The big differences are in "bank loans and other debt (net):" Differences in this category explain, on average, more than 80 percent of the gap. Residents of emerging markets place a considerable amount of money abroad, and how this money is recorded importantly affects the measure of "total private capital inflows (net)." Note that, when resident outflows are excluded, the average swings in bank loans into emerging markets decrease substantially from table 1.2. The absolute magnitude of swings more or less approaches the size of swings in portfolio flows. However, since the cumulative magnitude (1990-99) of portfolio flows is larger than the cumulative magnitude of bank loans, the relative volatility of bank loans remains much greater.

Scope of "Bank Loans and Other Debt (Net)"

In the IMF tables, "bank loans and other debt (net)" includes items such as loans, trade credits, currency and deposits, and kindred assets and liabilities—whether placed by banks or other financial institutions. "Portfolio investment (net)" includes both equity securities and debt securities (bonds and notes, money market instruments, and financial derivatives). "Bank loans and other debt (net)" in the IIF tables, however, only covers commercial bank lending. The approximately $200 billion difference between decade totals in the WB tables (panel 1) and the IIF tables in "bank loans and other debt (net)" stems from holdings by nonbank financial institutions of currency, trade credits, and other debt instruments. Below, we give additional comparisons based on the differing definitions of "bank loans and other debt (net)" in each table. The purpose of the additional comparisons is to highlight the role of banking activities.

Treatment of Interest Payments and Profit Remittances

In both the IMF tables and IIF tables, "interest payments" are not subtracted from "bank loans and other debt (net)." Likewise, "profit remittances" are

Table A.4 Net and net-net capital flows to emerging markets, by region, 1990-1999 (billions of dollars at current prices)

Flows	1990	1991	1992	1993	1994	1995
Panel 1						
Emerging Markets (net)						
Total private capital inflows (net)	59.2	82.6	135.9	202.4	222.8	270.7
Bank loans and other debt (net)[d]	31.1	29.9	64.7	48.7	60.6	98.9
Portfolio investment (net)[e]	3.9	18.3	25.1	87.7	73.3	66.9
Foreign direct investment (net)[f]	24.1	34.4	46.1	66.0	88.8	105.0
Net official flows	27.7	27.2	23.5	25.0	13.2	21.2
Panel 2						
Emerging Markets (net-net)						
Total private capital inflows(net-net)	(6.2)	15.9	73.3	137.0	147.1	176.6
Bank loans and other debt (net-net)[d]	(12.1)	(10.6)	30.8	15.8	24.0	52.6
Portfolio investment (net-net)[e]	(0.7)	10.5	17.2	78.1	59.2	45.5
Foreign direct investment (net-net)[f]	6.6	16.0	25.2	43.1	63.9	78.5
Net-net official flows	7.5	5.8	1.2	1.2	(12.4)	(9.3)

a. Estimated.
b. Average absolute value of year-to-year change.
c. The ratio of absolute deviation (note b) to the average flows for 1990-99. The "own" figure relates the absolute deviation to average annual capital flows of the same type. The "total" figure relates the absolute deviation to the absolute deviation of total private capital flows. Negative signs are ignored in calculating relative deviations.
d. In panel 1, interest payments on long-term and short-term debt are not subtracted from "bank loans and other debt (net)." Likewise, these payments are not subtracted in tables 1.2 and 1.3, nor in tables A.1 to A.3. In panel 2, by contrast, interest payments are subtracted. "Bank loans and other debt (net)" is the sum of short-term flows, commercial banks, and other private loans under net private flows in table A.6. "Bank loans and other debt (net-net)" is the sum of short-term flows, commercial banks, and other private loans under net-net private flows in table A.6.

1996	1997	1998	1999[a]	Flows, 1990–99		Absolute deviation[b]	Relative deviation (percent)[c]	
				Total	Average		Own	Total
325.1	324.3	220.1	227.5	2,071	207	42.0	20	
82.7	74.9	(6.1)	(17.1)	468	47	24.2	52	58
111.6	79.1	55.2	52.6	574	57	23.1	40	55
130.8	170.3	170.9	192.0	1,028	103	18.7	18	44
3.0	13.9	23.5	25.6	204	20	7.4		
221.9	210.6	96.2	87.3	1,160	116	40.3	35	
31.7	20.2	(63.8)	(81.4)	7	1	25.4	>100	63
89.3	52.0	24.3	18.3	394	39	25.1	64	62
100.9	138.5	135.7	150.4	759	76	16.6	22	41
(28.0)	(14.9)	(4.5)	(6.2)	(60)	(6)	7.5		

e. Net flows of debt securities (bonds and notes, etc.) are included under "portfolio invest-ment (net)," This is the sum of (4)', (6)' in table A.6. "Portfolio investment (net)" is the sum of bonds and portfolio equity under net private flows in table A.6. "Portfolio investment (net-net)" is the sum of bonds and portfolio equity under net-net private flows in table A.6.

f. In panel 1, profit remittances on FDI are not subtracted from "foreign direct investment (net)." Likewise, profit remittances are not subtracted in tables 1.2 and 1.3, nor in tables A.1 to A.4. In panel 2, by contrast, profit remittances are subtracted.

Note: Capital outflows such as net lending or acquisition of assets abroad by residents of emerging markets are not reflected in either panel 1 or panel 2. This explains the substantial difference between capital flows (net) as shown in panel 1 of this table and the figures in table 1.3. See the text of appendix A.

Sources: World Bank, Global Development Finance, 1997, 1998, 1999, 2000.

Table A.5 Net and net-net capital flows to emerging markets, by region, 1990-99
(World Bank estimates, percent of GDP)

Flows	1990	1991	1992	1993	1994	1995	1996	1997	1998	1999	Average percentage
Panel 1											
As share of GDP of the G-10											
Total private capital inflows (net)	0.6	0.7	0.9	1.3	1.2	1.4	1.5	1.7	1.3	1.2	1.2
Bank loans and other debt (net)[a]	0.4	0.4	0.5	0.4	0.4	0.6	0.4	0.5	0.3	0.0	0.4
Portfolio investment (net)[b]	0.0	0.1	0.1	0.5	0.4	0.3	0.5	0.4	0.2	0.3	0.3
Foreign direct investment (net)[c]	0.2	0.2	0.3	0.4	0.5	0.5	0.6	0.8	0.8	0.9	0.5
Net official flows	0.3	0.3	0.2	0.2	0.1	0.1	0.0	0.1	0.1	0.1	0.1
As share of GDP of all emerging markets											
Total private capital inflows (net)	1.9	2.3	3.3	4.6	4.4	5.3	5.3	5.4	4.0	3.9	4.0
Bank loans and other debt (net)[a]	1.3	1.2	1.8	1.5	1.4	2.2	1.4	1.6	0.9	0.1	1.3
Portfolio investment (net)[b]	0.1	0.4	0.5	1.8	1.4	1.2	1.7	1.2	0.7	0.8	1.0
Foreign direct investment (net)[c]	0.5	0.7	1.0	1.3	1.7	2.0	2.1	2.6	2.4	2.9	1.7
Net official flows	0.9	0.9	0.7	0.6	0.4	0.4	0.0	0.2	0.3	0.4	0.5
Panel 2											
As share of GDP of the G-10											
Total private capital inflows (net-net)	0.0	0.1	0.4	0.8	0.7	0.8	0.9	1.0	0.5	0.3	0.6
Bank loans and other debt (net)[a]	(0.1)	(0.1)	0.1	0.1	(0.0)	0.1	(0.1)	(0.0)	(0.3)	(0.6)	(0.1)
Portfolio investment (net)[b]	0.0	0.1	0.1	0.5	0.4	0.3	0.5	0.4	0.2	0.3	0.3
Foreign direct investment (net)[c]	0.0	0.1	0.1	0.3	0.3	0.4	0.5	0.7	0.6	0.7	0.4
Net-net official flows	0.3	0.3	0.2	0.2	0.1	0.1	0.0	0.1	0.1	0.1	0.1

As share of GDP of all emerging markets

Total private capital inflows (net)	0.0	1.5	2.8	2.5	3.0	3.0	3.2	1.6	1.1	1.9
Bank loans and other debt (net)[a]	(0.2)	0.5	0.2	(0.1)	0.3	(0.4)	(0.2)	(1.0)	(2.0)	(0.3)
Portfolio investment (net)[b]	0.1	0.5	1.8	1.4	1.2	1.7	1.2	0.7	0.8	1.0
Foreign direct investment (net)[c]	0.2	0.3	0.9	1.2	1.5	1.6	2.1	1.9	2.3	1.3
Net official flows	0.9	0.7	0.6	0.4	0.4	0.0	0.2	0.3	0.4	0.5

G-10 = Group of Ten countries; see note f to table A.1.

a. In panel 1, interest payments on long-term and short-term debt are not subtracted from "bank loans and other debt (net)." Likewise, these payments are not subtracted in tables 1.2 and 1.3, nor in tables A.1 to A.3. In panel 2, by contrast, interest payments are subtracted.

b. Net flows of debt securities (bonds and notes, etc.) are included under "portfolio investment (net)."

c. In panel 1, profit remittances on FDI are not subtracted from "foreign direct investment (net)." Likewise, profit remittances are not subtracted in tables 1.2 and 1.3, nor in tables A.1 to A.4. In panel 2, by contrast, profit remittances are subtracted.

Note: Capital outflows such as net lending or acquisition of assets abroad by residents of emerging markets are *not* reflected in either panel 1 or panel 2. This explains the substantial difference between capital flows (net) as shown in panel 1 of this table and the figures in table 1.2. See the text of appendix A.

Sources: World Bank, *Global Development Finance*, 1997, 1998, 1999, 2000.

Table A.6 Decomposition of net and net-net capital flows to emerging markets, by region, 1990-99
(billions of dollars at current prices)

Flows	1990	1991	1992	1993	1994	1995
All emerging markets						
Net private flows	59.2	82.6	135.9	202.4	270.7	325.1
Short-term flows (net)	16.5	22.1	37.6	36.6	48.4	67.5
Long-term private capital flows (net)	15.7	18.6	38.1	48.8	50.4	62.2
Commercial banks[c]	3.2	4.8	16.3	3.5	8.8	30.4
Bonds[d]	1.2	10.8	11.1	36.6	38.2	30.8
Other private[e]	11.3	3.0	10.7	8.7	3.5	1.0
Portfolio equity (net)	2.8	7.6	14.1	51.0	35.2	36.1
Foreign direct investment (net)	24.1	34.4	46.1	66.0	88.8	105.0
Memorandum: official flows (net)	27.7	27.2	23.5	25.0	13.2	21.2
Net-net private flows	(6.2)	15.9	73.3	137.0	147.1	176.6
Short-term flows (net-net)	3.3	7.0	27.5	22.6	32.7	46.5
Long-term private capital flows (net-net)	(18.8)	(14.7)	6.5	20.3	15.3	15.6
Commercial banks[c]	(19.7)	(13.2)	(1.2)	(10.1)	(5.5)	12.2
Bonds[d]	(3.4)	3.0	3.2	27.1	24.1	9.5
Other private[e]	4.3	(4.4)	4.5	3.3	(3.3)	(6.1)
Portfolio equity (net)	2.8	7.6	14.1	51.0	35.2	36.1
Foreign direct investment (net-net)	6.6	16.0	25.2	43.1	63.9	78.5
Memorandum: official flows (net-net)	7.5	5.8	1.2	1.2	(12.4)	(9.3)
Asia						
Net private flows	31.5	39.9	59.6	86.2	122.1	144.5
Short-term flows (net)	10.6	11.2	11.3	7.3	30.3	41.4
Long-term capital flows (net)	7.6	13.0	19.8	15.8	26.2	27.5
Commercial banks[c]	6.4	6.6	11.6	2.9	3.4	10.7
Bonds[d]	(0.6)	4.6	2.6	9.0	18.8	15.7
Other private[e]	1.8	1.8	5.6	3.9	4.0	1.1
Portfolio equity (net)	1.7	1.1	5.5	22.9	18.8	20.6
Foreign direct investment (net)	11.6	14.7	23.0	40.2	46.7	55.0
Memorandum: official flows (net)	10.8	11.9	11.3	11.6	8.6	9.2
Net-net private flows	11.4	19.1	39.0	64.8	97.4	111.9
Short-term flows (net-net)	5.8	6.1	7.3	3.2	25.3	32.7
Long-term capital flows (net-net)	(2.4)	2.6	9.9	5.7	14.6	13.0
Commercial banks[c]	(0.3)	(0.4)	5.5	(3.3)	(3.1)	2.7
Bonds[d]	(1.9)	3.4	1.2	7.3	16.4	12.0
Other private[e]	(0.2)	(0.4)	3.2	1.8	1.3	(1.7)
Portfolio equity (net)	1.7	1.1	5.5	22.9	18.8	20.6
Foreign direct investment (net-net)	6.4	9.3	16.3	33.0	38.7	45.6
Memorandum: official flows (net-net)	4.2	4.8	3.7	3.1	(0.7)	(0.6)

1996	1997	1998	1999	Flows, 1990-99		Absolute deviation[a]	Relative deviation (percent)[b]	
				Total	Average		Own	Total
325.1	324.3	220.1	227.5	2,071	207	42.0	20	
42.9	20.4	(47.6)	(11.2)	233	23	22.7	97	54
102.1	103.4	81.2	19.2	540	54	19.1	35	45
37.5	51.6	44.6	(11.4)	189	19	15.2	80	36
62.4	48.9	39.7	25.0	305	30	12.6	41	30
2.2	3.0	(3.1)	5.5	46	5	4.7	>100	11
49.2	30.2	15.6	27.6	269	27	13.7	51	33
130.8	170.3	170.9	192.0	1,028	103	18.7	18	44
3.0	13.9	23.5	25.6	204	20	7.4		
221.9	210.6	96.2	87.3	1,160	116	40.3	35	
19.7	(3.2)	(69.4)	(30.3)	56	6	23.1	>100	57
52.2	45.1	14.3	(60.4)	75	8	21.5	>100	53
16.4	26.3	14.0	(52.3)	(33)	(3)	15.8	>100	39
40.2	21.8	8.8	(9.3)	125	12	14.2	>100	35
(4.4)	(2.9)	(8.4)	1.2	(16)	(2)	5.2	>100	13
49.2	30.2	15.6	27.6	269	27	13.7	51	34
100.9	138.5	135.7	150.4	759	76	16.6	22	41
(28.0)	(14.9)	(4.5)	(6.2)	(60)	(6)	7.5		
163.3	115.7	35.8	67.2	866	87	32.3	37	
33.6	(3.4)	(39.1)	(11.7)	92	9	16.3	>100	50
43.0	38.4	(2.3)	(6.2)	183	18	10.3	56	32
12.5	8.0	(8.1)	(14.5)	40	4	5.6	>100	17
26.1	26.1	6.1	3.9	112	11	6.6	58	20
4.4	4.3	(0.3)	4.4	31	3	2.4	77	7
23.3	11.7	9.4	20.1	135	13	6.2	46	19
63.4	69.0	67.8	65.0	456	46	6.8	15	21
5.8	17.2	15.9	17.6	120	12	2.6		
126.6	74.6	(6.0)	22.8	562	56	30.7	55	
23.4	(13.9)	(47.4)	(17.1)	25	3	16.2	>100	53
27.3	19.2	(23.5)	(30.5)	36	4	11.0	>100	36
4.4	(1.6)	(19.4)	(28.9)	(45)	(4)	6.2	>100	20
21.1	19.4	(1.5)	(4.2)	73	7	6.8	93	22
1.7	1.5	(2.7)	2.6	7	1	2.4	>100	8
23.3	11.7	9.4	20.1	135	13	6.2	46	20
52.7	57.6	55.6	50.4	366	37	6.5	18	21
(3.2)	8.3	6.3	6.9	33	3	2.5		

(*table continues next page*)

Table A.6 Decomposition of net and net-net capital flows to emerging markets, by region, 1990-99

(billions of dollars at current prices) (*continued*)

Flows	1990	1991	1992	1993	1994	1995
Latin America						
Net private flows	21.5	31.4	44.4	80.2	72.9	78.7
Short-term flows (net)	9.1	8.2	13.4	20.1	12.5	15.9
Long-term capital flows (net)	3.3	4.1	8.1	19.2	18.9	25.3
Commercial banks[c]	2.8	1.3	4.3	0.3	6.2	15.0
Bonds[d]	0.1	4.1	4.7	20.5	15.0	11.5
Other private[e]	0.4	(1.3)	(0.9)	(1.6)	(2.3)	(1.2)
Portfolio equity (net)	0.9	6.2	8.2	27.2	13.2	7.6
Foreign direct investment (net)	8.2	12.8	14.6	13.7	28.4	29.8
Memorandum: official flows (net)	6.9	8.1	9.3	2.7	(1.4)	9.3
Net-net private flows	(0.9)	8.6	22.6	56.1	43.5	41.3
Short-term flows (net-net)	6.6	3.9	10.2	15.4	6.6	9.1
Long-term capital flows (net-net)	(9.3)	(7.2)	(2.9)	8.8	5.2	5.3
Commercial banks[c]	(6.2)	(3.3)	(0.6)	(3.2)	2.6	9.8
Bonds[d]	(2.3)	(1.4)	(0.4)	14.4	5.7	(2.4)
Other private[e]	(0.9)	(2.5)	(1.9)	(2.4)	(3.0)	(2.1)
Portfolio equity (net)	0.9	6.2	8.2	27.2	13.2	7.6
Foreign direct investment (net-net)	1.8	5.6	7.1	4.8	18.5	19.2
Memorandum: official flows (net-net)	0.8	(3.6)	(6.2)	(5.3)	(9.7)	(0.3)

a. Average absolute value of year-to-year change.
b. The ratio of absolute deviation (note a) to the average flows for 1990-99. The "own" figure relates the absolute deviation to average annual capital flows of the same type. The "total" figure relates the absolute deviation to the absolute deviation of total private capital flows. Negative signs are ignored in calculating relative deviations.
c. Commercial banks are loans from private banks and other private financial institutions.
d. Bonds include publicly issued or privately placed bonds.
e. Other private includes credits from manufacturers, exporters, and other suppliers of goods, and bank credits covered by the guarantee of an export credit agency.

1996	1997	1998	1999	Flows, 1990-99 Total	Average	Absolute deviation[a]	Relative deviation (percent)[b] Own	Total
105.4	128.1	112.3	97.0	772	77	16.9	22	
0.9	12.4	(14.5)	(0.9)	77	8	10.1	>100	60
47.2	41.1	55.8	4.9	228	23	12.9	57	76
15.9	31.5	40.4	(4.2)	113	11	10.4	91	61
32.4	10.6	17.6	9.6	126	13	9.7	77	57
(1.1)	(1.0)	(2.2)	(0.5)	(12)	(1)	0.9	75	5
13.9	9.9	1.7	3.6	93	9	7.3	79	43
43.4	64.7	69.3	89.4	374	37	9.2	25	54
(8.3)	(5.1)	6.9	6.3	35	3	6.3		
63.6	81.0	59.0	36.2	412	41	17.3	42	
(6.8)	5.3	(21.8)	(7.4)	21	2	10.6	>100	61
25.4	14.6	25.3	(31.1)	34	3	13.3	>100	77
8.5	22.2	28.9	(19.7)	39	4	10.2	>100	59
18.8	(6.1)	(0.9)	(10.4)	15	1	10.5	>100	61
(1.8)	(1.5)	(2.8)	(1.0)	(20)	(2)	0.9	45	5
13.9	9.9	1.7	3.6	93	9	7.3	79	43
31.0	51.2	53.8	71.2	264	26	8.2	31	48
(17.4)	(13.0)	(0.8)	(3.6)	(59)	(6)	6.5		

Note: Repayments of loan principal are subtracted to obtain net loans. Interest payments on long-term and short-term debt are subtracted from new loans to calculate the net-net amounts. Likewise, profit remittances on foreign direct investment are subtracted from new foreign direct investment flows to calculate the net-net foreign direct investment flows. Capital outflows such as net lending or acquisition of assets abroad by residents of emerging markets are not reflected in either net or net-net flows.

Sources: World Bank, *Global Development Finance,* 1997,1998,1999, 2000.

not subtracted from "foreign direct investment (net)." In the WB tables (panel 2), however, these payments and remittances are subtracted. The cumulative size of "interest payments" and "profit remittances" can best be seen by comparing the two panels of the WB tables. In panel 2, this distinction is made by labeling each category (net-net) as compared to (net) figures (the net figures only subtract repayments of principal, not income remittances). For "bank loans and other debt," the difference between (net) and (net-net) figures add up to a decadal magnitude of $460 billion. The decadal gap between "foreign direct investment (net)" and "foreign direct investment (net-net)" totals about $270 billion.

Additional Comparisons

Table A.6 presents the net capital-flows data with detailed decomposition, isolating commercial bank loans from portfolio bonds and equities. "Commercial banks" under "long-term private capital flows (net)" in table A.6 include only loans from private banks and other private financial institutions. However, "bank loans and other debt (net)" in table A.1 (IIF table) covers commercial bank lending, which refers to "transactions that relate to liabilities of residents of that economy, whether they refer to transactions in debt securities or to components of other investment, such as trade credit or other loans."

In short, bank activities other than loan making are included in table A.1, but not in table A.6. Thus, comparing the figures in tables A.1 and A.6 gives a very rough idea of how much volatility increases when additional activities of banks (trading in debt securities and other investment) are taken into account. Average absolute deviations ($34.9 billion) as a percentage of cumulative flows ($269.3 billion) are about 13 percent in table A.1 (including bank trading activities), but only 8 percent of cumulative flows ($15.2 billion vs. $18.9 billion) in table A.6. This comparison suggests that trading activity adds to the volatility of total bank portfolios. On top of these core definitional differences, the estimates in each table reflect different data sources and different coverage of financial institutions.

A Deeper Look at Bank Activity

Table A.7 summarizes gross flows of many forms of capital to emerging markets during the 1980s and the 1990s. It is useful to start by explaining the concept of "gross flows," Gross flows are recorded without subtracting flows in the opposite direction. The main analysis of this book is based on net flows, drawn from balance of payments data (table 1.2). By comparison, gross flow data (from IMF and BIS sources), while less complete in coverage, provide more information about the means by which capital is raised.

Table A.7 records the gross amount of all new capital issues that occur in the context of formal international offerings or facilities. However, the data in table A.7 excludes bank lending that is not syndicated (e.g., interbank lending) and loans that do not involve international public offerings (Mussa and Richards 1999). The figures also exclude purchases in secondary markets. By definition, the data do not reflect repayments of prior loans.

Looking at the gross numbers in table A.7, portfolio flows (bonds and equities) have now overtaken syndicated loan issues. The trend becomes apparent when compared with the respective flows in the 1980s (table A.7). On average, the share of syndicated loans declined from more than 80 percent of gross financing in the 1980s to less than 50 percent in the 1990s. Moreover, there is a distinct shift toward financing for private borrowers in emerging markets rather than financing for official borrowers (sovereigns and public corporations) (table A.7).

Despite their loss of market share, banks are still major players in the emerging markets. In terms of the size of external debt stock, banks hold about 30 percent of the external debt stock of the emerging-market economies overall, and a somewhat larger share in Latin America than in Asia (table A.8).[1]

Syndicated Loans

As noted above, the gross loan figures in table A.7 refer to syndicated loans, defined as loans issued by at least three financial institutions working together. The syndicated loan data, moreover, are limited to loans with a maturity of at least 1 year and for an amount more than $1 million. Announced syndicated loans to emerging markets are shown in table A.9. In principle, the figures for "All emerging markets" in table A.9 should be identical with the figures recorded under "Syndicated loans" in table A.7. In comparison with the size of cumulative flows during the part-decade period 1992-99, the volatility of syndicated loans is fairly small. The average absolute deviation of syndicated loans was less than 10 percent of the part-decade total of flows in each region. By contrast, the average absolute deviation of net bank loans and deposits in emerging markets was 32 percent of the cumulative *negative* flows (table 1.2).

The text of the book emphasizes volatility in net bank lending. However, one important segment of international banking, the syndicated loan market, appears to be insulated from extreme volatility. The implication is that other forms of international bank lending—short-term interbank loans, trade credits, and corporate loans—together with deposits

---

1. Note, however, the dramatic shift toward nonbank financing in Latin America. In 1982, before the Latin American debt crisis, banks held almost 70 percent of total external debt in Latin America. Now, the share is 33 percent.

Table A.7 Gross private market financing to emerging markets, by region, financing type, and borrower type, 1980-99
(billions of dollars)

Flows	Average, 1980-82	Average, 1983-89	1990	1991	1992	1993	1994	1995
All emerging markets	18.2	23.0	38.1	61.6	64.5	117.4	133.4	160.3
Asia	6.0	12.3	19.5	21.2	25.2	56.3	83.5	88.1
Latin America	8.8	3.1	4.7	14.3	21.5	41.2	25.8	36.3
Africa	0.9	1.8	1.2	4.7	3.4	1.4	3.6	9.4
Middle East	0.7	1.6	1.1	12.0	6.1	4.3	8.9	9.2
Europe	1.8	4.3	11.6	9.4	8.3	14.2	11.7	17.4
Bonds	2.2	6.1	8.7	14.4	25.7	65.0	53.8	59.2
Equities	n.a.	0.3	1.2	5.6	7.2	11.9	17.9	10.0
Syndicated loans	16.0	16.6	28.2	41.6	31.5	40.5	61.6	91.1
Sovereign	3.6	5.0	2.1	15.6	9.6	18.2	16.6	25.6
Public	11.5	13.1	23.2	25.6	25.7	35.1	39.0	49.0
Private	3.1	4.9	12.8	20.5	29.2	64.1	77.8	85.7

n.a. = not available

a. Average absolute value of year-to-year deviations.
b. The ratio of absolute deviation (note a) to the average flows for 1990-99. The "own" figure relates the absolute deviation to average annual capital flows of the same type. The "total" figure relates the absolute deviation to the absolute deviation of total private capital flows. Negative signs are ignored in calculating relative deviations.
Sources: IMF, *International Capital Markets,* September 2000; Mussa and Richards (1999).

				Flows, 1990-99		Absolute	Relative deviation (percent)[b]	
1996	1997	1998	1999	Total	Average	deviation[a]	Own	Total
226.1	297.2	157.4	178.5	1,435	143	46.7	33	
123.4	130.6	41.1	66.6	656	66	25.1	38	54
64.9	96.2	66.6	65.4	437	44	17.0	39	36
5.7	15.2	3.9	4.7	53	5	4.5	84	10
10.3	16.3	9.6	15.5	93	9	4.8	51	10
21.9	38.9	36.2	26.3	196	20	5.7	29	12
105.3	133.2	80.2	87.0	633	63	23.0	36	49
17.8	26.2	9.4	23.2	130	13	7.9	61	17
103.0	137.8	67.7	68.4	671	67	22.3	33	48
41.8	47.4	50.6	51.9	279	28	7.2	26	15
54.7	74.5	33.5	25.6	386	39	11.1	29	24
129.5	175.3	73.3	101.0	769	77	32.5	42	70

Table A.8 External debt stock in emerging markets, by maturity and type of creditor (billions of dollars)

Debt stock	1982	1990	1991	1992	1993	1994	1995	1996	1997	1998	1999	Average stock, 1990-99	Absolute deviation[a]	Relative deviations (percent)[b] Own	Total
All emerging markets	839	1,228	1,245	1,324	1,461	1,564	1,689	1,749	1,813	1,922	1,942	1,594	79	5	
By maturity															
Short-term	187	185	168	207	243	250	321	367	397	418	391	295	33	11	41
Long-term	652	1,043	1077	1,117	1,218	1,313	1,368	1,383	1,416	1,504	1551	1,299	56	4	71
By type of creditor															
Official	249	579	600	630	672	730	770	777	752	745	756	701	27	4	33
Banks	434	387	403	400	417	413	450	467	508	513	509	447	16	4	20
Other private	156	262	242	294	372	421	468	506	553	664	678	446	51	11	64
Asia		187	333	367	408	455	510	561	596	640	655	663	519	37	7
By maturity															
Short-term	40	46	47	57	67	74	96	114	110	98	92	80	10	12	27
Long-term	147	287	320	350	389	436	466	482	529	557	572	439	32	7	86
By type of creditor															
Official	75	172	184	203	224	251	256	267	270	247	257	233	15	6	40
Banks	82	101	101	112	122	142	165	190	190	173	167	146	13	9	34
Other private	31	60	82	93	110	116	140	140	180	236	239	139	20	14	55
Latin America		331	437	459	480	539	565	613	640	669	738	735	587	34	6
By maturity															
Short-term	63	73	63	80	86	101	139	159	182	208	203	129	18	14	53
Long-term	268	365	396	401	452	465	475	481	487	529	532	458	19	4	55
By type of creditor															
Official	41	144	160	161	161	168	193	184	169	178	179	170	9	5	27
Banks	224	198	200	184	186	165	172	178	216	229	229	196	12	6	35
Other private	66	95	99	135	191	232	249	279	283	331	327	222	27	12	79

a. Average absolute value of year-to-year deviations. Figures for 1982 are excluded in calculating average deviations.
b. The ratio of absolute deviation (note a) to the average stock for 1990-99. The "own" figure relates the absolute deviation to the average capital stock of the same type. The "total" figure relates the absolute deviation to the absolute deviation of total stock in the region. Negative signs are ignored in calculating relative deviations.

Source: IMF, World Economic Outlook, various issues.

Table A.9 Announced international syndicated credit facilities, by borrower region, 1992-99 (billions of dollars)

Region or country	1992	1993	1994	1995	1996	1997	1998	1999	Flows, 1992-99		Absolute deviation[a]	Relative deviations (percent)[b]	
									Total	Average		Own	Total
All emerging markets	27.6	22.7	42.5	70.6	84.0	129.2	71.6	54.9	503	63	26.5	42	42
Asia Pacific	13.5	16.8	33.6	41.2	49.6	54.4	20.2	16.6	246	31	11.2	18	42
Five affected countries	6.9	12.1	18.5	28.6	34.7	33.0	8.3	9.0	151	19	7.8	12	30
Indonesia	1.5	2.6	4.8	10.5	13.3	11.4	0.0	0.5	45	6	3.7	6	14
South Korea	2.0	2.6	3.1	5.9	11.2	10.2	0.4	2.5	38	5	3.2	5	12
Malaysia	1.2	2.4	4.1	4.1	3.0	3.5	2.9	3.8	25	3	0.9	1	3
Philippines	0.3	0.6	0.0	1.4	0.6	2.6	2.3	1.7	10	1	0.9	1	3
Thailand	1.9	3.9	6.5	6.7	6.6	5.3	2.7	0.5	34	4	1.6	2	6
Latin America	3.5	2.4	3.3	8.4	11.5	31.0	28.4	16.8	105	13	6.3	10	24
Africa and Middle East	7.5	0.7	3.0	12.1	10.2	19.6	11.1	11.0	75	9	5.4	9	21
Europe	2.9	2.8	2.4	8.8	12.9	24.0	12.0	10.4	76	10	5.1	8	19

a. Average absolute value of year-to-year deviations.
b. The ratio of absolute deviation (note a) to the average flows for 1992-99. The "own" figure relates the absolute deviation to average annual capital flows of the same type. The "total" figure relates the absolute deviation to the absolute deviation of total private capital flows. Negative signs are ignored in calculating relative deviations.

Source: Bank for International Settlements, *Quarterly International Banking and Financial Market Development*, June 2000.

by residents of emerging markets, are the main sources of volatility (BIS 1997).

A statement in the new IMF publication, *Emerging Market Financing*, sheds more light on the syndicated loan segment of the international banking market (IMF 2000a, 21):

> We expect the syndicated loan market to continue to be relatively resilient to fluctuations in global capital market . . . This is readily apparent from the behavior of the share of syndicated bank loans in total financing of emerging markets on international capital markets . . . The share peaked around each of the emerging markets crises—the Tequila, Asian, and Russian crises . . . representing at around half, the largest component of all fundraising by emerging markets on international capital markets.

Interbank Loans

Tables A.10 and A.11 give a detailed picture of banking activity, taken from BIS sources. Table A.10 draws on consolidated banking statistics from the asset side of bank balance sheets. The data mainly cover financial claims reported by domestic bank head offices, including exposures of their foreign affiliates. The data are collected on a consolidated worldwide basis for each bank, with inter-office positions being netted out (BIS 2000a). Thus the reporting system for consolidated positions does not conform to the methodology for reporting balance of payments data (table 1.2), or external debt data (tables A.4, A.5, and A.6).

Table A.11 draws on another set of banking data from the BIS, organized by the location of banking offices. In this dataset, both domestic and foreign-owned banking offices in 18 countries and 6 offshore centers record their positions, including positions vis-à-vis their own affiliates. Data reported under this system are consistent with the principles of reporting balance of payments data (table 1.2) and external debt statistics (Tables A.4, A.5, and A.6) (BIS 2000a).

In Table A.10, annual changes in the assets of industrial-country banks in the emerging markets sum up to $340 billion during the period 1990-99. These figures reflect net flows (after repayments), but do not reflect deposits by residents of emerging markets. About a third of the flows in table A.10 take the form of interbank loans. Interbank loans account for over half of overall volatility in bank lending to emerging markets. When the average absolute deviation of each flow is contrasted with its decadal total, the swings in interbank loans are about 25 percent of the cumulative flows to emerging markets, whereas the swings in loans to the nonbank private sector are about 7 percent. Volatility in short-term lending accounted for two-thirds of overall volatility in bank lending to emerging markets (table A.10).

In the latter part of the 1990s, when the Asian, Russian, and Brazilian crises took place, interbank loans dominated the run from emerging markets.

Table A.10 Change in assets for BIS consolidated bank lending, by maturity and type, 1990-99
(billions of dollars)

Change	1990	1991	1992	1993	1994	1995	1996	1997	1998	1999	Flows, 1990-99 Total	Average	Absolute deviation[a]	Relative deviations[b] (percent) Own	Total
Total flows															
All emerging markets	(14)	32	16	21	64	84	103	142	(59)	(52)	338	34	44	>100	
Asia Pacific	19	21	11	23	52	65	61	54	(85)	(34)	188	19	30	>100	68
Five affected countries	13	14	8	15	35	54	51	13	(73)	(27)	104	10	25	>100	57
Indonesia	6	3	1	2	4	10	11	5	(14)	(5)	23	2	5	>100	12
Malaysia	(1)	1	1	5	0	3	5	6	(7)	(3)	10	1	3	>100	8
Philippines	(0)	(1)	(2)	(1)	1	1	5	7	(4)	0	7	1	3	>100	6
South Korea	5	6	4	3	15	21	22	(2)	(30)	(4)	42	4	11	>100	25
Thailand	3	6	3	7	14	19	7	(3)	(19)	(15)	22	2	7	>100	16
Latin America	(20)	(3)	6	7	12	7	30	39	9	(13)	73	7	14	>100	31
Africa and Middle East	1	(2)	1	(3)	5	1	(5)	11	13	4	25	3	6	>100	14
Europe	(14)	16	(2)	(6)	(5)	12	17	37	4	(8)	51	5	16	>100	36

(table continues next page)

Table A.10 Change in assets for BIS consolidated bank lending, by maturity and type, 1990-99
(billions of dollars) (continued)

Change	1990	1991	1992	1993	1994	1995	1996	1997	1998	1999	Flows, 1990-99 Total	Average	Absolute deviation[a]	Relative deviations (percent)[b] Own	Total
Short-term lending (up to 1 year)															
All emerging markets	11	12	39	28	38	59	57	57	(79)	(38)	183	18	28	>100	79
Asia Pacific	17	16	15	16	32	43	31	3	(72)	(19)	82	8	22	>100	
Five affected countries	13	10	10	11	23	35	29	(8)	(63)	(12)	49	5	20	>100	72
Indonesia	5	2	2	2	2	6	7	1	(11)	(5)	11	1	4	>100	14
Malaysia	0	1	1	3	(1)	1	3	3	(5)	(2)	6	1	3	>100	9
Philippines	0	0	(0)	(1)	1	1	4	4	(3)	(1)	5	0	2	>100	6
South Korea	5	4	4	2	11	14	13	(9)	(29)	5	20	2	10	>100	37
Thailand	3	4	3	6	10	13	2	(7)	(15)	(10)	8	1	5	>100	18
Latin America	3	6	11	9	11	5	19	24	(6)	(15)	69	7	8	>100	30
Africa and Middle East	1	(7)	7	(2)	1	1	(6)	11	5	1	12	1	7	>100	26
Europe	(10)	(2)	7	5	(7)	9	12	18	(7)	(6)	20	2	9	>100	33
Interbank loans															
All emerging markets	(4)	31	21	14	17	44	34	47	(57)	(53)	94	9	23	>100	68
Asia Pacific	11	12	8	12	23	33	26	27	(52)	(27)	74	7	16	>100	
Five affected countries	10	7	7	7	15	27	24	(0)	(42)	(13)	42	4	13	>100	58
Indonesia	3	1	1	1	0	1	3	1	(7)	(1)	3	0	2	>100	10
Malaysia	0	1	1	2	(1)	1	2	3	(4)	(2)	3	0	2	>100	9
Philippines	0	0	(1)	(0)	0	1	3	4	(3)	(1)	4	0	2	>100	7

	1	2	3	4	5	6	7	8	9	10	11	12	13	14	15
South Korea	34	>100	8	3	28	(1)	(19)	(8)	16	13	11	2	4	5	5
Thailand	17	>100	4	0	5	(8)	(10)	(1)	0	12	5	2	1	1	2
Latin America	29	>100	7	1	8	(10)	(11)	14	7	1	(0)	4	7	3	(5)
Africa and Middle East	12	>100	3	1	5	(3)	1	(0)	(3)	2	3	0	4	0	0
Europe	44	>100	10	1	7	(14)	6	6	4	7	(9)	(2)	2	16	(10)
Loans to nonbank private sector															
All emerging markets	56	74	23	31	313	(10)	(3)	100	72	50	46	22	8	12	16
Asia Pacific		>100	13	11	109	(16)	(32)	24	37	36	28	12	7	8	6
Five affected countries	48	>100	11	6	64	(16)	(30)	11	28	27	19	8	5	8	5
Indonesia	13	>100	3	2	19	(5)	(7)	3	8	9	4	1	1	2	3
Malaysia	6	>100	1	1	9	(2)	(3)	2	4	3	3	2	1	0	(1)
Philippines	4	>100	1	1	6	0	(0)	3	7	1	1	0	(0)	(0)	(0)
South Korea	16	>100	4	2	11	(2)	(12)	6	7	7	3	1	0	0	0
Thailand	15	>100	4	12	18	(7)	(9)	(3)	24	8	9	4	2	5	2
Latin America	32	61	7		122	3	16	33		9	12	11	6	6	2
Africa and Middle East	15	>100	3	2	24	5	10	12	1	1	2	(2)	(4)	(3)	2
Europe	33	>100	8	6	58	(1)	3	32	10	4	4	1	0	1	4

BIS = Bank for International Settlements.

a. Average absolute value of year-to-year deviations.

b. The ratio of absolute deviation (note a) to the average flows for 1990-99. The "own" figure relates the absolute deviation to average annual capital flows of the same type. The "total" figure relates the absolute deviation to the absolute deviation of total private capital flows. Negative signs are ignored in calculating relative deviations.

Note: Consolidated banking statistics from the BIS cover the cross-border claims on, and liabilites to, individual countries, or groups of countries, of all the offices worldwide of banks with head offices in reporting countries. The figures exclude positions between different offices of the same bank. The figures for different maturies and type of lending presented here are overlapping and not comprehensive. E.g., most of interbank lending consists of short-term lending. The sum of interbank lending and loans to the non-bank private sector do not add up to total net flows.

Source: Bank for International Settlements, Quarterly Review International Banking and Financial Market Developments, table 9A, various issues.

Table A.11 Change in assets for BIS reporting banks in emerging markets, by type and sector[a], 1996-99 (billions of dollars)

	1996	1997	1998	1999	Average flows	Absolute deviation[a]	Relative deviations (percent)[b] Own	Relative deviations (percent)[b] Total
Panel A								
Changes in total assets,								
all sectors								
All emerging markets	126	91	(79)	(60)	19	74	>100	
Asia and Pacific	81	6	(97)	(54)	(16)	73	>100	98
Five affected countries	58	(10)	(83)	(32)	(17)	64	>100	87
Indonesia	9	7	(14)	(6)	(1)	11	>100	14
Malaysia	7	4	(7)	(4)	0	6	>100	7
Philippines	6	3	(1)	0	2	3	>100	3
South Korea	27	(4)	(33)	(5)	(4)	29	>100	39
Thailand	10	(20)	(29)	(33)	(14)	17	>100	22
Latin America	29	31	(8)	(29)	9	16	>100	22
Africa and Middle East	(0)	22	22	2	11	14	>100	19
Europe	17	32	4	8	15	16	>100	21
Panel B								
Changes in external								
loans, all sectors								
All emerging markets	110	73	(72)	(67)	11	63	>100	
Asia Pacific	71	4	(91)	(57)	(18)	65	>100	>100
Five affected countries	50	(10)	(79)	(28)	(17)	60	>100	96
Indonesia	9	7	(13)	(6)	(1)	10	>100	15
Malaysia	6	3	(5)	(4)	0	4	>100	7
Philippines	5	3	(2)	1	2	3	>100	6
South Korea	21	(5)	(31)	(2)	(4)	27	>100	43
Thailand	8	(19)	(28)	(31)	(14)	16	>100	25
Latin America	26	30	(6)	(28)	8	16	>100	26
Africa and Middle East	(1)	16	20	1	9	14	>100	22
Europe	14	20	4	5	11	7	70	12
Panel C								
(Panel A–Panel B),								
all sectors								
All emerging markets	16	18	(6)	7	9	14	>100	
Asia Pacific	9	2	(6)	3	2	8	>100	58
Five affected countries	8	0	(4)	(4)	0	4	>100	32
Indonesia	1	(0)	(1)	0	(0)	1	>100	7
Malaysia	1	0	(1)	(0)	(0)	1	>100	9
Philippines	0	1	1	(1)	0	1	>100	7
South Korea	5	1	(2)	(3)	0	3	>100	20
Thailand	1	(1)	(1)	(0)	(0)	1	>100	7
Latin America	3	1	(2)	(1)	0	2	>100	17
Africa and Middle East	0	6	1	1	2	4	>100	26
Europe	3	12	(0)	3	5	8	>100	62

BIS = Bank for International Settlements.

a. Average absolute value of year-to-year deviations.

b. The ratio of absolute deviation (note a) to the average flows for 1996-99. The "own" figure relates the absolute deviation to average annual capital flows of the same type. The "total" figure relates the absolute deviation to the absolute deviation of total private capital flows. Negative signs are ignored in calculating relative deviations.

Note: The locational banking statistics from the BIS are provided by reporting banks in 18 countries and 6 offshore centers. The figures report on-balance sheet assets and liabilities vis-à-vis nonresidents in any currency plus similar assets and liabilities vis-à-vis residents

	1996	1997	1998	1999	Absolute flows	Absolute deviation[a]	Relative deviations (percent)[b] Own	Total
Changes in total assets, interbank								
All emerging markets	77	24	(65)	(51)	(4)	52	>100	
Asia and Pacific	48	(3)	(60)	(43)	(14)	41	>100	80
Five affected countries	41	(15)	(69)	(26)	(17)	51	>100	98
Indonesia	3	3	(10)	(3)	(2)	7	>100	13
Malaysia	6	4	(6)	(3)	0	5	>100	9
Philippines	4	1	(1)	(1)	1	2	>100	4
South Korea	20	(5)	(25)	(3)	(3)	23	>100	44
Thailand	8	(17)	(27)	(16)	(13)	15	>100	30
Latin America	19	15	(13)	(8)	3	12	>100	23
Africa and Middle East	1	5	7	(1)	3	5	>100	10
Europe	10	7	0	1	5	3	>100	7
Changes in external loans, interbank								
All emerging markets	69	21	(64)	(58)	(8)	46	>100	
Asia and Pacific	42	(2)	(56)	(48)	(16)	36	>100	77
Five affected countries	36	(14)	(67)	(26)	(18)	48	>100	>100
Indonesia	2	3	(10)	(4)	(2)	6	>100	14
Malaysia	6	3	(5)	(3)	0	4	>100	9
Philippines	4	0	(2)	(0)	1	3	>100	6
South Korea	16	(4)	(24)	(2)	(3)	20	>100	44
Thailand	7	(17)	(27)	(16)	(13)	15	>100	32
Latin America	18	13	(12)	(9)	3	11	>100	24
Africa and Middle East	1	4	7	(1)	3	4	>100	10
Europe	8	5	(2)	(0)	2	4	167	9
(Panel A–Panel B), interbank								
All emerging markets	9	4	(1)	6	4	6	>100	
Asia and Pacific	6	(1)	(3)	5	1	6	>100	>100
Five affected countries	5	(1)	(2)	(0)	0	3	>100	47
Indonesia	0	(0)	(0)	1	0	1	>100	10
Malaysia	(0)	0	(0)	1	0	1	>100	14
Philippines	0	1	1	(1)	0	1	>100	17
South Korea	4	(1)	(1)	(1)	0	2	>100	38
Thailand	0	(1)	(1)	0	(0)	1	>100	11
Latin America	1	2	(1)	0	0	2	>100	29
Africa and Middle East	(0)	2	1	(0)	0	1	>100	20
Europe	2	2	3	1	2	1	24	9

denominated in foreign currencies. The locational banking statistics report data on the positions of all banking offices within the reporting area. Such offices report exclusively on their own (unconsolidated) business, which includes international transactions with any of their own affiliates located either inside or outside the reporting area. The basic organizing principle is the residence of the banking office, regardless of the nationality of ownership. This conforms with the methodology used for balance of payments data (IMF, table 1.2) and external debt data (World Bank, tables A.4, A.5, A.6).

Sources: Bank for International Settlements, *Guide to International Banking Statistics*, July 2000; BIS Quarterly Review, *International Banking and Financial Market Development*, August 2000.

Panel A in table A.11 (the locational statistics from BIS sources) shows clearly the regions and countries where bank outflows were largest. It also shows that changes in interbank assets dominated the overall changes in bank assets. Panel B in table A.11 shows that interbank loans (a *negative* total of $71 billions in 1996-99 in the case of the five affected Asian countries) accounted for more than 100 percent of the total *negative* loan flows to all sectors.

Panel C in table A.11 provides rough estimates of the size of international banking activity in emerging markets, other than loan activity. In other words, panel C provides a rough estimate of securities trades.[2] On the basis of these rough estimates, banks devote more than 80 percent of their asset activities to loan making in emerging markets. Bank trading in securities, however, added to the volatility of overall banking operations (table A.11).[3]

---

2. The estimates are made by subtracting changes in bank loans in emerging markets (panel B) from changes in their total assets (panel A).

3. Two factors help explain the high share of volatility accounted for by interbank loans in table A.11. First, the period under consideration in table A.11 was a period of high volatility. Second, the greater volatility portrayed in table A.11 (compared with table A.10) illustrates the difference in methodology. Interbank loans show more volatility when transactions between foreign affiliates and their head offices are recorded (the convention in table A.11).

Appendix B
G-10 Financial Regulations: Supervisors and Structure

The current trend in G-10 countries is to set up regulatory agencies with responsibility for consolidated oversight of banks and other financial institutions. Although many of these initiatives contemplate some form of "umbrella" supervision of financial conglomerates, there is no international consensus on what governmental authority should exercise this responsibility (Institute of International Bankers 1999). To augment the summary in table 2.9, this appendix provides brief descriptions of the regulatory structures in G-10 countries and Spain, and the existing mechanism for international coordination.[1]

Belgium

1. *Dominant authorities:* Banking and Finance Commission (BFC); Securities Regulation Fund (Fund); Office de Controle des Assurances.

2. *Degree of independence:* The Banking and Finance Commission is an autonomous public institution that has its own legal identity. The

---

1. The sources for this appendix are as follows. Web sites of Individual Financial Supervisors (see table 2.9 for references). Institute of International Bankers (1999, 2000). European Commission, *Institutional Arrangements for the Regulation and Supervision of the Financial Sector*, January 2000. Economist Intelligence Unit, *Country Finance: Individual Country Reports:* Belgium, February 2000; Canada, June 2000; France, October 2000; Germany, March 2000; Italy, September 2000; Japan, June 2000; the Netherlands, July 2000; Spain, October 2000; Sweden, October 2000; Switzerland, September 2000; the United Kingdom, August 2000; and the United States, March 2000. Bannock, Baxter, and Davis (1998); Barth, Caprio, Jr., and Levine (2001).

Commission is composed of a chairman and six other members appointed by royal decree. The Securities Regulation Fund is an independent public institution. The BFC monitors the way the Fund performs its tasks as market authority, and the National Bank of Belgium carries out the day-to-day management of the Fund.

3. *Definitions of principal financial institutions:* Four types of domestic banks are recognized under Belgian law: commercial banks, savings banks, securities banks (a category that brokers can use to broaden their sphere of activity), and local-authority savings banks. The distinction between commercial banks and savings banks has only historical significance. The major Belgian banks are universal banks, handling commercial and investment banking functions. All the leading banks have ties to the insurance companies, and to leasing and factoring organizations. Most have in-house brokerage divisions and investment arms or stakes in venture capital companies. Three factors have contributed to radical changes in the banking landscape in the past 5 years: the government's withdrawal from bank ownership; mergers, takeovers, and initiatives by domestic banks to extend their service areas; and foreign banks moving into the country.

4. *Supervisory responsibility by type of financial institution:* The Banking and Finance Commission has a central role in local financial affairs. It is responsible for prudential and supervisory control of credit institutions, asset management firms, stockbrokers, securities traders, investment funds, and foreign exchange traders. In addition, it has been endowed with supervisory responsibility for holding companies, the stock market and futures and options market, takeover bids for quoted companies, and detection of insider trading. The Insurance Control Office supervises insurance companies, mortgage lending, and pension funds. The Committee of the Securities Regulation Fund is a supervisory body for the institutions recognized for holding electronic accounts of public debt securities, and for transactions in bonds, strips, and Treasury certificates outside the Brussels Stock Exchange.

5. *Coordination among supervisors:* The Bank of Belgium has a systemic interest in the stability of the financial system as the lender of last resort, but the Banking and Finance Commission and the Securities Regulation Fund supervise institutions on a day-to-day basis. The two institutions exchange data. For example, the "Memorandum between the Banking and Finance Commission and the Securities Regulation Fund on the supervision of the holding of accounts in dematerialized securities of the Belgian public debt" defines ways in which data are shared between the two.

6. *Permissible activities for banking organizations:* See table B.1.

7. *Supervision over financial conglomerates:* Financial conglomerates operate without an umbrella regulator.

8. *Host country supervision of nondomestic banking organizations:* Belgium applies its own regulatory standards, in addition to any non-EU home-country regulations. The EU Second Banking Directive, extended to the European Economic Association (EEA) area, grants primary responsibility to home countries in the EU and EEA (including Iceland, Liechtenstein, Norway, and Switzerland). Financial authorities do not apply umbrella supervision to nondomestic banking organizations.

9. *Market risk capital requirements:* Banks and securities firms are subject to risk-based capital requirements for market risk. Banks are permitted to use internal models to measure market risk for the purpose of capital-adequacy requirements.

10. *Domestic legal framework:* Law on the Legal Status and Supervision of Investment Firms, on Intermediaries and Investment Advisors, 1995; Royal Decree on the Organization of the Secondary Off-Exchange Market in Linear Bonds, Strips, and Treasury Certificates, 1995; Royal Decree of 14 September 1997.

Canada

1. *Dominant authorities:* Office of the Superintendent of Financial Institutions (OSFI); Canada Deposit Insurance Corporation (CDIC).

2. *Degree of independence:* OSFI's supervisory mandate makes it independent. OSFI provides prudential review of proposed mergers of financial institutions (along with the competition authority) and makes recommendations to the minister of finance. The minister ultimately has the authority to approve mergers involving institutions under federal jurisdiction. The superintendent is a governor-in-council for seven years and can only be removed for cause. If removed, a report disclosing the reasons must be tabled in Parliament.

3. *Definitions of principal financial institutions:*

■ Commercial banks—banks in Canada are classified into two groups: Schedule I, which are broadly held, and Schedule II, which can have dominant shareholders. Historically, the domestic banks have been Schedule I banks and foreign banks have been Schedule II. A financial-sector policy framework, made public in June 2000, proposes to replace the current two-tier system of bank classification with a three-tier system including large, medium-sized, and small banks, defined by minimum equity limits: over C$5 billion,

Table B.1 Permissible activities for banking organizations in G-10 countries, 1999

Country	Securities[a]	Insurance[b]	Real estate[c]	Bank investment in industrial firms[d]	Industrial firm investment in banks
United Kingdom	Permitted; usually conducted through subsidiaries	Permitted through subsidiaries	Permitted	Permitted, subject to supervisory consultation	No statutory prohibition, controlling investment not favored
United States	Permitted	Permitted, but states may impose restrictions	Not permitted	Not permitted, except for grandfathered arrangements	Generally prohibited except for grandfathered arrangements
Japan	Permitted through subsidiaries	Not permitted until 2001	Not permitted	Limited to holding 5 percent interest	Permitted, provided total investment does not exceed investing firm's capital or net assets
Canada	Permitted through subsidiaries	Permitted through subsidiaries	Permitted through subsidiaries	Permitted up to 10 percent interest in industrial firm	Permitted, up to 10 percent interest
Germany	Permitted	Permitted, but only through insurance subsidiaries	Permitted, but subject to limits based on bank's capital	Permitted, but limited to 15 percent of bank's capital in each firm; aggregate limited to 60 percent	Permitted, subject to regulatory consent based on the suitability of the shareholder
Italy	Permitted	Limited to 10 percent of bank's capital in each firm; aggregate limited to 20 percent	Not permitted	Permitted, up to 15 percent of the bank's capital, subject to approval of the Bank of Italy	Permitted, up to 15 percent interest, subject to approval of the Bank of Italy

				Subject to regulatory approval for voting shares in excess of 10 percent	Subject to regulatory approval for voting shares in excess of 5 percent
Netherlands	Permitted	Permitted through subsidiaries	Permitted		Not prohibited
France	Permitted	Permitted, usually through subsidiaries	Permitted	Permitted, but limited to 15 percent of bank's capital in each firm; aggregate limited to 60 percent	
Switzerland	Permitted through specific license	Permitted through subsidiaries	Permitted	Permitted	Not prohibited, but unusual
Sweden	Permitted	Permitted	Not permitted	Limited	Not prohibited, but unusual
Belgium	Permitted	Permitted through subsidiaries	Not permitted	Permitted, but limited to 15 percent of bank's capital in each firm; aggregate limited to 60 percent	Permitted, but subject to prior approval
Spain	Permitted	Permitted	Permitted	Permitted	More than 5 percent interest requires the approval from the Bank of Spain

G-10 = Group of Ten countries; see note f to table A.1.

a. Securities activities include underwriting, dealing, and brokering all kinds of securities, and all aspects of the mutual fund business.

b. Insurance activities include underwriting and selling insurance as principal or agent.

c. Real estate includes real estate investment, development, and management. Banks are permitted to their own premises, and such ownership is not considered part of "real estate."

d. Including investment in industrial firms through holding company structures.

Note: The table does not summarize the complete range of prudential restrictions that apply to the enumerated activities.

Sources: Institute of International Bankers, *Global Survey 2000: Regulatory and Market Developments*, September 2000; Barth, Brumbaugh, and Wilcox (2000).

C$1-5 billion, and under C$1 billion. The five biggest Schedule I banks (Royal Bank of Canada, Canadian Imperial Bank of Commerce, Bank of Montreal, Bank of Nova Scotia, and Toronto Dominion Bank)—created by numerous mergers over the past century among smaller regional institutions—have been the dominant financial institutions in Canada throughout the postwar period. The Schedule I banks have diversified into other services, such as brokerage, fund management, and venture capital. Most of Canada's largest banks created or bought insurance operations after the Bank Act was relaxed in 1992. Regulatory curbs require that insurance subsidiaries be run at arm's length from banking operations and prohibit bank engagement in the auto leasing business.

■ Credit unions—owned and controlled by their members, credit unions are cooperative financial institutions and are particularly active in Canada. With about a third of the population belonging to a credit union, the country has the world's highest per capita membership. The credit unions deal mainly with mortgage and consumer finance, and are also a significant financing source for small and medium-sized businesses. Individual credit unions are provincially incorporated and regulated.

4. *Supervisory responsibility by type of financial institution:* OSFI is responsible for supervising the banking system, federally chartered insurance and trust companies, federally registered pension funds, and some credit unions. Deposit-taking institutions are subject to federal audit and regulatory control to the extent that deposits are insured by the CDIC. Securities dealers are regulated at the provincial level, but because banks now own securities dealers, the two levels of government have established an elaborate program of information sharing. Jurisdiction over trust and insurance companies is divided, but generally, the larger institutions come under federal statutes.

5. *Coordination among supervisors:* The minister of finance reports to Parliament on the activities of the Bank of Canada, as well as those of the Office of the Superintendent of Financial Institutions. OSFI is responsible for regulating and supervising "Federally Regulated Financial Institutions." The Bank of Canada is responsible for the oversight of the clearing and settlement systems, with a view to controlling systemic risk. The Bank of Canada, OSFI, and CDIC work closely, and trouble with one usually means trouble with all three. A financial-sector policy framework paper, tabled by the Finance Department in mid-1999, envisages no major change in the regulatory structure.

6. *Permissible activities for banking organizations:* See table B.1.

7. *Supervision over financial conglomerates:* The Office of the Superintendent of Financial Institutions oversees the operations of financial conglomerates at the federal level. Certain companies within a financial conglomerates (e.g., securities firms and insurance companies) may also be subject to supervision by provincial authorities.

8. *Host country supervision of nondomestic banking organizations:* The establishment of nonbank affiliates by nondomestic banks is subject to OSFI approval, but it does not supervise these affiliates on an ongoing basis. In a recent development, Bill C-2 (introduced in Parliament in early 2001) distinguishes between "real" foreign banks and "near" foreign banks. A "real" foreign bank will be permitted to conduct financial services activities with the same treatment as the domestic banks. "Near" foreign banks will be permitted to carry on financial services activities in Canada through unregulated entities unless they decide to carry on an insurance business in Canada or core banking activities (deposit-taking business).

9. *Market risk capital requirements:* Banks are subject to risk-based capital requirements for market risk. Banks are permitted to use internal models to measure market risk for the purpose of capital-adequacy requirements.

10. *Domestic legal framework:* Bank Act, 1980; Office of the Superintendent of Financial Institutions Act, 1987 (Amendments, 1996); Bill C-2, 2001.

France

1. *Dominant authorities:* Banking Commission; Banking and Financial Regulatory Committee; Credit Institutions and Investment Committee; National Credit and Securities Council; Commission des Operations des Bourse; and Commission de Contrôle des Assurances.

2. *Degree of independence:* Three major supervisors of credit institutions, the Banking Commission, the Banking and Financial Regulatory Committee, and the Credit Institutions and Investment Committee, are cross-managed by the Banque de France and the Ministry of Economic Affairs and Finance. The structure reflects the balance between the two. Supervisors are accountable to the Parliament.

3. *Definitions of principal financial institutions:* The largest French banks are the three main commercial banks, BNP Paribas, Société Générale, and Credit Lyonnais. The French financial system has been transformed in the past several years by mergers, privatization, and integration among banking, insurance, brokerage, and other suppliers of

services. Domestic consolidation, epitomized by the merger between the Banque Nationale Paris and investment bank Paribas in August 1999, has created a small number of large universal banks. The banking and insurance industries have absorbed the stock brokerage business since reforms in 1987 authorized them to acquire stockbrokerage companies. Banks or insurance companies now either partially or wholly own all of the 40 or so brokerage houses in Paris.

4. *Supervisory responsibility by type of financial institution:* The Banque de France, chairing the Banking Commission, is in charge of banking supervision. The National Credit and Securities Council advises the government on credit policies. The Council is composed of representatives from various banks, organized labor, industry and commerce, regional bodies, and so on. Council members serve on two important committees. The Credit Institutions and Investment Committee (chaired by the governor of the Banque de France) has the power to permit or refuse any type of credit, and it verifies compliance with legal and regulatory supervisions. The Banking and Financial Regulatory Committee (chaired by the minister for economic affairs and finance) authorizes the establishment of banking networks, enforces credit norms and accounting regulations, and monitors relations between credit establishments and clients (see also table 2.9). The committees' decisions are conveyed to banks and clients through the French Credit Establishments Association, to which all banks belong. The French stock market is regulated by the Commission des Operations des Bourse.

5. *Coordination among supervisors:* The National Credit and Securities Council, chaired by the minister of the economy and finance, and deputy-chaired by the governor of the Banque de France, studies and issues opinion on subjects such as customer relations and the means of payment. Members of supervisory institutions, other than the Banking Commission, are appointed from among the members of this council. The Monetary and Financial Authorities Liaison Committee, set up in 1988, provides an additional link among regulators.

6. *Permissible activities for banking organizations:* See table B.1.

7. *Supervision over financial conglomerates:* Financial conglomerates operate without an umbrella regulator.

8. *Host country supervision of nondomestic banking organizations:* France applies its own regulatory standards, in addition to any non-EU home-country regulations. The EU Second Banking Directive, extended to the EEA area, grants primary responsibility to home countries in the EU and EEA (including Iceland, Liechtenstein, Norway, and Switzerland). Financial authorities do not apply umbrella supervision to domestic or nondomestic banking organizations.

9. *Market risk capital requirements:* Banks and securities firms are subject to risk-based capital requirements for market risk. Banks are permitted to use internal models to measure market risk for the purpose of capital-adequacy requirements.

10. *Domestic legal framework:* Banking Act, 1984; Financial Activity Modernization Act, 1996.

Germany

1. *Dominant authorities:* Federal Banking Supervisory Office (FBSO); Federal Securities Supervisory Office (FSSO); Federal Insurance Supervisory Office (FISO); Bundesbank.

2. *Degree of independence:* The FBSO, FSSO, and FISO are independent, superior federal authorities within the ambit of the Federal Ministry of Finance. For example, the FBSO reports directly to the Federal Ministry of Finance. The president of the FBSO is nominated by the Ministry and appointed by the president of the Federal Republic.

3. *Definitions of principal financial institutions:*

■ Universal banks—Germany is known for its universal banks. These banks provide a wide range of financial services within a single corporate structure. In some continental European countries, like Germany and the Netherlands, universal banks have combined the roles of commercial banks, investment banks, insurance, and brokerage.

■ Savings banks—public-sector savings banks are mostly small and lend predominately to private individuals, but most have commercial-banking functions as well. Most of these savings banks are owned by regional or municipal government authorities.

■ Landesbanken—the public-sector Landesbanken are important commercial and investment banks. The Landesbanken are a primary source of long-term credit for international firms, they play a major role in the mortgage business and provide the public sector with long-term financing.

4. *Supervisory responsibility by type of financial institution:* Although monetary policy for Germany and the other 11 euro zone countries is run by the European Central Bank, financial institutions in Germany continue to report to the Bundesbank's supervisory authorities and the Federal Banking Supervisory Office (FBSC). The FBSC must approve the opening of any new bank, including foreign bank branches, and it is responsible for enforcing regulations that govern the banking

sector. Asset managers and financial brokers are subject to supervision by the Federal Securities Supervisory Office. Insurance companies, meanwhile, are regulated by the FISO. The Third Financial Markets Promotion Law, effective April 1998, allows financial services firms to offer a wider range of services without having to be registered as banks. They may, for example, combine brokerage operations, discretionary portfolio management, own-account trading in financial instruments, and financial transfer operations. Since April 1998, these firms require a license from and are regulated by the Federal Banking Supervisory Office.

5. *Coordination among supervisors:* When issuing guidelines concerning capital and liquidity ratios, the Federal Banking Supervisory Office is required to reach agreement with the Bundesbank. In other areas, the Bundesbank merely has to be consulted. The Bundesbank is fully involved in the day-to-day surveillance of credit and financial services institutions.

6. *Permissible activities for banking organizations:* See table B.1.

7. *Supervision over financial conglomerates:* Financial conglomerates operate without an umbrella regulator. However, because most financial conglomerates are universal banks, the de facto umbrella regulator is the Federal Banking Supervisory Office.

8. *Host country supervision of nondomestic banking organizations:* Germany applies its own regulatory standards, in addition to any non-EU home-country regulations. The EU Second Banking Directive, extended to the European Economic Association (EEA) area, grants primary responsibility to home countries in the EU and EEA (including Iceland, Liechtenstein, Norway, and Switzerland). Financial authorities do not apply umbrella supervision to domestic or nondomestic banking organizations.

9. *Market risk capital requirements:* Banks and securities firms are subject to risk-based capital requirements for market risk. Banks are permitted to use internal models to measure market risk for the purpose of capital-adequacy requirements.

10. *Domestic legal framework:* Banking Act, 1961; Sixth Act Amending Banking Act, 1998; Securities Trading Act, 1998.

Italy

1. *Dominant authorities:* Bank of Italy; Ministry of Finance; Commissione Nazionale per le Societa e la Borsa (Consob); Instituto per la Vigilanza Sulle Assicurazioni Private e di Interesse Colletivo (ISVAP).

2. *Degree of independence:* Different supervisors stand independent from each other. New rules were announced in September 1999 on central bank approval for mergers and takeovers involving listed banks. When the rules take effect (they are not yet finalized), approval will have to be sought before a merger or takeover bid is made public. The governor of the central bank is appointed by the Bank of Italy's Executive Board, with the concurrence of the president of the Republic and the prime minister.

3. *Definitions of principal financial institutions:*

■ Commercial banks—universal banks are emerging in Italy. As a result of mergers and acquisitions since the mid-1990s, all the leading banks combine retail and wholesale banking; short-, medium-, and long-term credit; funds management; investment banking; leasing; and insurance. Banks have been allowed since January 1999 to sell banking products through insurance companies. Banks have been moving into insurance much more than insurance companies into banking. Although they are permitted to do so, Italian banks have not taken equity stakes in industrial firms. Many banks have major industrial groups among their own shareholders.

■ Savings, popular, and cooperative banks—savings banks are indistinguishable from other commercial banks, although most have kept their original names. Many are being subsumed into partnership with commercial banks. "Popular" banks are still covered by separate legislation and are a major force. The key difference between popular banks and other institutions is that popular banks must have at least 200 shareholders, and no single shareholder may hold more than 0.5 percent of the shares. Institutions formerly in the rural and artisans' bank category have been reclassified as cooperative banks, similar to popular banks.

4. *Supervisory responsibility by type of financial institution:* The Bank of Italy is responsible for supervising the banking and asset-management system; wholesale markets in government securities; interbank funds; and clearing, settlement, and guarantee systems for transactions involving securities and derivatives. Approval from the Bank of Italy is needed to establish or acquire a bank or securities trading company. For listed financial institutions, the lead supervisor is the stock market regulator, the National Financial Markets Commission (Consob). The Institute for Supervision of Private and Collective Interest Insurance (ISVAP) has a regulatory role in the insurance markets similar to that of the central bank in its sector. ISVAP's activity is financed by a levy on insurers that amounts to 2 percent of premiums.

5. *Coordination among supervisors:* The Bank of Italy is charged with safeguarding stability, whereas Consob is responsible for transparent and proper conduct of individual institutions. The Bank is charged with defining the prudential rules for limiting risk. The supervision of bank holding companies temporarily lies in the Treasury.

6. *Permissible activities for banking organizations:* See table B.1.

7. *Supervision over financial conglomerates:* Financial conglomerates operate without an umbrella regulator.

8. *Host country supervision of nondomestic banking organizations:* Italy applies its own regulatory standards, in addition to any non-EU home-country regulations. The EU Second Banking Directive, extended to the EEA area, grants primary responsibility to home countries in the EU and EEA (including Iceland, Liechtenstein, Norway, and Switzerland).

9. *Market risk capital requirements:* Banks and securities firms are subject to risk-based capital requirements for market risk. Banks are permitted to use internal models to measure market risk for the purpose of capital-adequacy requirements.

10. *Domestic legal framework:* Amato-Carli, 1990; Consolidated Law on Financial Intermediation, 1998.

Japan

1. *Dominant authorities:* Financial Services Agency (FSA) (the Financial Supervisory Authority was renamed in January 2001); Financial Reconstruction Commission (FRC); Securities and Exchange Surveillance Commission (all under the Prime Minister's Office).

2. *Degree of independence:* The FSA reports directly to the Prime Minister's Office and is independent of the Ministry of Finance (MoF), although consultations occur if its action is deemed to have a "grave impact" on the financial system. The Bank of Japan is not part of the government but remains a semigovernment corporation, 55 percent of which is owned by the MoF. The Bank has no statutory role in the supervision of financial institutions, other than as a lender of last resort. The autonomy of the central bank from the government, especially the MoF, has been a contentious matter in recent years. The passage of a revised Bank of Japan Law in April 1998 laid a path toward a more independent central bank.

3. *Definitions of principal financial institutions:*

   ■ Commercial banks—Japan's commercial banking industry is made up of city banks, regional banks, trust banks, and long-term-credit banks. City banks, with assets accounting for about half the combined assets of all the commercial banks, are the most powerful private financial institutions in the country. They provide a wide range of services, including consumer credit, cash management, foreign exchange facilities, securities sales, and leasing services. In the past, city banks primarily served major corporations. Five of the larger city banks (Sakura, Bank of Tokyo-Mitsubishi, Sumitomo, Fuji, and Dai-Ichi Kangyo) are directly affiliated with corporate groups (keiretsu). However, the development of capital markets has decreased the loan demand from large corporations, and the city banks have shifted more of their attention to small companies and to other types of financing. The process of phasing in mutual entry of firms between banking, securities, and trust businesses was initiated in 1993. Through subsidiaries, the lines between city banks, long-term credit banks, trust banks, and securities companies are increasingly blurred.

■ Financial holding companies—as a precursor to a universal banking system, banks, securities companies, and insurers can organize financial holding companies under the Financial Holding Companies Law of March 1998. A bank holding company is permitted to hold more than 50 percent of the shares in each subsidiary in the areas of banking, securities, trust banking, insurance, and investment advisory services. Securities and insurance holding companies are permitted to have securities and insurance subsidiaries, respectively. However, a bank holding company must not have nonfinancial companies under its control.

■ Postal savings system—the Japanese postal savings system is the largest depository institution in the world, holding –260 trillion in personal deposits and savings (a size comparable to the nation's entire commercial banking sector, which had –288 trillion in personal deposits and savings). Postal accounts include savings, annuities, and insurance policies. The primary reason that the Japanese government, via the postal savings system, is in the banking business is to provide an inexpensive source of financing for its own projects. In fact, most of the funds are routed to the Trust Fund of the Bureau of the Ministry of Finance. Proposals for dismantling the system have been debated recently but only modest reforms are planned to scale back the size of the postal savings system.

4. *Supervisory responsibility by type of financial institution:* The creation of the FSA in June 1998 replaced traditional MoF guidance to financial institutions. The MoF now plays a policy role with respect to planning the overall working of the financial system. The FSA is responsible for the supervision of all possible financial activities and institutions, from retail banking to insurance.

5. *Coordination among supervisors:* With the prolonged banking crises of the 1990s, the resolution of failed banks became a headache issue. The FRC, established in October 1998, was given authority both for reorganizing and recapitalizing failed banks. With the exception of rights to issue and eliminate existing licenses, general supervision of financial institutions is delegated to the FSA. Financial crisis management required cooperation between the new FRC and the MoF. The FSA also cooperates with the MoF. The FRC was unsuccessful in this effort and was absorbed by the FSA in 2001.

6. *Permissible activities for banking organizations:* See table B.1.

7. *Supervision over financial conglomerates:* A single regulator (FSA) oversees the activities of all financial conglomerates.

8. *Host country supervision of nondomestic banking organizations:* Supervision of the capital adequacy of nondomestic banks relies on consolidated supervision by the home country, but Japanese standards are applied to the other financial activities of the branches or nondomestic banks. Japanese authorities do not apply their umbrella supervision to nondomestic banking organizations.

9. *Market risk capital requirements:* Banks are subject to risk-based capital requirements for market risk. Banks are permitted to use internal models to measure market risk for the purpose of capital-adequacy requirements.

10. *Domestic legal framework:* Financial Reconstruction Law, 1998; Financial Functions Early Strengthening Law, 1998; Law on the Establishment of the Financial Reconstruction Commission, 1998; Financial Holding Company Law, 1998.

The Netherlands

1. *Dominant authorities:* Netherlandsche Bank; Securities Board; Insurance Board.

2. *Degree of independence:* The Netherlandsche Bank is independent of the Ministry of Finance and other ministers. The governor of the bank is appointed by the royal decree and is not accountable to the ministry. The Bank Council is the decision-making body of the bank. The Securities and Insurance Boards are also independent agencies.

3. *Definitions of principal financial institutions:* Through their affiliates and their close ties with large institutional investors, domestic universal banks can provide financing of every type. The distinctions between different kinds of banks, especially between universal banks and savings

banks, have effectively disappeared. All the major bank groups operate as universal banks, offering a wide range of retail and wholesale banking services and financial products. There are also no restrictions on the lending practices of financial institutions.

4. *Supervisory responsibility by type of financial institution:* The Netherlandsche Bank supervises both retail and wholesale banks. Retail banking is classified under "credit institutions," which include universal banks, savings banks, cooperative banks, security credit institutions, and mortgage banks. Wholesale banking is classified under "investment institutions," which include securities-issuing institutions that deal in the primary market, and securities institutions that trade in the secondary market. The Securities Board of the Netherlands supervises securities trading in the country. Insurance companies and pension funds are supervised by the Insurance Board.

5. *Coordination among supervisors:* The Council of Financial Supervisors brings together the Netherlandsche Bank, the Securities Board, and the Insurance Board. The council has a coordinating function with respect to the supervision of conglomerates, the integrity of the financial sector, and providing of information to consumers.

6. *Permissible activities for banking organizations:* See table B.1.

7. *Supervision over financial conglomerates:* Financial conglomerates operate without an umbrella regulator. The Council of Financial Supervisors has a coordinating function.

8. *Host country supervision of nondomestic banking organizations:* The Netherlands applies its own regulatory standards, in addition to any non-EU home-country regulations. The EU Second Banking Directive, extended to the EEA area, grants primary responsibility to home countries in the EU and EEA (including Iceland, Liechtenstein, Norway, and Switzerland). Financial authorities do not apply umbrella supervision to domestic or nondomestic banking organizations.

9. *Market risk capital requirements:* Banks are subject to risk-based capital requirements for market risk. Banks are permitted to use internal models to measure market risk for the purpose of capital-adequacy requirements.

10. *Domestic legal framework:* Act on the Supervision of the Credit System, 1992; Exchange Offices Act, 1995; Banking Act, 1998.

Spain

1. *Dominant authorities:* Banco de España; Comision Nacional del Mercado de Valores (CNMV); and Directorate General Insurance of the Ministry of Economy and Finance.

2. *Degree of independence:* Supervision is ultimately the responsibility of the government and the Ministry of Finance (Ministerio de Hacienda). A direct supervisory role is assigned to the Banco de España and the other financial regulators. All supervisors are fully independent, but are obliged to cooperate with each other when necessary (see below).

3. *Definitions of principal financial institutions:*

■ Commercial banks—Spain's financial markets have long been dominated by a number of large private commercial banks, which engage in a variety of financial operations, ranging from extending short-term credit to investing in manufacturing companies. Spanish commercial banks are primarily active in short-term credits and discounting of commercial bills. They supply about 40 percent of the total credit volume in Spain. Commercial banks offer a full range of banking services, including the financing and management of syndicated loans in foreign currencies, and investment banking operations. Although smaller in size than their European counterparts, Spanish commercial banks are now among the most profitable in Europe. The two Spanish banking giants—Grupo Banco Santander Central Hispano (BSCH) and Grupo Banco Bilbao Vizcaya Argentaria (BBVA)—control almost one-third of the lending and deposit markets.

■ Savings banks—cajas de ahorro—are an important source of medium- and long-term loans, though they tend to concentrate on specific sectors, such as agriculture, small business, and construction. They play an important role in retail banking and in the mortgage-lending market. Spanish savings banks, led by La Caixa, accounted for 40 percent of total lending, 52 percent of deposits and 52 percent of all mortgage lending in 1999. Although traditionally concentrated on long-term housing and agriculture projects, savings banks now compete with commercial banks in most business segments.

4. *Supervisory responsibility by type of financial institution:* The Banco de España supervises all credit institutions (commercial banks, saving banks, credit cooperatives, and finance companies) and monitors the interbank, foreign exchange, and book-entry public debt markets. Securities firms and collective investment undertakings are supervised by the Comision Nacional del Mercado de Valores. The CNMV is exclusively responsible for overseeing financial markets (stock, private bond, and derivative markets) and entities operating in those markets. Insurance companies and pension funds are supervised by the Directorate General Insurance of the Ministry of Economy and Finance.

5. *Coordination among supervisors:* The Banco de España cooperates with the Comision Nacional del Mercado de Valores, and the Directorate General Insurance of the Ministry of Economy and Finance, whenever undertakings included in a banking group are subject to supervision by these authorities on an individual basis. Specifically, when book-entry trading in public debt, which in principle falls under the supervision of the Banco de España, is considered an official market, there is supervisory coordination between the Banco and the CNMV.

6. *Permissible activities for banking organizations:* See table B.1.

7. *Supervision over financial conglomerates:* The lead regulator for a financial conglomerate is determined on the basis of the financial conglomerate's principal activity.

8. *Host country supervision of nondomestic banking organizations:* Spain applies its own regulatory standards, in addition to any non-EU home-country regulations. The EU Second Banking Directive, extended to the EEA area, grants primary responsibility to home countries in the EU and EEA (including Iceland, Liechtenstein, Norway, and Switzerland). Financial authorities do not apply umbrella supervision to nondomestic banking organizations.

9. *Market risk capital requirements:* Banks and securities firms are subject to risk-based capital requirements for market risk. Banks are permitted to use internal models to measure market risk for the purpose of capital-adequacy requirements.

10. *Domestic legal framework:* Law on Discipline and Intervention of Credit Institutions, 1998; Law of Autonomy of the Banco de España, 1994 (First Amendments, 1997; Second Amendments, 1998); Securities Market Law, 1988 (Amendments, 1999).

Sweden

1. *Dominant authorities:* Financial Supervisory Authority (FSA); Riksbank; Ministry of Finance.

2. *Degree of independence:* The Riksbank is directly responsible to the Riksdag (parliament), not to the government. The FSA is funded by levies on the regulated industries rather than by general government revenues. Such funding secures the agency's independence from the Ministry of Finance, to which the FSA ultimately reports.

3. *Definitions of principal financial institutions:* In Sweden, the lines of demarcation between commercial banks and savings banks have

largely faded away. The four most important banks in Sweden are Svenska Handelsbanken, Skandinaviska Enskilda Banken (SEB), ForeningsSparbanken, and MeritaNordbanken. Consolidation in the banking-financial-insurance sector continues as well. Insurance companies are taking an increasingly aggressive role and have become integrated with banks, both through direct mergers and by starting their own banks.

4. *Supervisory responsibility by type of financial institution:* The Riksbank has the general responsibility of steering credit policies. The dominant supervisory authority is the Financial Supervisory Authority. Through its Banking, Securities, and Insurance departments, the FSA supervises banks and other credit institutions, securities companies and fund management companies, stock exchanges and clearinghouses, insurance companies, brokers, and friendly societies.

5. *Coordination among supervisors:* The Riksbank is responsible for oversight, and the Financial Supervisory Authority is responsible for direct supervision. The Riksbank influences the supervisory system either by contacting bank executives and simultaneously informing the FSA, or by providing general analysis of the financial system through its annual publication, *Financial Market Report.*

6. *Permissible activities for banking organizations:* See table B.1.

7. *Supervision over financial conglomerates:* A single regulator, the Financial Supervisory Authority, oversees the activities of all financial conglomerates.

8. *Host country supervision of nondomestic banking organizations:* Sweden applies its own regulatory standards, in addition to any non-EU home-country regulations. The EU Second Banking Directive, extended to the EEA area, grants primary responsibility to home countries in the EU and EEA (including Iceland, Liechtenstein, Norway, and Switzerland). Financial authorities do not apply umbrella supervision to nondomestic banking organizations.

9. *Market risk capital requirements:* Banks and securities firms are subject to risk-based capital requirements for market risk. Banks are permitted to use internal models to measure market risk for the purpose of capital-adequacy requirements.

10. *Domestic legal framework:* Banking Act, 1987; Swedish Insider Legislation, 2001.

Switzerland

1. *Dominant authorities:* Swiss National Bank; Swiss Federal Banking Commission (SFBC); Federal Office of Private Insurance.

2. *Degree of independence:* The Swiss Federal Banking Commission is an administrative authority of Switzerland, which is independent of the individual directives of the Federal Council and is not a part of the central government administration. Administratively, however, it is integrated within the Federal Department of Finance.

3. *Definitions of principal financial institutions:* The two biggest universal banks are UBS and Credit Suisse, which rank among the world's largest 10 banks. Within Switzerland, UBS and Credit Suisse compete with cantonal banks, regional and savings banks, and cooperatives. In recent years, the number of big banks has continued to decline through mergers, while boundaries have faded between national, cantonal, and private banks, as well as between insurers and capital-market participants.

4. *Supervisory responsibility by type of financial institutions:* The Swiss National Bank's regulatory authority is limited to the imposition of minimum-reserve requirements on banks and the supervision of domestic bond issues. The dominant authority is the Swiss Federal Banking Commission. It is elected by the Federal Council and oversees the banks, investment trusts, and the SWX Swiss Exchange. No bank may operate without the SFBC's authorization, which may be withdrawn if a bank ceases to fulfill required conditions. The blurring of lines between traditional banking and insurance resulted in close cooperation between the SFBC and the Federal Office of Private Insurance—the federal insurance supervisor.

5. *Coordination among supervisors:* The Swiss Federal Banking Commission is in permanent contact with the Federal Department of Finance and other federal departments, as well as the Swiss National Bank. In addition, the SFBC maintains regular contacts with various associations, foremost the Swiss Bankers' Association, the Association of Investment Funds, and the Swiss Institute of Certified Accountants and Tax Consultants.

6. *Permissible activities for banking organizations:* See table B.1.

7. *Supervision over financial conglomerates:* Financial conglomerates operate without an umbrella regulator.

8. *Host country supervision of nondomestic banking organizations:* Switzerland applies its own regulatory standards, in addition to any non-EU home-country regulations. The EU Second Banking Directive, extended to the EEA area, grants primary responsibility to home countries in the EU and EEA (including Iceland, Liechtenstein, Norway, and Switzerland). Financial authorities do not apply umbrella supervision to domestic or nondomestic banking organizations.

9. *Market risk capital requirements:* Banks and securities firms are subject to risk-based capital requirements for market risk. Banks are permitted to use internal models to measure market risk for the purpose of capital-adequacy requirements.

10. *Domestic legal framework:* Stock Exchange Act, 1997; Last Amendments to the Banking Law (1934), 1999.

United Kingdom

1. *Dominant authority:* Financial Services Authority (FSA).

2. *Degree of independence:* The Head of the FSA is appointed and removed by Her Majesty's Treasury. The FSA is accountable to the Ministry of Finance, and independent from the Bank of England.

3. *Definitions of principal financial institutions:*

   ■ Commercial banks—privately owned banks that operate checking ac-counts, receive deposits, take in and pay out notes and coin, and make loans domestically through their branches.

   ■ Building societies—institutions that accept deposit, upon which they pay interest, and make loans for house purchases secured by mortgages. They are owned by its members, who also represent their customers. Elsewhere, similar functions are performed by savings banks, and savings and loan associations (in the United States).

   ■ Clearinghouse—an institution that settles mutual indebtedness between a number of organizations. In England and Wales, the Cheque and Credit Clearing Company Ltd operates a bulk clearing system for cheques and other paper credit items paid into banks other than those upon which they were drawn.

   ■ Unit trust—an organization that invests funds subscribed by the public in securities, and in return issues units that it will repurchase at any time (similar to a mutual fund in the United States). The units, which represent equal shares in the trust's investment portfolio, produce income and fluctuate in value according to the interest and dividends paid and the stock exchange prices of the underlying investments. The trustees that actually hold the securities are usually banks or insurance companies, and are distinct from the management company.

4. *Supervisory responsibility by type of financial institution:* The FSA has been assigned supervisory responsibility over all possible financial activities and institutions, from retail banking to insurance. Various

commissions and boards that regulate different financial sectors are now in the process of merging into the FSA.

5. *Coordination among supervisors:* Since 1997, the Bank of England no longer has supervisory powers over individual financial institutions. It remains responsible for the overall stability of the financial system. The FSA is the primary supervisor for all financial institutions. The joint Committee of Treasury/Bank/FSA has been the coordinating body since March 1998.

6. *Permissible activities for banking organizations:* See table B.1.

7. *Supervision over financial conglomerates:* A single regulator, FSA, oversees the activities of all financial conglomerates as a whole.

8. *Host country supervision of nondomestic banking organizations:* The United Kingdom applies its own supervisory standards apart from the home coun-try. However, within the European Union, relationships among bank supervisors are governed by the Second Banking Directive, which establishes a "home-country" supervisory system for banks incorporated in a member state. Under these arrangements, a member (home) state permits a bank to branch throughout the European Union, and the home-country supervisor has the primary responsibility for the operation of the bank throughout the European Union. The UK financial authorities apply their umbrella supervision to nondomestic banking organizations.

9. *Market risk capital requirements:* Banks and securities firms are subject to risk-based capital requirements for market risk. Banks are permitted to use internal models to measure market risk for risk-based capital-adequacy requirements.

10. *Domestic legal framework:* First Banking Act, 1979; Financial Services Act 1986; Bank of England Act 1998; Financial Services and Market Bills 1999.

United States

1. *Dominant authorities:* The Federal Reserve, Office of the Comptroller of the Currency (OCC—Treasury Department); Office of Thrift Supervision (OTS—Treasury Department); Federal Deposit Insurance Corporation (FDIC); Securities and Exchange Commission (SEC).

2. *Degree of independence:* The Federal Reserve, FDIC, and SEC are independent from the Treasury Department. However, supervision of important financial institutions is the responsibility either of the central bank (Fed) or Treasury.

3. *Definitions of principal financial institutions:* The US banking system was historically a diverse collection of institutions with limited geographical service areas, generally confined to a single state. US banks were prohibited from several important financial activities that were permitted for banks in other major countries. As a consequence of ingenious legal strategies and regulatory tolerance, the geographical and activity boundaries became increasingly blurred in the 1980s and 1990s. The Financial Services Modernization Act, also known as the Gramm-Leach-Bliley Act (GLBA) of October 1999 made it easier for banks, insurers, and securities firms to enter each other's businesses. GLBA permits the creation of a "financial holding company" (FHC), which can have subsidiary corporations that engage in any activity considered "financial in nature," "incidental" to finance, or "complementary" to it. The new law does away with the 25 percent revenue ceiling for nonbanking financial activities that was a core feature of the former bank holding company statute. Proponents of the bill (almost the entire financial industry) see this as a breakthrough that enables them to compete with the universal banks of Europe and the post-1998 "Big Bang" banks of Japan.

4. *Supervisory responsibility by type of financial institution:* The Federal Reserve has primary responsibility for supervising and regulating all bank holding companies, their nonbank subsidiaries, and their foreign subsidiaries together with state-chartered banks that are members of the Federal Reserve System (state member banks) and their foreign branches and subsidiaries. Depending on whether the bank is part of a holding company or conducts securities or insurance activities in an operating subsidiary, other supervisors, such as the FDIC or the SEC, may have some supervisory authority. The Federal Reserve shares supervisory and regulatory responsibilities with the OCC (national banks), the FDIC (state nonmember banks), and the OTS (thrift holding companies, savings and loan associations).

5. *Coordination among supervisors:* The Federal Financial Institutions Examination Council (FFIEC), established by statute in 1978, consists of the chairpersons of the FDIC and the National Credit Union Administration, the comptroller of the currency, the director of the OTS, and a governor of the Federal Reserve Board appointed by the board chairman. Its goal is to harmonize federal principles and standards, and to promote coordination both among federal agencies and between federal and state agencies. GLBA conferred the lead supervisory role on the Federal Reserve.

6. *Permissible activities for banking organizations:* See table B.1.

7. *Supervision over financial conglomerates:* The Federal Reserve oversees the activities of all financial conglomerates as the "umbrella" supervisor. Before passage of GLBA, nonbank financial conglomerates were not

regulated at the group level. Since the new law, banks have been able to affiliate through holding companies with all types of financial institutions, and the Federal Reserve is the "umbrella" supervisor for the group.

8. *Host country supervision of nondomestic banking organizations:* The United States applies its own supervisory standards in addition to whatever standards may be applied by the home country. As with domestic banks, the OCC is the primary regulator for federal branches and agencies, and the states are the primary regulator for branches and agencies licensed under their laws. The Federal Reserve has examination authority over the combined US operations of international banks, including their branches and agencies. The Federal Reserve is also the umbrella supervisor of non-domestic banking organizations. In determining whether to permit an international bank to conduct activities in the United States, the Federal Reserve makes its own assessment of the adequacy of an international bank's global capital.

9. *Market risk capital requirements:* Banks are subject to risk-based capital requirements for market risk. Banks are permitted to use internal models to measure market risk for the purpose of capital-adequacy requirements.

10. *Domestic legal framework:* International Banking Act, 1978; Financial Services Modernization Act, 1999.

The European Union and International Coordination

As shown in table 2.9, the mechanism for regulatory coordination over the financial sector exists at the European and international levels. In contrast to the provisions of the Banking Directive of the European Common Market, financial-market liberalization under NAFTA was not directed toward regulatory harmonization (Haar and Dandapani 1999). Through provisions such as de jure national treatment and MFN, however, there was increased pressure for more deregulation in the US market, culminating in the passage of the Financial Services Modernization Act of 1999.

Banking

European Union

- European Commission Banking Advisory Committee (BAC): The BAC was established in 1978 under the First Banking Coordination

Directive. The BAC assists the Commission in the proper implementation of the European Banking Directives. Its tasks range from authorization requirements for banks to establishing ratios for the solvency, liquidity, and profitability of credit institutions. However, the BAC does not discuss specific problems relating to individual credit institutions. This remains the exclusive competence of the national banking supervisory authorities. Its members include 15 EU countries as well as the European Commission. The European Central Bank, Norway, Iceland, and Liechtenstein participate as observers.

International

■ Basel Committee on Banking Supervision (BCBS): The Basel Committee was established in 1974 after serious disruptions in international banking and currency market (notably the failure of Bankhaus Herstatt in Germany). The committee does not—and never was intended to—have legal force. It formulates and recommends best practices; national authorities are then left to implement what is best suited to their national systems. The BCBS is one of three committees of the Bank for International Settlements; the other two are the Committee on Payment and Settlement System, and the Committee on Global Financial System. The BCBS is best known for its recommendations on bank capital ratios and its development of the 1997 *Core Principles for Effective Banking Supervision*.

Securities

European Union

■ The High Level Securities Supervisors Committee (HLSSC): At the EU level, four groups exist for coordination over securities and derivatives market regulations (table 2.9). The HLSSC is one of the four and assists the European Commission in the preparation of new proposals of securities legislation, which cover listing conditions, access to markets, investor compensation schemes, and so on. The HLSSC is an informal working group with no legal basis. Its membership includes national securities supervisor of the EU countries and officials of finance ministries.

International

■ International Organization of Securities Commissions (IOSCO): IOSCO was created in the early 1980s as a forum for securities regulators around the world. Its main tasks are to establish standards, exchange information, and provide mutual assistance to promote the integrity of the markets. Through its permanent committee structure and joint activities with other institutions, it aims to promote high standards and implement them. The need for monitoring the adoption of best practices led to the addition of an Implementation Committee in 1998. In 1999, the Technical Committee set up a special task force on Hedge Funds and Other Highly Leveraged Institutions.

Insurance

European Union

- Insurance Committee (IC): The IC was set up by an EU Directive in 1992. It is attached to the European Commission and assists the Commission in preparing legislation for the supervision of the EU insurance sector. Prudential issues related to the supervision of financial conglomerates provided strong motivation for creating the IC, as an analogue to the existing system of coordination between banking and securities regulators.

International

- International Association of Insurance Supervisors (IAIS): The IAIS was established in 1994 to provide insurance regulators around the world with an official forum to discuss regulatory issues. Before its inception, an informal forum existed under the National Association of Insurance Commissioners (NAIC), the umbrella organization of US state insurance regulators. Its main functions are standard setting and information gathering, like its counterparts in banking and securities sectors. In 1997, the IAIS issued its first four reports: *Insurance Supervisory Principles*; *Guidance on Insurance Regulation and Supervision for Emerging Market Economies*; *Insurance Concordat*; and *Model Memorandum of Understanding*. Additional standards on licensing, on-site inspection, and derivatives were issued in 1998.

Cross-Sector

European Union

- Banking Advisory Committee/Insurance Committee/High Level Securities Supervisors Committee (BAC/IC/HLSSC): No single cross-sector forum exists in the European Union to discuss specific supervisory issues arising from cross-border financial conglomerates. On a pragmatic basis, however, three sectoral regulatory bodies under the

European Commission have been coordinating supervision on financial conglomerates since 1991. A first meeting of the three bodies took place in 1994. After consulting the BAC, IC, and HLSSC, the Commission set up and mandated under these three parental bodies a new technical group on possible EU legislative response to financial conglomerates.

International

- The Joint Forum on Financial Conglomerates: The Forum was constituted in 1996 to advance the work of the Tripartite Group of banking, securities, and insurance supervisors that was established in 1994. It operates under the aegis of the BCBS, IOSCO, and IAIS. It was mandated to facilitate the exchange of information between supervisors and to enhance supervisory coordination, and to develop principles toward the more effective supervision of financial conglomerates.

- Financial Stability Forum: See box 3.2.

- Committee on Global Financial System (CGFS): It has been a forum since 1960s—formerly called the Euro-Currency Standing Committee—for the regular exchange of views among senior central bank officials. It has been responsible for developing and overseeing the implementation of BIS statistics on banking, derivatives, and foreign exchange market activities. Its work focuses on financial stability, especially the potential impact of financial innovations on systemic risk.

References

Ahearne, Alan G., William L. Griever, and Francis E. Warnock. 2000. *Information Costs and Home Bias: An Analysis of U.S. Holdings of Foreign Equities.* International Finance Discussion Papers 691. Washington: Board of Governors of the Federal Reserve System.

Aitken, Brian, and Ann E. Harrison. 1999. Do Domestic Firms Benefit from Direct Foreign Investment? Evidence from Venezuela. *American Economic Review* 89, no. 3 (June): 605-18.

Aitken, Brian, Gordon H. Hanson, and Ann E. Harrison. 1997. Spillovers, Foreign Investment, and Export Behavior. *Journal of International Economics* 43: 103-32.

Albuquerque, Rui. 2000. The Composition of International Capital Flows: Risk-Sharing through Foreign Direct Investment. University of Rochester, NY. Photocopy.

American Federation of Labor and Congress of Industrial Organizations (AFL-CIO). 2000. *Industrialized Country Financial Markets: The Missing Dimension in the Stabilizing Global Finance Debate.* Economic Policy Paper E040. Washington: Public Policy Department, AFL-CIO.

Ammer, John, and Frank Packer. 2000. *How Consistent Are Credit Ratings? A Geographic and Sectoral Analysis of Default Risk.* International Finance Discussion Papers 668. Washington: Board of Governors of the Federal Reserve System.

Auerback, Marshall. 2001. The New Basle [*sic*] Accord: Self-Regulation Run Amok. From *PrudentBear.com*, http://216.46.231.211 (23 January).

Bagehot, Walter. 1962. *Lombard Street: A Description of the Money Market.* Homewood, IL: Richard D. Irwin (originally published in 1873 in London).

Baily, Martin N., Diana Farrell, and Susan Lund. 2000. The Color of Hot Money. *Foreign Affairs* 79, no. 2 (March/April): 99-109.

Bank for International Settlements (BIS). 1988. *International Convergence of Capital Measurement and Capital Standards.* Basel: Committee on Banking Supervision.

Bank for International Settlements (BIS). 1997. *Quarterly Review: International Banking and Financial Market Development.* Basel: Bank for International Settlements.

Bank for International Settlements (BIS). 1999. *A New Capital Adequacy Framework.* Consultative paper issued by the Basel Committee on Banking Supervision. http://www.bis.org/publ/ (June).

Bank for International Settlements (BIS). 2000a. *Quarterly Review: International Banking and Financial Market Development.* Basel: Bank for International Settlements.

Bank for International Settlements (BIS). 2000b. *70th Annual Report.* Basel: Bank for International Settlements.

Bannock, Graham, R. E. Baxter, and Evan Davis. 1998. *Dictionary of Economics: The Economist Book.* New York: John Wiley & Sons (first published in 1972).

Baran, Paul A., and Paul Sweezy. 1966. *Monopoly Capitalism.* New York: Monthly Review Press.

Barth, Michael, and Xin Zhang. 1999. Foreign Equity Flows and the Asian Financial Crisis. In *Financial Markets and Development: The Crisis in Emerging Markets,* ed. Alison Harwood, Robert E. Litan, and Michael Pomerleano. Washington: Brookings Institution.

Barth, James R., Dan Brumbaugh, Jr., and James A. Wilcox. 2000. Policy Watch: The Repeal of Glass-Steagall and the Advent of Broad Banking. *Journal of Economic Perspectives* 14, no. 2 (Spring): 191-204.

Barth, James R., Gerard Caprio, Jr., and Ross Levine. 2000. Banking Systems around the Globe: Do Regulation and Ownership Affect Performance and Stability? World Bank, Washington. Photocopy (February).

Barth, James R., Gerard Caprio, Jr., and Ross Levine. 2001. The Regulation and Supervision of Banks Around the World: A New Database. Manuscript. Washington: World Bank (February).

Barth, James R., Daniel E. Nolle, and Tara N. Rice. 2000. Commercial Banking Structure, Regulation and Performance: An International Comparison. In *Modernizing Financial Systems,* ed. Dimitri B. Papadimitriou. New York: St. Martin's Press.

Barth, James R., Daniel E. Noelle, Hilton L. Root, and Glenn Yago. 2000. *Choosing the Right Financial System for Growth.* Policy Brief 8. Santa Monica, CA: Milken Institute.

Basel Committee on Banking Supervision. 1998. Sound Practices for Loan Accounting, Credit Risk Disclosure and Related Matters. Basel: Bank for International Settlements.

Basel Committee on Banking Supervision. 1999. *A New Capital Adequacy Framework: Consultative Paper.* Basel: Bank for International Settlements.

Basel Committee on Banking Supervision. 2001. *The New Basel Capital Accord: Consultative Document.* Basel: Bank for International Settlements.

Bayoumi, Tamim, Barry Eichengreen, and Paolo Mauro. 2000. *On Regional Monetary Arrangements For ASEAN.* CEPR Discussion Paper 2411. London: Center for Economic and Policy Research.

Beck, Thorsten. 2000. Deposit Insurance as a Private Club: The Case of Germany. Paper presented at a World Bank conference on deposit insurance, Washington (8-9 June). http://www.worldbank.org/research/interest/confs/upcoming/deposit_insurance/home.htm.

Beck, Thorsten, Asli Demirgüç-Kunt, and Ross Levine. 1999. A New Database on Financial Development and Structure. World Bank, Washington. Photocopy (June).

Beck, Thorsten, Norman Loayza, and Ross Levine. 2000. Finance and Sources of Growth. *Journal of Financial Economics* 58, no. 1 (October): 261-300.

Bekaert, Geert, Campbell R. Harvey, and Robin Lumsdaine. 1998. *Dating the Integration of World Equity Markets.* NBER Working Paper 6724. Cambridge, MA: National Bureau of Economic Research.

Bekaert, Geert, Campbell R. Harvey, and Christian Lundblad. 2000. *Emerging Equity Markets and Economic Development.* NBER Working Paper 7763. Cambridge, MA: National Bureau of Economic Research.

Benston, George, Richard Herring, and Robert Litan. 1999. The Basel Committee's New Capital Adequacy Framework. Statement No. 156 of the Shadow Financial Regulatory Committee. Photocopy (27 September).

Bergsten, C. Fred, and John Williamson. 1983. Exchange Rates and Trade Policy. In

Trade Policy in the 1980s, ed. William R. Cline. Washington: Institute for International Economics.

Bergsten, C. Fred, Thomas Horst, and Theodore H. Moran. 1978. *American Multinationals and American Interests.* Washington: Brookings Institution.

Berlin, Mitchell. 2000. Why Don't Banks Take Stock? *Business Review.* Federal Reserve Bank of Philadelphia (May/June).

Berry, John M. 2000. Dr. Bill. *The International Economy* 14, no. 6: 8-13.

Bhagwati, Jagdish. 1998. Yes to Free Trade, Maybe to Capital Controls. *Wall Street Journal,* 16 November, A38.

Blustein, Paul. 2001. *Chastening.* Washington: Institute for International Economics.

Boehne, Edward G. 2000. Financial Modernization: Vastly Different or Fundamentally the Same? *Business Review.* Federal Reserve Bank of Philadelphia (July/August).

Boland, Vincent. 2000. Time for the Fainted-Hearted to Beware. *Financial Times Survey: International Capital Markets.* Supplement (19 May).

Borensztein, E., J. De Gregorio, and J-W. Lee. 1998. How Does Foreign Direct Investment Affect Economic Growth? *Journal of International Economics* 45: 115-35.

Brown, Drusilla K., Alan V. Deardorff, and Robert M. Stern. 2001. CGE Modeling and Analysis of Multilateral and Regional Negotiating Options. In *Issues and Options for U.S.-Japan Trade Policies,* ed. Robert M. Stern. Ann Arbor, MI: University of Michigan Press.

Brown, S., W. Goetzmann, and J. Park. 1998. Hedge Funds and the Asian Currency Crisis of 1997. NBER Working Paper 6427. Cambridge, MA: National Bureau of Economic Research.

Buiter, Willem H., and Anne C. Sibert. 1999. UNDROP: A Small Contribution to the New Magnitude of Speculative Attacks. *Journal of International Economics* 23: 221-39.

Calomiris, Charles W. 1997. *The Postmodern Bank Safety Net.* Washington: AEI Press.

Calomiris, Charles W. 1998. Blueprints for a New Global Financial Architecture. Columbia University, NY. Photocopy.

Calomiris, Charles W., and Robert Litan. 1999. Statement of the Shadow Financial Regulatory Committee on Revising the Basel Capital Standards. Statement No. 154 Photocopy (26 April).

Calvo, Guillermo A., and Enrique G. Mendoza. 1999. *Rational Contagion and the Globalization of Securities Markets.* NBER Working Paper 7153. Cambridge, MA: National Bureau of Economic Research.

Camdessus, Michel. 2000a. *IMF Morning Press.* Washington: International Monetary Fund. http://www.mpress.com (2 February).

Camdessus, Michel. 2000b. *IMF Survey.* Washington: International Monetary Fund (10 January).

Camdessus, Michel. 2000c. *IMF Survey* and *Special Supplement.* Washington: International Monetary Fund (21 February).

Caprio, Gerard, and Daniela Klingebiel. 1996. Bank Insolvencies: Cross-Country Experience. World Bank, Washington. Photocopy.

Caramazza, Francesco, Luca Ricci, and Ranil Salgado. 2000. *Trade and Financial Contagion in Currency Crises.* International Monetary Fund Working Paper 55. Washington: International Monetary Fund.

Caves, Richard E. 1996. *Multinational Enterprise and Economic Analysis,* 2d ed. Cambridge, UK: Cambridge University Press (first published in 1982).

Chenery, Hollis B. 1986. Growth and Transformation. In *Industrialization and Growth,* ed. Hollis B. Chenery, Sherman Robinson, and Moshe Syrquin. New York: Oxford University Press.

Choe, Hyuk, Bong-Chan Kho, and Rene M. Stulz. 1999. Do Foreign Investors Destabilize Stock Markets? The Korean Experience in 1997. *Journal of Financial Economics* 54, no. 2 (November): 227-64.

Chuhan, Punam, Stijin Claessens, and Nlandu Mamingi. 1998. Equity and Bond Flows to Latin America and Asia: The Role of Global and Country Factors. *Journal of Development Economics* 55: 439-63 (original version published in 1993).

Chuhan, Punam, Gabriel Perez-Quiros, and Helen Popper. 1996. *International Capital Flows: Do Short-Term Investment and Direct Investment Differ?* Policy Research Working Paper 1669. Washington: World Bank.

Claessens, Stijin, and Daniela Klingebiel. 1999. *Alternative Frameworks for the Provision of Financial Services: Economic Analysis and Country Experiences.* Policy Research Working Paper 2189. Washington: World Bank.

Claessens, Stijin, Michael P. Dooley, and Andrew Warner. 1995. Portfolio Capital Flows: Hot or Cold? *World Bank Economic Review* 9, no. 1: 153-74.

Cline, William R. 1995. *International Debt Reexamined.* Washington: Institute for International Economics.

Cline, William R. 2000. The Management of Financial Crises. Institute of International Finance, Washington. Photocopy (June).

Cline, William, David Folkerts-Landau, and Manuel Medina-Mora. 1999. Roundtable: Prospects for the Future. In *Financial Markets and Development: The Crisis in Emerging Markets,* ed. Alison Harwood, Robert E. Litan, and Michael Pomerleano. Washington: Brookings Institution.

Coppejans, Mark, and Ian Domowitz. 2000. The Impact of Foreign Equity Ownership on Emerging Market Share Price Volatility. *International Finance* 3, no. 1: 95-122.

Corrigan, Gerald E. 1982. Are Banks Special? 1982 Annual Report Essay. *The Region.* Minneapolis, MN: Federal Reserve Bank of Minneapolis.

Corrigan, Gerald E. 2000. Are Banks Special? A Revisitation. *The Region* (Special Issue) 14, no 1. Minneapolis, MN: Federal Reserve Bank of Minneapolis.

Council on Foreign Relations. 1999. *Safeguarding Prosperity in a Global Financial System: The Future International Financial Architecture.* Task Force Report. Carla A. Hills and Peter G. Peterson, co-chairs; Morris Goldstein, project director. New York: Council on Foreign Relations, and Washington: Institute for International Economics.

Council on Foreign Relations. 2000. A Financial Architecture for Middle-Class-Oriented Development. A Report of the Project on Development, Trade, and International Finance. Walter Russell Mead, project director. Sherle R. Schwenninger, senior program coordinator. New York: Council on Foreign Relations.

Cull, Robert, Lemma Senbet, and March Sorge. 2000. Deposit Insurance and Financial Development. Paper presented at World Bank conference on deposit insurance, Washington (8-9 June). http://www.worldbank.org/research/interest/confs/upcoming/deposit_insurance/home.htm.

Dai Xianglong. 1999. Statement. Meeting of the Interim Committee of the Board of Governors of the IMF, Washington. Photocopy (26 September).

De Gregorio, Jose, Sebastian Edwards, and Rodrigo O. Valdes. 2000. *Controls on Capital Inflows: Do They Work?* NBER Working Paper 7645. Cambridge, MA: National Bureau of Economic Research.

De Gregorio, Jose, Barry Eichengreen, Takatoshi Ito, and Charles Wyplosz. 1999. *An Independent and Accountable IMF.* Chapter 4 of the Geneva Report on the World Economy. International Center for Monetary and Banking Studies (Geneva) and Center for Economic and Policy Research (London).

Demirgüç-Kunt, Asli, and Enrica Detragiache. 1998. The Determinants of Banking Crises in Developing and Developed Countries. *IMF Staff Papers* 45, no. 1: 81-109.

Demirgüç-Kunt, Asli, and Enrica Detragiache. 2000. Does Deposit Insurance Increase Banking System Stability? An Empirical Investigation. Paper presented at a World Bank conference on deposit insurance, Washington (8-9 June). http://www.worldbank.org/research/interest/confs/upcoming/deposit_insurance/home.htm.

Demirgüç-Kunt, Asli, and Harry Huizinga. 1999. *Market Discipline and Financial Safety Net Design.* Policy Research Working Paper 2183. Washington: World Bank.

Demirgüç-Kunt, Asli, and Ross Levine. 1999. *Bank–Based and Market-Based Financial Systems: Cross-Country Comparisons.* Washington: Development Review Group, World Bank, and Finance Department, University of Minnesota.

Demirgüç-Kunt, Asli, and Tolga Sabaci. 2000. Deposit Insurance around the World: A Database. World Bank Financial Sector Research Data. Washington: World Bank.

Denizer, Cevdet, Murat F. Iyigun, and Ann L. Owen. 2000. *Finance and Macroeconomic Volatility.* International Finance Discussion Paper 670. Board of Governors of the Federal Reserve System. http://www.bog.frb.fed.us (June).

De Soto, Hernando. 2000. *The Mystery of Capital: Why Capitalism Triumphs in the West and Fails Everywhere Else.* New York: Basic Books.

Diamond, Douglas W., and Raghuram G. Rajan. 2000. *Banks, Short Term Debt and Financial Crises: Theory, Policy Implications and Applications.* NBER Working Paper 7764. Cambridge MA: National Bureau of Economic Research.

Dobson, Wendy, and Pierre Jacquet. 1998. *Financial Services Liberalization in the WTO.* Washington: Institute for International Economics.

Dooley, Michael P. 1994. *Are Capital Inflows to Developing Countries a Vote for or against Economic Policy Reforms?* Working Paper. University of California, Santa Cruz. Photocopy.

Dooley, Michael P. 2000. *Can Output Loss Following International Financial Crises Be Avoided?* NBER Working Paper 7531. Cambridge, MA: National Bureau of Economic Research.

Dunning, John H. 1988. *Explaining International Production.* London: Unwin Hyman Ltd.

Eatwell, John, and Lance Taylor. 1999. Capital Flows and the International Financial Architecture. Working Group on Development, Trade, and International Finance. Council on Foreign Relations, New York. Photocopy (July).

Eatwell, John, and Lance Taylor. 2000. *Global Finance at Risk: The Case for International Regulation.* New York: New Press.

Edison, Hali J., and Carmen M. Reinhart. 2000. *Capital Controls During Financial Crises: The Case of Malaysia and Thailand.* International Finance Discussion Paper 662. Washington: Board of Governors of the Federal Reserve System.

Edwards, Franklin R. 1999. Hedge Funds and the Collapse of Long-Term Capital Management. *Journal of Economic Perspective* 13, no. 2 (Spring).

Edwards, Sebastian. 1997. *Openness, Productivity and Growth: What Do We Really Know?* NBER Working Paper 5978. Cambridge, MA: National Bureau of Economic Research.

Edwards, Sebastian. 1998. *Capital Flows, Real Exchange Rates, and Capital Controls: Some Latin American Experiences.* NBER Working Paper 6800. Cambridge, MA: National Bureau of Economic Research.

Edwards, Sebastian, ed. 2000a. *Capital Flows and the Emerging Economies.* Chicago: University of Chicago Press.

Edwards, Sebastian. 2000b. Contagion. Revised from the World Economy Lecture at the University of Nottingham, October 1999. Photocopy (March).

Eichengreen, Barry. 1994. *International Monetary Arrangements for the 21st Century.* Washington: Brookings Institution.

Eichengreen, Barry. 1999a. The Regulator's Dilemma: Hedge Funds in the International Financial Architecture. *International Finance* 2, no. 3: 411-40.

Eichengreen, Barry. 1999b. Solving the Currency Conundrum. Paper delivered to the Council on Foreign Relations Study Group on Economic and Financial Development, New York (September).

Eichengreen, Barry. 1999c. *Toward a New International Financial Architecture.* Washington: Institute for International Economics.

Eichengreen, Barry. 2000. *Can the Moral Hazard Caused by IMF Bailouts Be Reduced?* Geneva Reports on the World Economy Special Report 1. London: Center for Economic and Policy Research.

Eichengreen, Barry, and Albert Fishlow. 1996. *Contending with Capital Flows: What Is Different About the 1990s?* Occasional Paper. New York: Council on Foreign Relations. (Revised and extended version published in Miles Kahler, ed., *Capital Flows and Financial Crises*; Ithaca, NY: Cornell University Press, 1998.)

Eichengreen, Barry, and D. Mathieson. 1998. *Hedge Funds and Financial Market Dynamics.* IMF Occasional Paper 166. Washington: International Monetary Fund.

Eichengreen, Barry, and Ashoka Mody. 2000. Would Collective Action Clauses Raise Borrowing Cost? An Update and Additional Results. World Bank, Washington. Photocopy (May).

Eichengreen, Barry, and Andrew Rose. 1997. Staying Afloat When the Wind Shifts: External Factors and Emerging-Market Banking Crises. In *Money, Capital Mobility, and Trade: Essays in Honor of Robert A. Mundell*, ed. Guillermo Calvo, Rudiger Dornbusch, and Maurice Obstfeld. Cambridge, MA: MIT Press.

Eichengreen, Barry, and Christof Ruehl. 2000. *The Bail-in Problem: Systematic Goals, Ad Hoc Means.* CEPR Discussion Paper 2427. London: Center for Economic and Policy Research.

Engelen, Klaus C. 2000. Shoot-Out at the Basel Corral. *The International Economy* 14, no. 1 (January/February): 46-49.

Esrella, Arturo, Sangkyun Park, and Stavros Peristiani. 2000. Capital Ratios as Predictors of Bank Failure. *FRBNY Economic Policy Review.* New York: Federal Reserve Bank of New York (July).

Evenett, Simon J. 2000. Capital Controls: Theory, Evidence, and Policy Advice. World Bank, Washington. Photocopy.

Federal Reserve Board. 1999. *Using Subordinated Debt as an Instrument of Market Discipline.* Staff Studies 172. Washington: Federal Reserve Board.

Feis, Herbert. 1961. *Europe: The World's Banker 1870-1914. An Account of European Foreign Investment and the Connection of World Finance with Diplomacy before the War.* Published for Council on Foreign Relations. New York: Augustus M. Keiley. (Originally published in 1930 by Yale University Press.)

Feldstein, Martin. 1998. Refocusing the IMF. *Foreign Affairs* 77, no. 2 (March/April): 20-33.

Ferguson, Roger. 1999. Financial Market Lessons for Bankers and Bank Supervisors. Speech before the Bond Market Association, New York. http://www.federalreserve.gov/boarddocs/speeches/1999/default.htm (28 October).

Fernandez-Arias, Eduardo, and Ricardo Hausmann. 2000. Is FDI a Safer Form of Financing? Working Paper 416. Washington: Inter-American Development Bank.

Finance Canada. 2000. Minister of Finance Calls for Renewed Focus on Making Globalization Work to the Benefit of All. Government of Canada, Ottawa. Photocopy (14 April).

Financial Stability Forum (FSF). 2000a. Report of the Study Group on Deposit Insurance, Basel, Switzerland. Photocopy (June).

Financial Stability Forum (FSF). 2000b. Report of the Working Group on Highly Leveraged Institution. Basel, Switzerland. Photocopy (March).

Fischer, Stanley. 1999. On the Need for an International Lender of Last Resort. *Journal of Economic Perspectives* 13, no. 4 (Fall).

Fishlow, Albert. 2000. International Financial Reform: The Morning After. *Milken Institute Review*, first quarter. Santa Monica, CA: Milken Institute.

Folkerts-Landau, David, and Peter M. Garber. 1998. Capital Flows from Emerging Markets in a Closing Environment. *Global Emerging Markets* 1, no. 3. (October): 69-79.

Forbes, Kristin, and Roberto Rigobon. 1999. *No Contagion, Only Interdependence: Measuring Stock Market Co-Movements.* NBER Working Paper 7267. Cambridge, MA: National Bureau of Economic Research.

Françoise, Joseph F., and Ludger Schuknecht. 1999. *Trade in Financial Services: Procompetitive Effects and Growth Performance.* CEPR Discussion Paper 2144. London: Center for Economic and Policy Research.

Frankel, Jeffrey A. 1999. *No Single Currency Regime Is Right for All Countries or at All Times*. Essays in International Finance No. 215. Princeton, NJ: Princeton University, Department of Economics, International Finance Section.

Frankel, Jeffrey A. 1999/2000. International Finance and Macroeconomics. *NBER Reporter*. http://www.nber.org/reporter (Winter).

Frankel, Jeffrey, and David Romer. 1999. Does Trade Cause Growth? *American Economic Review* 98, no. 3: 179-99.

Frankel, Jeffrey A., and Andrew K. Rose. 1996. Currency Crashes in Emerging Markets: An Empirical Treatment. *Journal of International Economics* 41: 351-66.

Frankel, Jeffrey, and Andrew K. Rose. 2000. *Estimating the Effect of Currency Unions on Trade and Output*. NBER Working Paper 7857. Cambridge, MA: National Bureau of Economic Research.

Frankel, Jeffrey, and Nouriel Roubini. 2000. The Role of Industrial Country Policies in Emerging Market Crises. Paper for the NBER Conference on Economic and Financial Crises in Emerging Market Economies, Woodstock, VT (19-21 October).

Frankel, Jeffrey, and S. Schmukler. 1996. *Country Fund Discounts, Asymmetric Information, and the Mexican Crisis of 1994: Did Local Residents Turn Pessimistic before International Investors?* NBER Working Paper 5714. Cambridge, MA: National Bureau of Economic Research.

Frankel, Jeffrey, and S. Schmukler. 1998. Crisis, Contagion, and Country Funds. In *Managing Capital Flows and Exchange Rates*, ed. R. Glick. Cambridge: Cambridge University Press.

Fraser, Robert. 1987. *The World Financial System*. London: Longman.

Fratianni, Michele, and John Pattison. 2000. Reconciling Global Financial Markets and National Regulation: The Role of the Bank for International Settlements. Center for German and European Studies, University of California, Berkeley. Photocopy (January).

Fratzscher, Marcel. 2000. *On Currency Crises and Contagion*. Working Paper 00-9. Washington: Institute for International Economics.

Froot, Kenneth, Paul O'Connell, and Mark Seasholes. 1998. *The Portfolio Flows of International Investors: Part 1*. NBER Working Paper 6687. Cambridge, MA: National Bureau of Economic Research.

Furfine, Craig. 2000. *Evidence on the Response of US Banks to Changes in Capital Requirements*. BIS Working Paper 88. Basel: Bank for International Settlements.

Furlong, Frederick. 1997. *Federal Subsidies in Banking: The Link to Financial Modernization*. FRBSF Economic Letter 97-31. San Francisco: Federal Reserve Bank of San Francisco.

Gavin, Michael. 1997. *A Decade of Reform in Latin America: Has It Delivered Lower Volatility?* Working Paper Green Series 349, Office of the Chief Economist. Washington: Inter-American Development Bank.

Gavin, Michael, and Ricardo Hausmann. 1998. *The Roots of Banking Crises: The Macroeconomic Context*. Working Paper 318, Office of the Chief Economist. Washington: Inter-American Development Bank.

Gavin, Michael, and Ricardo Hausmann. 1999. Preventing Crisis and Contagion: Fiscal and Financial Dimension. Inter-American Development Bank, Office of the Chief Economist, Washington: Inter-American Development Bank. Photocopy (March).

Giannini, Curzio. 1999. *Enemy of None But a Common Friend of All? An International Perspective on the Lender-of-Last-Resort Function*. Essays in International Finance No. 214. Princeton, NJ: Princeton University, Department of Economics, International Finance Section.

Gilibert, Pier-Luigi, and Alfred Steinherr. 1996. Private Capital Flows to Emerging Markets after the Mexican Crisis. In *Private Capital Flows to Emerging Markets after the Mexican Crisis*, ed. Guillermo Calvo, Morris Goldstein, and Eduard Hochreiter. Washington: Institute for International Economics.

Goeltom, Miranda S. 1998. Financial Market and Macroeconomic Policies. Paper presented at a conference on the economic issues facing the new government, sponsored by LPEM FEUI, US Agency for International Development, and PEG, Jakarta (18-19 August).

Goldberg, Linda, B. Gerard Dages, and Daniel Kinney. 2000. Foreign and Domestic Bank Participation in Emerging Markets: Lessons from Mexico and Argentina. Paper presented at a World Bank conference on contagion: how it spreads and how it can be stopped, Washington (3-4 February).

Goldsmith, Raymond. 1969. *Financial Structure and Development.* New Haven: Yale University Press.

Goldstein, Michael A., and Kenneth A. Kavajecz. 2000. Liquidity Provision during Circuit Breakers and Extreme Market Movements. Wharton School of the University of Pennsylvania, Rodney White Center for Financial Research, Philadelphia. Photocopy.

Goldstein, Morris. 1997. *The Case for an International Banking Standard.* POLICY ANALYSES IN INTERNATIONAL ECONOMICS 47. Washington: Institute for International Economics.

Goldstein, Morris. 2000. Strengthening the International Financial Architecture: Where Do We Stand? Paper presented at a KIEP/NEAEF Conference on regional financial arrangements in East Asia: issues and prospects, Honolulu (August).

Goldstein, Morris, Graciela L. Kaminsky, and Carmen M. Reinhart. 2000. *Assessing Financial Vulnerability: An Early Warning System for Emerging Markets.* Washington: Institute for International Economics.

Goodhart, C. A. E. 1995. *The Central Bank and the Financial System.* London: Macmillan.

Gould, David M., and Steven B. Kamin. 2000. *The Impact of Monetary Policy on Exchange Rates during Financial Crises.* International Finance Discussion Paper 669. Washington: Board of Governors of the Federal Reserve System.

Grilli, Vittorio, and Gian Maria Milesi-Ferretti. 1995. Economic Effects and Structural Determinants of Capital Controls. *IMF Staff Papers* 42, no. 3 (September): 517-51.

Group of Seven (G-7). 2000. *Strengthening the International Financial Architecture.* Report from G-7 Finance Ministers to the Heads of State and Government.

Group of Ten (G-10). 1998. *The Macroeconomic and Financial Implications of Aging Populations.* Basel: Bank for International Settlements. http://www.bis.org/publ/gten04.htm (April).

Gruber, Jonathan, and David Wise, eds. 1999. *Social Security and Retirement Around the World.* Chicago: University of Chicago Press.

Gruber, Jonathan, and David Wise, eds. 2001. *The Effect of Social Security and Retirement: Evidence from Around the World.* University of Chicago Press.

Haar, Jerry and Krishnan Dandapani. 1999. Banking in North America, NAFTA and Beyond. New York: Pergamon.

Habib, Michel, and Alexander P. Ljungqvist. 2000. *Financial Value and Managerial Incentives: A Stochaistic Frontier Approach.* CEPR Discussion Paper 2564. London: Center for Economic andPolicy Research.

Haddad, Mona, and Ann Harrison. 1993. Are There Positive Spillovers from Direct Foreign Investment? Evidence from Panel Data for Morocco. *Journal of Development Economics* 42: 51-74.

Haggard, Stephan. 2000. *The Political Economy of the Asian Financial Crisis.* Washington: Institute for International Economics.

Hamilton, Alexander. 1781. Hamilton, Alexander: *The Works of;* ed., H.C. Lodge; 1904, Putnam's, NY). Quoted in *Banks and Politics in America: From the Revolution to the Civil War* by Bray Hammond. Princeton, NJ: Princeton University Press, 1991.

Hammond, Bray. 1991. *Banks and Politics in America: From the Revolution to the Civil War.* Princeton, NJ: Princeton University Press.

Hargreaves, Deborah. 2001. Capital Rules Geared to Business. *Financial Times* (22 January).

Harrison, Ann. 1996. Determinants and Effects of Direct Foreign Investment in Côte d'Ivoire, Morocco, and Venezuela. In *Industrial Evolution in Developing Countries:*

Micro Patterns of Turnover, Productivity, and Market Structure, ed. Mark J. Roberts and James R. Tybout. New York: Oxford University.

Harvey, Campbell R., and Andrew H. Roper. 1999. The Asian Bet. In *Financial Markets and Development: The Crisis in Emerging Markets*, ed. Alison Harwood, Robert E. Litan, and Michael Pomerleano. Washington: Brookings Institution.

Harwood, Alison, Robert E. Litan, and Michael Pomerleano, eds. 1999. *Financial Markets and Development: The Crisis in Emerging Markets*. Washington: Brookings Institution.

Hausmann, Ricardo, and Eduardo Fernandez-Arias. 2000. *Foreign Direct Investment: Good Cholesterol?* Inter-American Development Bank Working Paper 417. Washington: Inter-American Development Bank.

Hawke, John D., Jr. 1998. Testimony before the Senate Banking, Housing and Urban Affairs Subcommittee on Securities. *Treasury News*. RR-2180. 29 January.

Hawkins, John, and Philip Turner. 2000. International Financial Reform: Regulatory and Other Issues. Paper presented at a conference on international financial contagion: how it spreads and how it can be stopped, sponsored by African Development Bank, IMF, MIT, WIDER, and World Bank, Washington (3-4 February).

Hellmann, Thomas F., Kevin C. Murdock, and Joseph E. Stiglitz. 2000. Liberalization, Moral Hazard in Banking and Prudential Regulation: Are Capital Requirements Enough? *American Economic Review* 90, no. 1 (March).

Henning, C. Randall. 1999. *The Exchange Stabilization Fund: Slush Money or War Chest?* Washington: Institute for International Economics.

Henry, Peter Blair. 2000. Stock Market Liberalization, Economic Reform, and Emerging Market Equity Prices. *Journal of Finance* 55, no. 2 (April).

Higgins, Matthew. 1998. Demography, National Savings, and International Capital Flows. *International Economic Review* 39, no. 2 (May): 343-69.

Hirtle, Beverly J., and Jose A. Lopez. 1999. Supervisory Information and the Frequency of Bank Examination. *Federal Reserve Bank of New York Economic Policy Review* (April).

Hobson, John. 1902. *Imperialism*. London: Allen & Unwin.

Hufbauer, Gary Clyde, and Edward A. Fogarty. 1998. Bring on a Bigger, Meaner IMF. *Journal of Commerce* (13 April): 7A.

Hufbauer, Gary Clyde, and Erika Wada. 1999a. Can Financiers Learn from Traders? *Journal of International Economic Law* 2, no. 4 (December).

Hufbauer, Gary Clyde, and Erika Wada. 1999b. *Hazards and Precautions: Tales of International Finance*. Working Paper 99-11. Washington: Institute for International Economics.

Hufbauer, Gary Claude, and Erika Wada. 1999c. Impact of Dollarization on Trade, Prices, Finance. Paper for conference sponsored by Strategic Assessments Group (November).

Hufbauer, Gary, Erika Wada, and Tory Warren. 2001. The Benefit of Price Convergence. Institute for International Economics, Washington. Photocopy (April).

Hymer, Stephan H. 1976. *The International Operations of National Firms*. Cambridge, MA: MIT Press. (Originally Ph.D. dissertation, Massachusetts Institute of Technology, accepted 1959).

Institute of International Finance (IIF). 1999a. *Report of the Task Force on Risk Assessment*. Washington: Institute of International Finance.

Institute of International Finance (IIF). 1999b. *Report of Working Group on Financial Crises in Emerging Markets*. Washington: Institute of International Finance.

International Monetary Fund (IMF). 1993. *Balance of Payment Manual*, 5th ed. Washington: International Monetary Fund.

International Monetary Fund (IMF). 1996. *Coordinated Portfolio Investment Survey: Survey Guide*. Washington: International Monetary Fund.

International Monetary Fund (IMF). 1998. Turbulence in Mature Financial Markets. *World Economic Outlook and International Capital Markets: Interim Assessment* (September).

International Monetary Fund (IMF). 1999a. *Coordinated Portfolio Investment Survey*. Washington: IMF.

International Monetary Fund (IMF). 1999b. *External Evaluation of Surveillance Report.* Members of the Evaluation Team: John Crow (Chairman), Richard Arriazu, and Niels Thygesen. Washington: International Monetary Fund.

International Monetary Fund (IMF). 1999c. *International Capital Markets.* Washington: International Monetary Fund (September).

International Monetary Fund (IMF). 1999d. International Financial Contagion. In *World Economic Outlook.* Washington: International Monetary Fund (May).

International Monetary Fund (IMF). 1999e. *International Financial Statistics,* CD-ROM version (June). Washington: International Monetary Fund.

International Monetary Fund (IMF). 1999f. *International Standards and Fund Surveillance— Progress and Issues.* http://www.imf.org/external/np/rosc/stand.htm (16 August).

International Monetary Fund (IMF). 1999g. *Results of the 1997 Coordinated Portfolio Investment Survey.* Washington: International Monetary Fund.

International Monetary Fund (IMF). 2000a. *Emerging Market Financing: Quarterly Report on Developments and Prospects.* Washington: International Monetary Fund (Second Quarter 2000).

International Monetary Fund (IMF). 2000b. *Emerging Market Financing: Quarterly Report on Developments and Prospects.* Washington: International Monetary Fund (Third Quarter 2000).

International Monetary Fund (IMF). 2000c. *International Capital Markets.* Washington: International Monetary Fund.

International Financial Institution Advisory Commission. 2000. Alan H. Meltzer, chairman. *Report of the International Financial Institution Advisory Commission.* Washington.

Institute of International Bankers. 1999. *Global Survey 1999: Regulatory and Market Developments.* New York.

Institute of International Bankers. 2000. *Global Survey 2000: Regulatory and Market Developments.* New York. http://www.ibs.org.

Ito, Takatoshi. 1999. *Capital Flows in Asia.* NBER Working Paper 7134. Cambridge, MA: National Bureau of Economic Research.

Jeanne, Olivier. 2000. *Debt Maturity and the Global Financial Architecture.* CEPR Discussion Paper 2520. London: Center for Economic and Policy Research.

Johnston, R. Barry, and V. Sundararajan, eds. 1999. *Sequencing Financial Sector Reforms: Country Experiences and Issues.* Washington: International Monetary Fund.

Jones, Kenneth, and Barry Kolatch. 1999. The Federal Safety Net, Banking Subsidies, and Implications for Financial Modernization. *FDIC Banking Review* 12, no. 1: 1-17.

Kaminsky, Graciela, K., and Carmen M. Reinhart. 1999. The Twin Crises: The Causes of Banking and Balance-of-Payments Problems. *American Economic Review* 93, no. 3 (June): 473-500.

Kaminsky, Graciela L., and Carmen M. Reinhart. 2000. On Crises, Contagion and Confusion. *Journal of International Economics* 51, no. 1 (June): 145-68.

Kaminsky, Graciela, Richard Lyons, and Sergio Schmukler. 2000. Managers, Investors, and Crises: Mutual Fund Strategies in Emerging Markets. Paper presented at a World Bank conference on contagion: how it spreads and how it can be stopped? Washington (3-4 February).

Kane, Edward J. 1989. *The S&L Insurance Mess: How Did it Happen?* Washington: Urban Institute Press.

Kane, Edward J. 2000. Architecture of Supra-Governmental International Financial Regulation. *Journal of Financial Services Research* 18, no. 2/3 (December): 301-18.

Kaufman, George. 1999. *Banking and Currency Crises and Systemic Risk: A Taxonomy and Review.* College of Business Administration Working Paper 99-11-03. Chicago: Loyola University.

Kaufman, George. 2000. Comments. "The Subsidy Provided by the Federal Safety Net: Theory and Measurement." *Journal of Financial Services Research* 17, no. 1 (February): 57-62.

Khan, Aubhik. 2000. The Finance and Growth Nexus. *Business Review*. Federal Reserve Bank of Philadelphia (January/February).

Kim, Woochan, and Shang-Jin Wei. 1999. *Foreign Portfolio Investors Before and During a Crisis*. NBER Working Paper 6968. Cambridge, MA: National Bureau of Economic Research.

Kim, Woochan, and Shang-Jin Wei. 2000. Foreign Portfolio Investors: Before and During a Crisis. Paper prepared for a research project on corruption and poor public governance, sponsored by the Brookings Institution, Washington (October).

Kindleberger, Charles P. 1996. *Manias, Panics, and Crashes*, 3d ed. New York: Wiley.

King, Mervyn. 1999. Reforming the International Financial System: The Middle Way. Speech delivered at Federal Reserve Bank of New York (9 September).

King, R. G., and Ross Levine. 1993. Finance and Growth: Schumpeter Might Be Right. *Quarterly Journal of Economics*, no. 108 (August): 715-37.

Kletzer, Kenneth. 2000. Capital Inflows and Developing Country Financial Crises: Implications of Competing Explanations for Policy Interventions. http://econ.ucsc.edu/~kkletzer (January).

Kletzer, Kenneth, and Ashoka Mody. 2000. Will Self-Protection Policies Safeguard Emerging Markets from Crises? Paper prepared as background for chapter 5 of the World Bank's *Global Development Finance 2000*. http://econ.ucsc.edu/~kkletzer (February).

Knight, Malcolm, Lawrence Schembri, and James Powell. 2000. Reforming the Global Financial Architecture: Just Tinkering Around the Edges? Paper presented at Bank of England conference, London (5-6 May).

Kohler, Horst. 2000a. *IMF Survey* 29, no. 11 (5 June).

Kohler, Horst. 2000b. Toward a More Focused IMF. Address to International Monetary Conference, Paris (30 May).

Kraay, Aart. 1998. In Search of the Macroeconomic Effects of Capital Account Liberalization. World Bank, Washington. Photocopy.

Kraay, Aart, Norman Loayza, Luis Serven, and Jaume Ventura. 2000. *Country Portfolios*. NBER Working Paper 7795. Cambridge, MA: National Bureau of Economic Research.

Krugman, Paul. 1997. No Free Lunch; Seven Habits of Highly Defective Investors. *Fortune* 136, no. 2 (29 December): 44-45.

Krugman, Paul. 1998. Saving Asia: It's Time to Get Radical. *Fortune*. http://www.fortune.com/fortune/investor/1998/980907/sol5.html (7 September).

Kwast, Myron L., and S. Wayne Passmore. 2000. The Subsidy Provided by the Federal Safety Net: Theory and Evidence. *Journal of Financial Services* 17, no. 1 (February): 35-55.

Lall, Sanjaya, and Paul Streeten. 1977. *Foreign Investment, Transnationals, and Developing Countries*. Boulder, CO: Westview Press.

Lane, Philip, and Gian-Maria Milesi-Ferretti. 2000. *External Capital Structure: Theory and Evidence*. CEPR Discussion Paper 2583. London: Center for Economic and Policy Research.

Lenin, Vladimir I. 1939. *Imperialism: The Highest Stage of Capitalism*. New York: International Publishers (originally published in 1917).

Levine, Ross. 1997. Financial Development and Economic Growth: Views and Agenda. *Journal of Economic Literature* 35, no. 2 (June): 688-726.

Levine, Ross. 1998. The Legal Environment, Banks, and Economic Growth. *Journal of Money, Credit, and Banking* 30 (2): 592-620 (August).

Levine, Ross. 2000. Bank-Based or Market-Based Financial Systems: Which Is Better? University of Minnesota, MN. Photocopy (January).

Levine, Ross, and S. Zervos. 1998. Stock Markets, Banks, and Growth. *American Economic Review* 88, no. 3 (June): 537-58.

Levine, Ross, Norman Loayza, and Thorsten Beck. 2000. Financial Intermediation and Growth: Causality and Causes. *Journal of Monetary Economics* 46, no. 1 (August): 31-77.

Levonian, M., and F. Furlong. 1995. Reduced Deposit Insurance Risk. *FRBSF Newsletter* 95-08. San Francisco: Federal Reserve Bank of San Francisco.

Lipsey, Robert E. 2000. *Interpreting Developed Countries' Foreign Direct Investment.* NBER Working Paper 7810. Cambridge, MA: National Bureau of Economic Research.

Litan, Robert, and Jonathan Rauch. 1997. *American Finance for the 21st Century.* Washington: US Department of the Treasury.

Longin, François, and Bruno H. Solnik. 2000. *Extreme Correlation of International Equity Markets.* CEPR Discussion Paper 2538. London: Center for Economic and Policy Research.

Loretan, Mico, and William B. English. 2000. *Evaluating "Correlation Breakdowns" During Periods of Market Volatility.* International Finance Discussion Papers 658. Washington: Board of Governors of the Federal Reserve System.

Lowenstein, Roger. 2000. *When Genius Failed: The Rise and Fall of Long Term Capital Management.* New York: Random House.

Lucas, Robert. 1990. Why Doesn't Capital Flow from Rich to Poor Countries? *American Economic Review.* Papers and Proceedings of the 102nd Annual Meeting of the American Economic Association (May).

McKinnon, Ronald I. 1973. *Money and Capital in Economic Development.* Washington: Brookings Institution.

McKinnon, Ronald I. 1984. *An International Standard for Monetary Stabilization.* POLICY ANALYSES IN INTERNATIONAL ECONOMICS 8. Washington: Institute for International Economics.

Mann, Catherine L. 1999. *Is the US Trade Deficit Sustainable?* Washington: Institute for International Economics.

Marris, Stephen. 1987. *Deficits and the Dollar: The World Economy at Risk.* POLICY ANALYSES IN INTERNATIONAL ECONOMICS 14. Washington: Institute for International Economics.

Martin, Paul. 2000. Statement by the Honorable Paul Matin, Minister of Finance for Canada, to the Institute for International Economics. http://www.fin.gc.ca/newse00/00-031e.html (14 April).

Marx, Karl, and Friedrich Engels. 1959. *Das Kapital: A Critique of Political Economy,* ed. Serge L. Levitsky. Chicago: Regnery (originally published between 1867).

Maxfield, Sylvia. 1998. Effects of International Portfolio Flows on Government Policy Choice. In *Capital Flows and Financial Crises,* ed. Miles Kahler. New York: Council on Foreign Relations.

Mayer, Martin. 1999. *Risk Reduction in the New Financial Architecture.* Levy Institute Public Policy Brief 56. Annandale-on-Hudson, NY: Bard College.

Meltzer, Alan. 1998. Asian Problems and the IMF. Testimony before Joint Economic Committee of US Congress, Washington (24 February).

Meyer, Laurence H. 1999a. An Agenda for Bank Supervision and Regulation. Speech to Institute of International Bankers meeting, Washington. http://www.federalreserve.gov/boarddocs/speeches/1999/default.htm (27 September).

Meyer, Laurence H. 1999b. Market Discipline as a Complement to Bank Supervision and Regulation. Speech to a conference on reforming bank capital standards, Council on Foreign Relations, New York. http://www.federalreserve.gov/boarddocs/speeches/1999/default.htm (14 June).

Meyer, Laurence H. 2000a. The Challenges of Global Financial Institution Supervision. Speech to Federal Financial Institutions Examination Council. International Banking Conference, Arlington, VA. http://www.federalreserve.gov/boarddocs/speeches/2000/default.htm (31 May).

Meyer, Laurence H. 2000b. Supervising LCBOs: Adapting to Change. Speech to National Bureau of Economic Research conference on prudential supervision: what works and what doesn't, Islamorada, FL. http://www.federalreserve.gov/boarddocs/speeches/2000/default.htm (14 January).

Miller, Marcus, and Lei Zhang. 1999. *Sovereign Liquidity Crisis: The Strategic Case for a Payments Standstill.* Working Paper 99-9. Washington: Institute for International Economics.

Minsky, Hyman P. 1982. *Can "It" Happen Again?* Armonk, NY: M. E. Sharpe.

Mishkin, Frederic S. 1998. The Dangers of Exchange-Rate Pegging in Emerging-Market Countries. *International Finance* 1, no. 1 (October): 81-101.

Mishkin, Frederic S. 2000. *Prudential Supervision: Why Is It Important and What Are the Issues?* NBER Working Paper 7926. Cambridge, MA: National Bureau of Economic Research.

Moran, Theodore H. 1998. *Foreign Direct Investment and Development: The New Policy Agenda for Developing Countries and Countries in Transition.* Washington: Institute for International Economics.

Moran, Theodore H. 2001. *Parental Supervision: The New Paradigm for Foreign Direct Investment and Development.* Forthcoming. Washington: Institute for International Economics.

Morck, Randall, Bernard Yeung, and Wayne Yu. 2000. The Information Content of Stock Markets: Why Do Emerging Markets Have Synchronous Stock Price Movements? *Journal of Financial Economics* (January): 215-60.

Mussa, Michael, and Anthony Richards. 1999. Capital Flows in the 1990s Before and After the Asian Crisis. International Monetary Fund, Washington. Photocopy (April).

Neal, Larry. 1990. *The Rise of Financial Capitalism: International Capital Markets in the Age of Reason.* Cambridge, UK: Cambridge University Press.

Noland, Marcus. 2000. *How the Sick Man Avoided Pneumonia: The Phillippines in the Asian Financial Crisis.* Working Paper 00-5. Washington: Institute for International Economics.

Obstfeld, Maurice. 1994. Risk, Diversification, and Growth. *American Economic Review* 84, no. 5 (December): 1310-29.

Obstfeld, Maurice. 1998. The Global Capital Market: Benefactor or Menace? *Journal of Economic Perspectives* 12, no. 4 (Fall): 9-30.

Obstfeld, Maurice, and Alan M. Taylor. 1997. *The Great Depression as a Watershed: International Capital Mobility Over the Long Run.* NBER Working Paper 5960. Cambridge, MA: National Bureau of Economic Research.

Organization for Economic Cooperation and Development (OECD). 2000. *OECD Economic Outlook 67.* Paris: Organization for Economic Cooperation and Development.

Overseas Development Council (ODC). 2000. *The Future Role of the IMF in Development.* ODC Task Force Report. John W. Sewell and Sylvia Saborio, co-chairs; Kevin Morrison, project director. Washington.

Palley, Thomas I. 2000. Stabilizing Finance: The Case for Asset-Based Reserve Requirements. *Financial Markets and Society* (August).

Peek, Joe, Eric S. Rosengren, and Geoffrey M. B. Tootell. 1999. Is Bank Supervision Central to Central Banking? *Quarterly Journal of Economics* 114, no. 2 (May): 629-53.

Perot, Ross, and Pat Choate. 1993. *Save Your Job, Save Our Country: Why NAFTA Must Be Stopped—Now!* New York: Hyperion.

Persaud, Avinash. 2000. *The Disturbing Interaction between the Madness of Crowds and the Risk Management of Banks.* Winning essay for Institute of International Finance's 2000 essay competition in honor of Jacques de Larosiere. http://www.iif.com/public.htm (June).

Peterson, Peter G. 1999. *Gray Dawn: How the Coming Age Wave Will Transform America and the World.* New York: Random House.

Pomerleano, Michael, and Xin Zhang. 1999. Corporate Fundamentals and the Behavior of Capital Markets in Asia. In *Financial Markets and Development: The Crisis in Emerging Markets,* ed. Alison Harwood, Robert E. Litan, and Michael Pomerleano. Washington: Brookings Institution.

Portes, Richard, and Helene Rey. 1999. *The Determinants of Cross-Border Equity Flows.* CEPR Discussion Paper 2225. London: Center for Economic and Policy Research.

Pratti, Alessandro, and Garry J. Schinasi. 1999. *Financial Stability in European Economic and Monetary Union.* Essays in International Finance 86. Princeton, NJ: Princeton University, Department of Economics, International Finance Section.

Quinn, Dennis. 1997. The Correlates of Change in International Financial Regulation. *American Political Science Review* 91, no. 3 (September): 531-51.

Radelet, Steven. 1998. Indonesia's Implosion. *Harvard Asia Pacific Review* 2, no. 2 (Summer): 87-88.

Radelet, Steven. 1999. *Orderly Workouts for Cross-Border Private Debt.* HIID Development Discussion Paper 721. Cambridge, MA: Harvard University.

Radelet, Steven, and Jeffrey Sachs. 1998. The East Asian Financial Crisis: Diagnosis, Remedies, Prospects. *Brookings Papers on Economic Activity* 1: 1-90. Washington: Brookings Institution.

Rajan, R. G., and L. Zingales. 1998. Financial Dependence and Growth. *American Economic Review* 88, no. 3 (June): 559-86.

Ramey, Garey, and Valerie A. Ramey. 1995. Cross-Country Evidence on the Link between Volatility and Growth. *American Economic Review* 85, no. 5: 1138-51.

Reineke, Wolfgang H. 1998. *Global Public Policy.* Washington: Brookings Institution.

Reisen, Helmut, and Julia von Maltzan. 1999. Boom and Bust and Sovereign Ratings. *International Finance* 2, no. 2: 273-93.

Rodrik, Dani. 1998. Who Needs Capital-Account Convertibility? In *Should the IMF Pursue Capital-Account Convertibility?* ed. Stanley Fischer, Richard N. Cooper, Rudiger Dornbusch, Peter M. Garber, Carlos Massad, Jacques J. Polak, Dani Rodrik, and Savak S. Tarapore. Essays in International Finance 207. Princeton, NJ: Princeton University, Department of Economics, International Finance Section.

Rodrik, Dani. 1999. *The New Global Economy and Developing Countries: Making Openness Work.* Baltimore: Johns Hopkins University Press for Overseas Development Council.

Rodrik, Dani, and Andres Velasco. 1999. *Short-Term Capital Flows.* NBER Working Paper 7364. Cambridge, MA: National Bureau of Economic Research.

Rogoff, Kenneth. 1999. International Institutions for Reducing Global Financial Instability. *Journal of Economic Perspectives* 13, no. 4: 21-42.

Roubini, Nouriel. 2000. *Bail-In, Burden-Sharing, Private Sector Involvement (PSI) in Crisis Resolution and Constructive Engagement of the Private Sector. A Primer: Evolving Definitions, Doctrine, Practice, and Case Law.* Stern School of Business, New York University. http://www.stern.nyu.edu/globalmacro (July).

Sachs, Jeffrey, and Andrew Werner. 1995. Economic Reform and the Process of Global Inte-gration. *Brookings Papers on Economic Activity 1995,* 1. Washington: Brookings Institution.

Sachs, Jeffrey, Aaron Tornell, and Andres Velasco. 1996. *Financial Crises in Emerging Markets: The Lessons from 1995.* NBER Working Paper 5576. Cambridge, MA: National Bureau of Economic Research.

Sarno, Lucio, and Mark P. Taylor. 1999. Hot Money, Accounting Labels and the Permanence of Capital Flows to Developing Countries: An Empirical Investigation. *Journal of Development Economics* 59: 337-64.

Schulze, Gunter G. 2000. *The Political Economy of Capital Controls.* Cambridge, UK: Cambridge University Press.

Schumpeter, Joseph A. 1934. *A Theory of Economic Development.* Translated by Redvers Opie. Cambridge, MA: Harvard University Press (original version published in 1912).

Shull, Bernard, and Lawrence J. White. 1998. Of Firewalls and Subsidiaries: The Right Stuff for Expanded Bank Activities. *The Banking Law Journal* (May).

Smalhout, James. 2001. Backing up the Banks. *Euromoney.* http://www.euromoney.com (January).

Smarzynska, Beata, and Shang-Jin Wei. 2000. *Corruption and Composition of Foreign Direct Investment: Firm-Level Evidence.* NBER Working Paper 7969. Cambridge, MA: National Bureau of Economic Research.

Solomon, Robert. 1982. *The International Monetary System, 1945-1981.* New York: Harper & Row.

Solomon, Robert. 1999. *Money on the Move: The Revolution in International Finance Since 1980*. Princeton, NJ: Princeton University Press.

Solow, Robert. 1956. A Contribution to the Theory of Economic Growth. *Quarterly Journal of Economics* 70, no. 1 (February): 65-94.

Solow, Robert. 1957. Technical Change and the Aggregate Production Function. *Review of Economics and Statistics* 39 (August): 312-20.

Soros, George. 1998. *The Crisis of Global Capitalism*. New York: Public Affairs Press.

Soto, Marcelo. 2000. *Capital Flows and Growth in Developing Countries: Recent Empirical Evidence*. OECD Development Center Technical Paper 160. http://www.oecd.org/dev/publication/tp1a.htm (July).

Stiglitz, Joseph. 1999. What Have We Learned from the Recent Crises? Implications for Banks. Remarks at conference on global financial crises: implications for banking and regulation, sponsored by Federal Reserve Bank of Chicago, Chicago (6 May).

Stulz, Rene M. 1999. *International Portfolio Flows and Security Markets*. Working Paper 99-3. Columbus: Department of Finance, Ohio State University. http://www.cob.ohio-state.edu/fin/dice/1999.htm (March).

Summers, Lawrence H. 1999a. The Right Kind of IMF for a Stable Global Financial System. Remarks delivered at London Business School, London (14 December).

Summers, Lawrence H. 1999b. Roots of the Asian Crises and the Road to a Stronger Global Financial System. Remarks to Institute of International Finance, Washington (25 April).

Summers, Lawrence H. 2000. International Financial Crises: Causes, Prevention, and Cures. Richard T. Ely Lecture. American Economic Association Papers and Proceedings (May).

Taylor, Alan M., and Jeffrey G. Williamson. 1994. Capital Flows to the New World as an Intergenerational Transfer. *Journal of Political Economy* 102, no. 2 (April): 348-71.

Taylor, Mark P., and Lucio Sarno. 1997. *Capital Flows to Developing Countries: Long- and Short-Term Determinants*. Washington: World Bank.

Tesar, Linda L., and Ingrid M. Werner. 1995. US Equity Investment in Emerging Stock Markets. *World Bank Economic Review* 9, no. 1 (January): 109-30.

Truglia, Vincent J. 2000. Can Industrialized Countries Afford Their Pension System? *Washington Quarterly* (Summer): 201-11.

United Nations Conference on Trade and Development (UNCTAD). 1998. *World Investment Report: Trends and Determinants*. New York and Geneva: United Nations.

United Nations Conference on Trade and Development (UNCTAD). 1999. *World Investment Report: Foreign Direct Investment and the Challenge of Development*. New York and Geneva: United Nations.

Van Rijckeghem, Caroline, and Beatrice Weder. 1999. *Sources of Contagion: Finance or Trade?* International Monetary Fund Working Paper 146. Washington: International Monetary Fund.

Vernon, Raymond. 1998. *In the Hurricane's Eye: The Troubled Prospects of Multinational Enterprises*. Cambridge, MA: Harvard University Press.

Wei, Shang-Jin. 2000. Local Corruption and Global Capital Flows. *Brookings Papers on Economic Activity* 2. Washington: Brookings Institution.

Whalen, Gary. 1999a. The Risks and Returns Associated with the Insurance Activities of Foreign Subsidiaries of US Banking Organizations. Economics Department, US Comptroller of the Currency, Washington. Photocopy (January).

Whalen, Gary. 1999b. Trends in Organizational Form and Their Relationship to Performance: The Case of Foreign Securities Subsidiaries of US Banking Organizations. Economics Department, US Comptroller of the Currency, Washington. Photocopy (March).

Williamson, John. 1983. *The Exchange Rate System*. Washington: Institute for International Economics.

Williamson, John. 1996. *The Crawling Band as an Exchange Rate Regime: Lessons from Chile, Colombia and Israel*. Washington: Institute for International Economics.

Williamson, John. 1998. Crawling Bands or Monitoring Bands: How to Manage Exchange Rates in a World of Capital Mobility. *International Finance* 1, no. 1 (October): 59-79.

Williamson, John. 2000. *The Role of the IMF: A Guide to the Reports.* International Economics Policy Brief 00-5. Washington: Institute for International Economics.

Williamson, John, and Molly Mahar. 1998. Current Account Targets. In *Real Exchange Rates for the Year 2000*, ed. Simon Wren-Lewis and Rebecca L. Driver. POLICY ANALYSES IN INTERNATIONAL ECONOMICS 54. Washington: Institute for International Economics.

World Bank. 2000a. *Global Development Finance: Analysis and Summary Tables.* Washington: World Bank.

World Bank. 2000b. *World Development Indicators.* CD-ROM version. Washington: World Bank.

Index

financial giants, 90*t*
GDP losses from banking and currency
  crises, 68*t*
gross private market financing, 186*t*-187*t*
largest banks, 80, 81*t*-83*t*
largest commercial banks, 81*t*
net bank lending to, 41*t*-42*t*
net capital flows, IIF figures, 173*t*, 174*t*
net-net capital flows, 9*t*-10*t*
nonfinancial giants, 91*t*
private investment, 14*t*-15*t*
  as percentage of GDP, 17*t*
syndicated loans, 189*t*
European Commission Banking Advisory
  Committee, 219-20
European expansion, 1
predatory practices, 40
European Union (EU)
capital rules established, 125
deposit insurance, 143
European Commission Banking Advisory
  Committee, 219-20
FDI inward stock per capita, 32*t*
financial institutions and their supervisors,
  119*t*
High Level Securities Supervisors
  Committee (HLSSC), 220
International Organization of Securities
  Commissions (IOSCO), 220-21
regulatory standards, 199
regulatory structures, 219-22

FDI. *See* foreign direct investment (FDI)
FDIC. *See* Federal Deposit Insurance
  Corporation
FDICIA. *See* FDIC Improvement Act of 1991
  (FDICIA)
FDIC Improvement Act of 1991 (FDICIA), 106,
  109
principal-agent problem, 109
Federal Bank Supervisory Office (FBSC,
  Germany), 205-06
Federal Deposit Insurance Corporation
  (FDIC), 106
Federal Financial Institutions Examination
  Council (FFIEC), 218
Federal Reserve
described, 217, 218-19
umbrella supervisor, 105
financial crises
arguments to moderate, 3
Basel I, record of, 126-27
characterized, 43
as complement to international capital
  flows, 57-58
as costs of foreign capital, 67, 68*t*, 69
deposit insurance, 109-10
early warning system, 155*b*
G-10 (Group of Ten) responsibilities, 129
GDP losses by region, 68*t*

goal of attenuating, 29
hedge funds, 47
history, 43-44
IMF count, 43*n*
IMF and government role, 131
interbank loans, 95, 190, 196
international capital flows, 43-44
liberalization and potential for, 61
losses, calculating impact, 68*n*
manias and panics, 40-45
  banks in a crisis, 45-46
portfolio investors, 46, 111-12
securities regulators, 121
short-term capital flows, 24*b*
syndicated loans, 190
who should pay for, 2
world-class panics, 43
financial derivatives, 18*b*
financial development
income growth, 58-61
  direction of causality, 59-60
sequencing, 60-61
volatility, 60
financial firms, in 100 largest companies, 90*t*
financial holding companies, 209
financial holding company (FHC), 218
financial institutions, 37-40, 83-88
capital accumulation strategies, 37
inefficient capital markets, 38
  Rx for, 38-40
insurance companies, 88
investment banks, 83, 85
wealth-management firms, 85-87
financial instruments, innovation, 96-97
financial openness, costs for emerging
  markets, 138
Financial Sector Assessment Program (FSAP),
  joint Bank-Fund, 154, 155*b*
financial sequencing, 61
Financial Services Agency (FSA, Japan), 208
Financial Services Agency (FSA, United
  Kingdom), 141
Financial Services Authority (FSA, United
  Kingdom), 216-17
Financial Services Modernization Act (1999)
deregulation response, 103
geographical and activity boundaries
  blurred, 218
pressure for deregulation, 219
as subsidy, 102
Financial Stability Forum (FSF)
financial institutions and their supervisors,
  119*t*, 127-28, 128*n*
standard-setting bodies, 158*b*
study group on deposit insurance, 144*n*
Working Group on HLIs, 137*n*
financial structures
in emerging markets, 71*t*
safety versus innovation, 121-22
Financing Corporation, 102, 102*n*

gross foreign assets, 6
Group of Twenty-Two (G-22) working
groups, 147

hedge funds
Asian financial crisis, 47
described, 86-87
disclosure requirements, 165n
largest, according to capitalization, 87t
numbers of, 47n
portfolio capital strategies, 112
positive and negative roles, 88
risk weights, 137
Russian financial crisis, 78-79
trends, 165
hedging
MNE operations, 52
portfolio investors, 46
herding
chances for, 140
defined, 140n
emerging markets, 132
evidence of, 139
information, 140
standstills, 148
strategic capital requirements on banks,
142
High Level Securities Supervisors Committee
(HLSSC), 119t, 220
highly leveraged institutions (HLIs), 88
risk weights, 137
high scenarios, 8t-9t, 21t, 27-28
"home country bias," 27n
Hong Kong, hedge funds, 88
hostile takeovers, 39n
human capital
differences in, 6
external economies in use, 6

IMF. See International Monetary Fund
imperialist critique, 40
income growth, changes in liberalization, 61
Indonesia, defaults, 58
industrial countries
assets vs. wealth, 6
investment forecasts, 28
inefficient capital markets, 38
information
advance, on large portfolio investments in
emerging markets, 142
asymmetric, 95, 95n
risk and leverage, 99n
disclosure and risk management, 141
"herding," 110
quality, 62
measured, 62n
quantity, 62n
requirements by US banking examiners,
122
transparency, 140

innovation, financial system safety trade-off,
121-22
insider trading, 142
Institute of International Finance (IIF), 7
joint crisis resolution, 149
methodology for G-10 bank operations, 11
on moral hazard, 131
net capital flows to emerging markets,
170t-171t
tables compared to IMF data, 174
institutional portfolio investors, 46
contagion, 51
institutional reforms, changes proposed, 28-29
insurance
G-10 regulation, 113t-20t
Insurance Committee (IC), 221
International Association of Insurance
Supervisors (IAIS), 119t, 221
investment coordination, 221
Insurance Committee (IC), 119t, 221
insurance companies, 88, 88n
large (listed), 89t
mergers, 103
interbank lending
Asian financial crisis, 77
BIS sources, 190, 192t-193t, 195t, 196
financial crises related, 49, 95
as least stable, 48n
moral hazard, 75n
overnight, 165
South Korea, 124, 124n
unsecured credits, 136n
interest payment, 175, 184
interest-rate risk, 99
internal-ratings model, 137
International Accounting Standards
Committee (IASC), standard-setting
bodies, 157b
International Association of Insurance
Supervisors (IAIS), 221
financial institutions and their supervisors,
119t
standard-setting bodies, 157b
international capital flows
activity indicators influenced, 55-56, 55t
advocated, 58
before 1970s, 5
theoretical explanations, 5-6
between rich nations, significance, 27
costs, 67, 68t, 69
costs and benefits, sizing up, 56-57
critics of, 57
during 1990s, 6, 8t-10t, 11
horrific side effects, 57
offsetting tendencies, 53n
standard deviations, 55-56
volatility year to year, 52-54
warnings of crisis, 49-50
International Federation of Accountants
(IFAC), standard-setting bodies, 158b

Sizing Up U.S. Export Disincentives*
J. David Richardson
September 1993   ISBN 0-88132-107-9
NAFTA: An Assessment
Gary Clyde Hufbauer and Jeffrey J. Schott/rev. ed.
October 1993   ISBN 0-88132-199-0
Adjusting to Volatile Energy Prices
Philip K. Verleger, Jr.
November 1993   ISBN 0-88132-069-2
The Political Economy of Policy Reform
John Williamson, editor
January 1994   ISBN 0-88132-195-8
Measuring the Costs of Protection
in the United States
Gary Clyde Hufbauer and Kimberly Ann Elliott
January 1994   ISBN 0-88132-108-7
The Dynamics of Korean Economic
Development*   Cho Soon
March 1994   ISBN 0-88132-162-1
Reviving the European Union*
C. Randall Henning, Eduard Hochreiter, and Gary
Clyde Hufbauer, Editors
April 1994   ISBN 0-88132-208-3
China in the World Economy   Nicholas R. Lardy
April 1994   ISBN 0-88132-200-8
Greening the GATT: Trade, Environment, and the
Future   Daniel C. Esty
July 1994   ISBN 0-88132-205-9
Western Hemisphere Economic Integration*
Gary Clyde Hufbauer and Jeffrey J. Schott
July 1994   ISBN 0-88132-159-1
Currencies and Politics in the United States,
Germany, and Japan
C. Randall Henning
September 1994   ISBN 0-88132-127-3
Estimating Equilibrium Exchange Rates
John Williamson, editor
September 1994   ISBN 0-88132-076-5
Managing the World Economy: Fifty Years After
Bretton Woods   Peter B. Kenen, editor
September 1994   ISBN 0-88132-212-1
Reciprocity and Retaliation in U.S. Trade Policy
Thomas O. Bayard and Kimberly Ann Elliott
September 1994   ISBN 0-88132-084-6
The Uruguay Round: An Assessment*
Jeffrey J. Schott, assisted by Johanna W. Buurman
November 1994   ISBN 0-88132-206-7
Measuring the Costs of Protection in Japan*
Yoko Sazanami, Shujiro Urata, and Hiroki Kawai
January 1995   ISBN 0-88132-211-3
Foreign Direct Investment in the United States,
3rd Ed.   Edward M. Graham and Paul R. Krugman
January 1995   ISBN 0-88132-204-0
The Political Economy of Korea-United States
Cooperation*
C. Fred Bergsten and Il SaKong, editors
February 1995   ISBN 0-88132-213-X

International Debt Reexamined* William R. Cline
February 1995   ISBN 0-88132-083-8
American Trade Politics, 3rd Ed.   I.M. Destler
April 1995   ISBN 0-88132-215-6
Managing Official Export Credits: The Quest for a
Global Regime*   John E. Ray
July 1995   ISBN 0-88132-207-5
Asia Pacific Fusion: Japan's Role in APEC*
Yoichi Funabashi
October 1995   ISBN 0-88132-224-5
Korea-United States Cooperation in the New
World Order*
C. Fred Bergsten and Il SaKong, editors
February 1996   ISBN 0-88132-226-1
Why Exports Really Matter! * ISBN 0-88132-221-C
Why Exports Matter More!* ISBN 0-88132-229-6
J. David Richardson and Karin Rindal
July 1995; February 1996
Global Corporations and National Governments
Edward M. Graham
May 1996   ISBN 0-88132-111-7
Global Economic Leadership and the Group of
Seven   C. Fred Bergsten and C. Randall Henning
May 1996   ISBN 0-88132-218-0
The Trading System After the Uruguay Round*
John Whalley and Colleen Hamilton
July 1996   ISBN 0-88132-131-1
Private Capital Flows to Emerging Markets After
the Mexican Crisis*   Guillermo A. Calvo,
Morris Goldstein, and Eduard Hochreiter
September 1996   ISBN 0-88132-232-6
The Crawling Band as an Exchange Rate Regime:
Lessons from Chile, Colombia, and Israel
John Williamson
September 1996   ISBN 0-88132-231-8
Flying High: Liberalizing Civil Aviation in the
Asia Pacific*
Gary Clyde Hufbauer and Christopher Findlay
November 1996   ISBN 0-88132-227-X
Measuring the Costs of Visible Protection in
Korea*   Namdoo Kim
November 1996   ISBN 0-88132-236-9
The World Trading System: Challenges Ahead
Jeffrey J. Schott
December 1996   ISBN 0-88132-235-0
Has Globalization Gone Too Far?   Dani Rodrik
March 1997   ISBN cloth 0-88132-243-1
Korea-United States Economic Relationship*
C. Fred Bergsten and Il SaKong, editors
March 1997   ISBN 0-88132-240-7
Summitry in the Americas: A Progress Report
Richard E. Feinberg
April 1997   ISBN 0-88132-242-3
Corruption and the Global Economy
Kimberly Ann Elliott
June 1997   ISBN 0-88132-233-4

Australia, New Zealand, and Papua New Guinea
D.A. Information Services
648 Whitehorse Road
Mitcham, Victoria 3132, Australia
tel: 61-3-9210-7777
fax: 61-3-9210-7788
e-mail: service@dadirect.com.au
http://www.dadirect.com.au

Canada
Renouf Bookstore
5369 Canotek Road, Unit 1
Ottawa, Ontario K1J 9J3, Canada
tel: 613-745-2665
fax: 613-745-7660
http://www.renoufbooks.com

United Kingdom and Europe
(including Russia and Turkey)
The Eurospan Group
3 Henrietta Street, Covent Garden
London WC2E 8LU England
tel: 44-20-7240-0856
fax: 44-20-7379-0609
http://www.eurospan.co.uk

India, Bangladesh, Nepal, and Sri Lanka
Viva Books Pvt.
Mr. Vinod Vasishtha
4325/3, Ansari Rd.
Daryaganj, New Delhi-110002
India
tel: 91-11-327-9280
fax: 91-11-326-7224
e-mail: vinod.viva@gndel.globalnet.
ems.vsnl.net.in

Japan and the Republic of Korea
United Publishers Services, Ltd.
Kenkyu-Sha Bldg.
9, Kanda Surugadai 2-Chome
Chiyoda-Ku, Tokyo 101
Japan
tel: 81-3-3291-4541
fax: 81-3-3292-8610
e-mail: saito@ups.co.jp
For trade accounts only.
Individuals will find IIE books in
leading Tokyo bookstores.

Southeast Asia (Brunei, Cambodia,
China, Malaysia, Hong Kong, Indonesia,
Laos, Myanmar, the Philippines, Singapore,
Taiwan, and Vietnam)
Hemisphere Publication Services
1 Kallang Pudding Rd. #04-03
Golden Wheel Building
Singapore 349316
tel: 65-741-5166
fax: 65-742-9356

Thailand
Asia Books
5 Sukhumvit Rd. Soi 61
Bangkok 10110 Thailand
tel: 662-714-0740-2 Ext: 221, 222, 223
fax: 662-391-2277
e-mail: purchase@asiabooks.co.th
http://www/asiabooksonline.com

Visit our Web site at:
http://www.iie.com
E-mail orders to:
orders@iie.com

WORLD CAPITAL MARKETS
CHALLENGE TO THE G-10

It is often pointed out that "for every bad borrower, and for every failed project, there is also a culpable lender or investor." This observation is particularly apt for the debate now raging in the capital markets: should private bankers and investment managers bear a greater share of the costs when financial crises erupt in emerging economies? Critics who have analyzed the "plumbing" of the world's financial architecture have thus far devoted enormous attention to the demand side-structural weaknesses in emerging markets. They have excoriated the IMF for ineptitude and policy mistakes.

But the authors of this study argue that financial leaders of the G-10 nations (industrial nations that were hardly affected by the crises of 1997-98) have a responsibility—both to their own citizens and the emerging markets—to take a far more vigilant stance. Dobson and Hufbauer criticize the supply side of world capital markets and ask how G-10 capital suppliers can reform their own financial systems to make the world safe for large-scale international capital flows. They draw a comprehensive picture of international finance through an extensive review of capital flows, the major financial players behind these flows, and the balance between costs and benefits of international capital movements. The authors analyze the implications of changing the rules of the game and recommend specific policy measures.

Wendy Dobson is professor at and director of the Institute for International Business at the University of Toronto. She was a visiting fellow at the Institute for International Economics in 1990-91. Between 1981 and 1987 she was president of the C.D. Howe Institute in Canada. From 1987 to 1989, she served as associate deputy minister of finance in the Canadian government with responsibility for international monetary affairs. Her most recent publications include *Financial Services Liberalization in the WTO* (Institute for International Economics, 1998) coauthored with Pierre Jacquet; *Fiscal frameworks and financial systems in East Asia: How much do they matter?* (University of Toronto Press, 1998); and *Multinationals and East Asia Integration* (1997) edited with Chia Siow Yue, which won the 1998 Ohira Prize.

Gary Clyde Hufbauer, Reginald Jones Senior Fellow, was formerly the Marcus Wallenberg Professor of International Finance Diplomacy at Georgetown University (1985-92); deputy director of the International Law Institute at Georgetown University (1979-81); deputy assistant secretary for international trade and investment policy of the US Treasury (1977-79); and director of the International Tax Staff at the Treasury (1974-76). He has written extensively on international trade, investment, and tax issues. He is coauthor of *NAFTA and the Environment: Seven Years Later* (2000); coeditor of *Unfinished Business: Telecommunications after the Uruguay Round* (1997); and coauthor of *Economic Sanctions Reconsidered* (2nd edition, 1990).

Hyun Koo Cho, research assistant at the Institute for International Economics, received his MA from the Johns Hopkins School of Advanced International Studies in Washington, DC.

ISBN 0-88132-301-2

INSTITUTE FOR INTERNATIONAL ECONOMICS

11 Dupont Circle, NW
Washington, DC 20036-1207
(202) 328-9000
FAX: (202) 328-5432
http://www.iie.com

DATE DUE

DEMCO 38-297